BLACK FATHERS

An Invisible Presence in America

BLACK FATHERS

An Invisible Presence in America

Edited by

Michael E. Connor
California State University, Long Beach

Joseph L. White
University of California, Irvine

 LAWRENCE ERLBAUM ASSOCIATES, PUBLISHERS
2006   Mahwah, New Jersey   London

Lawrence Erlbaum Associates, Inc., Publishers
10 Industrial Avenue
Mahwah, New Jersey 07430
www.erlbaum.com

Cover design by Tomai Maridou

Library of Congress Cataloging-in-Publication Data

Connor, Michael E.
Black fathers : an invisible presence in America / Michael E. Connor, Joseph L. White.
p. cm.
Includes bibliographical references and index.
ISBN 0-8058-4509-7 (cloth : alk. paper)
ISBN 0-8058-4510-0 (pbk. : alk. paper)
1. African American fathers. 2. Fatherhood—United States. I. White, Joseph L., 1932-
II. Title.

HQ756.C667   2005
306.874′2′08996073—dc22   200051237
                                                                      CIP

Books published by Lawrence Erlbaum Associates are printed on acid-free paper,
and their bindings are chosen for strength and durability.

Printed in the United States of America
10 9 8 7 6 5 4 3 2

This book is dedicated to the memory of my late father, Russell T. Connor (1908–1988), and all the other "invisible" African American men/fathers who toiled daily in a segregated, hostile America to attempt to provide a better life for their families, their children, and their communities. Men like my father who worked whatever jobs they could find, often two or three jobs at one time; men who cared for their children and for the mothers of their children; men who participated in household chores and were available to their families daily; men who worked to maintain their marriages, who problem solved and negotiated, who recognized successful marriages are partnerships and appreciated the strength and beauty of their wives; men who are gentle and strong, quiet and forceful, spiritual and worldly. Men like my dad and all the others who are ignored but present. These men are routinely ignored in studies focusing on African descended families—likely because they do not fit America's stereotypes of Black men. I thank you for showing us the way.

—**Michael E. Connor**

Contents

Introduction

In the parlance of social psychology, social work, and urban social scientists, African American fathers have often been described as "absent," "missing," "nonresidential," "noncustodial," "unavailable," "nonmarried," "irresponsible," and "immature." We have wondered why it is/was so difficult to find literature, research, and comments regarding positive attributes of African American families in general and African American fathers in particular. Surely to have survived and have such a major impact on popular culture (i.e., language, music, style of dress, athletics, and so forth), there must be some inherent and obvious strengths. For some years, the first author attempted to publish comments, observations, and findings regarding involved Black dads to no avail. Although he has presented at numerous major conferences, he was unable to publish his work on involved African American fathers. This book fills a void in attempting to offer a broader picture regarding the status of African American males in a fathering role. The purpose of this book is to get beyond the African American father "invisibility" syndrome and gloom and doom pathology oriented labels and tell another side of the story about the power of fathering in the African American experience.

It is a father story that is for the most part invisible to census takers, welfare officials, survey researchers, popular media, service providers, university professors, and others. But nonetheless, father figures are actively present in the lives of many African American children as mentors, teachers, preachers, "old heads," maternal partners, stepfathers, uncles, older male friends, social fathers, and, of course, biological fathers who contribute in a constructive way to the lives of African American children.

The voices of Black men as fathers, father figures, social fathers, absent fathers, and nonresidential fathers were a powerful presence in the Million Man March in October 1995. Some observers call the Million Man March the largest family values rally America has ever witnessed. The 800,000 Black men (some say a million) who assembled on the Mall in Washington, D.C., on that sunny autumn afternoon publicly pledged to take care of their children and guide them away from the destruction of inner-city crime and drugs. Husbands and boyfriends promised to respect their wives and girlfriends and take responsibility for their families and improving their communities.

Who are these *invisible* men who provide male nurturance and support to boys and girls and young men and women in the Black community? Who are these invisible men who provide guidance, mentoring, supervision, and discipline that translate into opportunities, skill building, knowledge, and often-financial resources for their biological and nonbiological children? Who are these men who assume the role of social fathers when the biological father is not available and augment fatherhood support systems when the biological father is present?

This book will try to bring these invisible social and biological fathers to life. We tell their stories and let the reader hear and feel the vibrancy of their voices as they struggle to meet the challenges of being fathers and Black men in America. The editors are intimately connected to the topic of Black fatherhood in several ways. Our experience with Black fatherhood spans three generations. The first editor was reared in a home with active and consistent male involvement including his father, his maternal grandfather, several uncles, a large extended family, male cousins, and family friends. The second editor's father was not present in his childhood family, nor was he closely connected on a day-to-day or, for that matter, month-to-month relationship. Census takers would probably ignore one of us and describe the other as growing up in a father-absent home. Pathology oriented psychoanalysts would probably say that in our adult lives we are still suffering from suppressed father hunger (the first editor remembers being "informed" by a history professor during his second year of college that he was "deficient" due to the lack of positive male role involvement). Yet there were Black men available to us as biological fathers, social fathers in roles as uncles, grandfathers, older male cousins, playground directors, camp counselors, teachers, preachers, and the proverbial "old heads." In our current lives as college teachers, counselors, mentors, community workers, and social activists, we now fulfill the social fatherhood role for many young Black men and women.

The first editor, Michael Connor, was the younger child in a two-parent intact household, where he was impacted by the love, nurturing, training/

teaching, and involvement of numerous solid, consistent adult African American males. As a child, Connor actively sought out and was reinforced by uncles, cousins, grandfathers, extended family members, and other older men (including his father) who were coaches, mentors, teachers, preachers, priests, disciplinarians, and old heads to provide him with the guidance he needed to grow, develop, and thrive. His father and uncles were his primary coaches as he developed athletically. Other extended male family members regularly attended his football, basketball, baseball games, and track meets. His parents and several uncles were supportive and instrumental in his academic pursuits. Other family members were invaluable in offering direction and advice as he navigated the tense racial climate of the 1950s and 1960s. Dr. Connor met the second editor in 1965, commencing a personal and professional relationship that continues. He is married with two adult children.

The so-called father absence phenomenon repeated itself with the children of the second editor, Joseph White, who was divorced from the mother of his three daughters almost 40 years ago. Despite his absence from the day-to-day household, he was very much psychologically present in the lives of his daughters, if often unseen. Two of his three daughters, who are now university teachers and administrators, describe him as their role model for how to develop and conduct a career in higher education.

In this volume, African American scholars and those doing scholarly work with African American fathers offer insights, bits of wisdom, experiences, and suggestions about the population. The book is divided into four sections. In Part I, we offer some research and theory regarding the impact of fathers on the lives of their children. In chapter 1, Connor and White note that many Black men fulfill a paternal role, but they tend to be ignored by social science literature. Although these men may or may not be the biological father, their impact on "their" children is significant. This chapter sets the tone for the following chapters where specific examples of "invisible" African American fathers and men are offered. In chapter 2, Hrabowski, Maton, and Grief consider the backgrounds of fathers whose sons became high-achieving college educated professionals. They found the fathers were present. Educated, married, hard working, and engaged with their families. The authors suggest Six Strategies of Successful Parenting. Chapter 3 by Caldwell and White discusses the concept of generative fathering and how it applies to African American men. They suggest that social fathering is a more accurate fit for the generative fathering activities in many African American communities.

In Part II, reactions and experiences from those men who had active, involved, and committed Black men in their lives as they were growing up are shared. In chapter 4, Connor discusses growing up in small town (actually a village) Ohio with active and involved appropriate male role models. He was unaware that other young Blacks were not reared similarly until he went to college. Although his small community was largely socially segregated and there was little interaction with Whites outside the school environment, the African American community was tight, close, supportive, and nurturing. He did not experience a sense of "being deprived"—and, in fact, was told by several males that "no one could beat me but me."

Claytie Davies and Percy Abrams' chapter 5 shares experiences living in father-involved homes. They are each cognizant and appreciative of the impact their dads' daily interaction had on their lives. They discuss their fathers' expectations related to education and responsibilities and are aware of the sacrifices their dads made for them and their families. Their dads were role models, they loved unconditionally, and they offered direction and guidance. Both of the authors are friends and young fathers themselves now and vow to remain close to one another, to their own children, and to one another's children.

In chapter 6, Kenneth Bentley shares thoughts and perceptions he derived via conversations with several successful professional African American men regarding their notions and perceptions of fatherhood, their perceptions of their own fathers, and some potential lessons for other African American fathers and fathers-to-be. Thomas Parham acknowledges the importance of having a positive Black man in his life in chapter 7. He shares that while his strong, committed, loving, and nurturing single mother did an amazing job of rearing her children to be thoughtful, kind, competent, and caring, there are limitations in what women can teach their sons about becoming men. Parham notes the importance of his father-in-law in his life. Through this man, he learned that family comes first and the importance of faith, kinship bonds, education, and a strong work ethic. Part II ends with Anne Chan's discussion of Bill Cosby, "an enduring icon of the ideal American father." Through Cosby's work on national television, America was exposed to successful Black parents who care about their children. White and Black responses to the show and the impact on the country are discussed.

In Part III, we share stories from African American men who had problematic relationships with their fathers, but who put forth the time, energy, and effort to work through the issues. In chapter 9, father and son psychologists (Ivory L. and Ivory A. Toldson) discuss their history, the pain and anguish and the healing. This powerful and moving account of a relationship in trouble uses the African tradition of call and response to tell the story of mistakes, miscues, growth, forgiveness, and healing. As the younger Dr. Toldson writes, "a man never outgrows the simple pleasure of receiving simple words from his father's heart." In chapter 10, Caldwell and Reese discuss how men who did not have a biological father residing in their home while they were growing up struggle with the meaning of fatherhood as they become fathers themselves. Each of the authors acknowledges that numerous surrogate fathers were present and they make a commitment to remain in the lives of their children (and one another's offspring). They note that many "fatherless" men become productive members of the community and competent fathers. Nnamdi Pole (chap. 11) shares some experiences, frustrations, and feelings pertaining to his own father's role and activities while growing up. Although anger, disappointment, and hurt were experienced, Pole is able to glean some ideas and notions as to what he learned from those negatives, which might be used to enable him to be a better father, male role model, husband, and friend. He is aware of what he does not want to be.

The primary focus of Part IV is on how to strengthen the role of Black fathers, father figures, and social fathers in family life and child rearing by discovering and internalizing psychological strengths anchored in African American psychological themes, African values, and spirituality. Consciousness-raising groups, fatherhood training programs, and parent education classes that are being utilized around the country to bring Black men into the orbit of children and help them understand the power of father presence in helping children grow up to be confident and capable people are offered. Practitioners and service delivery professionals discuss several programs and services African American men are providing to other African American men and to the Black community. Some of these authors experienced difficulties while growing up, but were able to get their lives turned around in order to be of service to others in the community. These final chapters offer excellent examples of viable programs to help improve the situation in our communities.

Julie Landsman tells the story of Shane Price in chapter 12. Although Mr. Price was reared by his grandparents the importance of friends and mentors is noted. As an adolescent and young adult, Shane fell by the wayside, deviated from his family's teachings and got involved in "life on the streets." Through a series of activities he found himself (the spiritual side prevailed) and he commenced a more responsible lifestyle, caring for his own children and others in the community. He notes the importance of male influences in the activities of the African American Men Project.

In chapter 13, Gary Cunningham discusses the plight of too many young urban Black males. This concern led him to develop the African American Men Project. His focus is on how Black men can help each other succeed. The author shares that during his early years he was without his father or strong male role models. At the age of 13, an uncle took him in and commenced parenting him. In this stable home with a caring, respectful father figure (and other appropriate role models), he was introduced to his culture and history. This interaction provided the background that led to educational and vocational success. His program offers broad services and works to partner with other service-oriented programs. Interestingly, at the age of 46, the author met his biological family and half siblings.

In chapter 14, Clarence Jones discusses fragile families. Mr. Jones is cognizant that fathers' involvement extends beyond financial contributions and he suggests other males in the community can "father" (e.g., uncles, male friends, brothers, grandfathers). As relates to his community activities, Mr. Jones indicates service programs must go beyond jobs training and mentor, nurture, and support the formal education of the young men they serve. Additionally, he states that mothers *and* fathers must be included in the training.

Part IV ends with Connor's chapter 15. The focus is on The Role of Men, a program developed for and available to underserved communities in California. The Program originated in Long Beach and is now in several health care jurisdictions throughout the state.

Prior to each part section is a piece of poetry offered by Malia Connor, a Katherine Dunham trained dancer (San Francisco State University) who has performed extensively throughout the Bay Area (1985–2005) as a dancer, choreographer, and poet with numerous companies. She began her own company in 1991, the Malia Movement Company, dedicating herself to the healing of women through movement. Her poetry is featured on both Mingus Amungus' CDs, having been one of the original members of the jazz group. Malia currently lives in Northern California with her 6-year-old daughter.

—*Michael E. Connor*
—*Joseph L. White*

RESEARCH AND THEORY

Onimasai*

Baby girl born into the sign of Leo
made a 2 month early appearance
maybe you liked the way the ocean felt
when mommy swam backstrokes in the Pacific
whatever it was, water broke on the Ave
with contractions starting 5 mins apart

Little head lodged in my ribs and
it doesn't matter if i'm completely dilated
except you're coming out too fast
little feet dangling out to greet your daddy
and by his expression i know
things have turned serious
as they wheel me away

19 mins later you appeared
4 pounds 9 ounces
with everything perfectly intact (asé)
and as i'm led to you

---

*The original poetry used in this volume, "Onimasai," "Honeywine," "Sunrise to Sunset," and "Mingus," was written and self-published by Malia Connor, copyright © 2001. Used by permission of Malia Connor.

i am welcomed by your strong cries
as the nurse places you on my chest

You lift your tiny head
to study your mommy and
now i silently weep with utter amazement
reaching out to my pretty Brown
honey warrior . . .

—Malia, July 28, 1998

Chapter 1

Fatherhood in Contemporary Black America: Invisible but Present*

Michael E. Connor
Emeritus, California State University, Long Beach

Joseph L. White
Emeritus, University of California, Irvine

When considering fathers and fathers' roles in the United States, the image that is usually conjured up is that of a breadwinner, disciplinarian, head-of-household. Those who "father" reside within a household that includes mother, children, and perhaps a family pet. Men who live outside the home and who father and the manner in which they father are routinely ignored. Allen and Connor (1997) noted in their discussion regarding generative fathering, that those men who may not be the biological father can have significant impact on children with whom they interact.

To more fully (perhaps truly) understand fathering in the African American community, social scientists might need to expand the views and scopes of investigation. Also, they may have to include a focus outside the community to determine what forces control said community (i.e., educational policies, the legal system, imposed limited economic opportunity, drug trade, etc.).

In this chapter, we discuss African American men who fulfill a fathering role, but who are not considered by those who research fathering. These males include the everyday men who are highly visible in the community, but who tend to be ignored. Some of these men have jobs, some reside in households with children, some are seen on street corners and on porches, some are in barbershops, others live with their parent or parents, some are

---

*The terms African American and Black are used interchangeably.

married, some spend considerable time in church, and others put a lot of
work toward honing their athletic skills.

DEMOGRAPHIC TRENDS CONCEAL FATHER
PARTICIPATION IN THE BLACK COMMUNITY

Historically, Black fathers have been either invisible in the study of child development and family life or characterized in negative terms such as *deadbeat*
dads and absent fathers who are financially irresponsible and rarely involved
in their children's lives (Coley, 2001). According to demographic data, most
African American children growing up in contemporary society do not live in
the same household with their biological fathers or reside with them only periodically. Only a minority of African American biological fathers live continuously with their children throughout childhood. Approximately 64% of African American children are growing up in one-parent households; one half
of Black families are headed by single mothers (U.S. Bureau of the Census,
1996). Although households without the biological or legal fathers present
are a growing concern in all ethnic groups in America, the problem is particularly acute in the African American community.

The demographic trends outlined earlier tend to conceal the variety of
ways Black men participate in the fathering experience although they may
not be legally part of the nuclear family. There seem to be major discrepan-
cies between the negative absent father images of Black men described in
demographic studies and the picture of Black men in fathering roles which
emerges from structured interviews, narratives, biographical sketches, community-based observations, and ethnographic investigations. These more
qualitative approaches of ordinary Black men who are not often celebrated
and whose voices are seldom heard indicate that Black men have always
risen to assume special places in the lives of children, families, and the
Black community (Hutchinson, 1995; Wade-Gayles, 1997).

In his book, *Black Fatherhood: The Guide to Male Parenting* (1995), Professor Earl Ofari Hutchinson, a Los Angeles-based sociologist, consultant, TV
commentator, newspaper columnist and teacher, conducted extensive interviews with five African American men who were actively involved with
their families and kids. The men who ranged in age from 26 to 88 included
Hutchinson's father. The interviewees were married, single, divorced, remarried, stepfathers, grandfathers, uncles, and older brothers. Inter-
spersed throughout the book are Hutchinson's views about his life experiences as a son and as a father who has been married, divorced, single, and
remarried. The men challenged the image of Black fathers as irresponsible
by highlighting what they were doing right as African American males to

enrich family life and support their children's healthy development. There was a consensus among the fathers about the importance of education, teaching values, guiding children through the pitfalls of sex, gangs and drugs, and developing constructive family and marital conflict resolution strategies. The core of the men's psychological strengths were anchored in African American cultural values such as spirituality, improvisation, resilience, and connectedness to others through the extended family and the larger African American community.

Commitment: Fatherhood in Black America, a book of photo essays and brief biological sketches of Black men in fathering roles, shows another side to the negative images of Black men as fathers (Perchinske, 1998). The aim of *Commitment* is to represent Black fathers performing responsibly at work, church, play, and in family and community settings. Young fathers, old fathers, single fathers, not married fathers, and fathers across a range of different socioeconomic levels are presented as supportive, nurturing men who don't conform to stereotypical views of African American fathers. One of the stories highlighted in *Commitment* is that of a widowed elderly great-grandfather who is raising his 10-year-old great-grandson alone. The great-grandfather is a retired farm laborer, who worked in a grove 6 days a week for 50 years picking oranges by hand, fertilizing trees, and pulling moss off trees. He raises his great-grandson with faith in God, a structured life with clear rules, and passes along the wisdom that can only come from life experiences. The great-grandfather feels the boy has filled his life with joy and purpose.

Ira Thomas (1997) in interviews conducted for his doctoral dissertation at Harvard with a sample of 26 middle-school African American boys confirmed the presence of Black male adults in father figure roles. The youth provided information about their social network of relationships with adult African Americans, the meaning of the relationships in their lives, and how relationships with adult males guided their behavior, values, and goals for the future. Using a combination of qualitative and quantitative data analyses methods, the author uncovered five basic dimensions that characterized the relationship between the boys and the adult men in their networks: relationship ideal or closeness of the relationship, physical presence, empowerment, communication, and teaching and learning. The boys described the relationships with adult males as being "tight." They valued spending time together, active engagement, instructive talk about conflict resolution, emotional and social support, and learning about life and family values from the experiences of the adults. The adult men in whom the boys shared rich relationships involved older friends, uncles, adult cousins, ministers, godfathers, stepfathers, coaches, older brothers, and some biological fathers.

SOCIAL FATHERHOOD IN THE AFRICAN AMERICAN COMMUNITY

Some of the confusion about fathering in the African American community is due to the lack of a clear definition of what a father is or is not. Traditional definitions of fatherhood underestimate the role of Black fathers and do not adequately capture the cultural nuances that surround the fathering role in the African American experience. A more fluent and inclusive term is needed to capture the essence of the fathering role in African American social and family networks.

Coley (2001) and others use the term *social fatherhood* to include men who assume some or all of the roles fathers are expected to perform in a child's life whether or not they are biological fathers. As a more inclusive term, social fatherhood encompasses biological fathers, but also extends to men who are not biological fathers who provide a significant degree of nurturance, moral and ethical guidance, companionship, emotional support, and financial responsibility in the lives of children. Because of high rates of divorce, out of wedlock births, separation, dissociation and reconstruction of families, more men are assuming father-like roles to children who are not their biological offspring. Black youth are well aware of the impact of social fathers in their lives. For example, in a recent research study when African American girls were asked to name a man who was "most like their father to me," 24% of the respondents named a nonbiological father (Coley & Chase-Lansdale, 2001). Similar rates of nonbiological father involvement have been reported in other studies (Coley, 2001). In his research with Black adolescent boys reviewed earlier, Thomas (1997) found that many of the adults which the youth shared rich relationships with were not their biological fathers. An example is the case of BJ.

At 12, BJ was heading for trouble. He was residing with his father in a high-crime area in Los Angeles. Unfortunately, his father was unable to provide proper support or supervision and BJ was having difficulties at home, at school, and in the community. Soon, the Department of Social Services revoked custody from the father and BJ and a younger sister were sent to live with their half brother, a former Marine. The older brother had gone through a period of adjustment as he was growing up and the Marines had helped to get him on track. He was concerned that his younger siblings were experiencing some of the issues he had gone through and thought he had the responsibility to help them. Although the older brother was married with two young children and lived in a two-bedroom apartment, he willingly accepted the younger siblings into his home. BJ now had rules, responsibilities, and structure. He wanted to be treated like a man, but had no sense of discipline or integrity. He now had to earn things. Five years later, BJ is a senior at a local high school where he is a solid student and a gifted football player (quarterback) who has received scholarship offers from several Division I programs. He "matured into a trustworthy, respectful 17-year old" under his brother's guidance. BJ states: "If it weren't for him, I wouldn't be here. I'd be locked up or dead. I can't thank him enough for allowing me to become the person I am." BJ's biological father is thankful that his younger son was placed with his older son. Although letting his son go was a painfully difficult task, the father recognized he was not up to the task of properly rearing his children. He was able to maintain contact with BJ over the years and is very supportive of his son's activities. BJ is not upset with or critical of his biological father. He says: "I don't want to tell you he's a bad person because he's not. I love my father to death. He wasn't ready for it." As relates to his brother, BJ says: "My brother has taught me to be a man. I don't know how to explain it, but it's great" (Sondheimer, 2002, p. B1 and B4).

The overlapping community, social, and family networks that make up the extended family in the African American community have always been a primary source of social fatherhood. The extended family provided a plethora of men as uncles, godfathers, brothers and half brothers, cousins, stepfathers, ministers, grandfathers, and biological fathers who assumed the responsibility for raising children. Most African American men learned the meaning of fatherhood through a circle of kin networks and community affiliations that provided a variety of men to be observed and emulated and from whom a frame of reference for viewing the world could be acquired. Through interactions of extended family members, young men have the opportunity to practice fathering by caring for younger siblings and participating in decision making. Social fathers as extended family members can augment the biological father role and provide adequate role models when the biological fathers are absent (Allen & Connor, 1997).

THE AFRICAN AMERICAN EXTENDED FAMILY SYSTEM

The origins of the African American extended family system can be traced back to Africa before Africans were enslaved in the New World. In the traditional African kinship network, guiding children did not only rest with the biological parents, but was also part of communal responsibility. Throughout childhood, adolescence, and young adulthood, African youth were surrounded by a network of adults in the family and community who took on the responsibility for teaching values that involved collective survival, building harmonious relationships, spirituality, and respect for others (Billingsley, 1992). The ancient African proverb states that it "takes a village to raise a child."

Despite centuries of slavery, de facto and de jure segregation, economic depressions, the rural to urban migration, and continuing traces of racism which are evident in employment, education, and the legal system, the African American cultural values, which are the foundation of the African American family, have persisted (Billingsley, 1992). Historically, in the communal tradition of African American life, powerful Black males were looked upon as role models and father figures. Men like Nat Turner, Congressman Adam Clayton Powell, Malcolm X, Jackie Robinson, Frederick Douglass, Reverend Martin Luther King, Jr., Richard Wright, and Ralph Ellison, as well as church deacons, older Black men sitting on the bench in parks, and the community elders who carried the hopes and aspirations of the African American community were claimed as father figures for their strength and commitment to uplifting the race (Morrison, 1998).

CHANGING DEFINITIONS OF FATHERHOOD

Not only has the definition of who should be included in the term *fatherhood* changed, there is also a growing lack of agreement among experts on the primary role of fathers in America. In the early history of America, Euro-American fathers were depicted as stern, emotionally insulated, moral overseers who autocratically ruled their wives and children with an iron hand. The new Euro-American fathers who have appeared in popular culture in the last 25 years are buddies with children, diaper changers, childbirth attendants, nursery school volunteers, and supportive companions to mom. The so-called "new nurturant" father is closely attuned to the needs of his children, offers hugs and expressions of affection, listens, reads bedtime stories, and is democratic and patient. The new dads are likely to be highly educated men living in the suburbs, which suggests that cultural and economic forces are shaping images of modern fatherhood. Despite the apparent changes in fatherhood roles, the economic provider role, which has always been dominant throughout Euro-American history, remains central to most definitions of fatherhood. "Deadbeat dads" who do not financially support their children or cannot master the breadwinner role are not held in high esteem in any segment of American society (Lamb, 1997; Pleck & Pleck, 1997).

Because Black men have always been connected to two cultural arenas in America, African American and Euro-American, they are, no doubt, influenced by dominant cultural definitions of fatherhood roles. Historically, Black men in America have experienced a dual cultural consciousness. The great African American civil rights leader and social philosopher, W. E. B. Dubois (1903) spoke of this duality as a "twoness," a double consciousness, feeling part of America and its values, yet excluded from full participation in mainstream America. With respect to fatherhood roles, the majority of Black males understand and accept the provider or "breadwinner" role

(Hunter & Davis, 1994). The dilemma for African American men is how to overcome the structural and institutional barriers that inhibit landing, keeping, and being promoted on jobs that pay the kind of wages that can support a family. Ethnographic research suggests that for many young inner-city African American fathers, even strong motivation to provide for or "do for" their children is difficult to sustain when fathers face bleak employment prospects because of a dearth of jobs combined with inadequate educational preparation in ghetto schools (Furstenberg, 1995).

Faced with dim employment prospects to support their children, some young Black fathers get caught up in the consequences of maladaptive choices. With drugs as the largest economy in the inner cities, it is not difficult to get caught up in drug business transactions that pay more than minimum wage jobs. As anyone can see who visits America's prisons or urban courts, thousands of Black men are caught up in the drug economy, which has consequences that further restrict their ability as providers. Dropping out of the work world or not contributing at all to economically provide for one's children will bring censure from the courts and the community.

To resolve the duality of being part of two cultures and perform effectively as breadwinners, African American men must draw on African cultural strengths which have sustained us from Slavery, through the Civil War, Reconstruction, the Great Migration to Urban America, and the Civil Rights Movement. Additionally, we may want to more fully examine DuBois' "twoness" (referred to here as biculturalism) mentioned earlier. One can argue that regardless of the level of knowledge, having some (even limited) bicultural ability has value over being limited to monocultural skills. Thus, what has too often been considered a weakness or a deficit may in fact be a strength. One possibility deriving from this perspective is that we likely know more about the wider community than the wider community knows about us, and we have survived in the face of enormous obstacles. We likely do not use this knowledge to our individual or collective advantage. Perhaps we might consider redefining ourselves, as a people—as fathers, from a position of positive affirmation. The implications of such a redefinition can be considerable. These cultural and psychological strengths, which will be discussed in greater detail in the last section of this book, involves spirituality, resilience, collective survival through extended family networks, emotional vitality, and the ability to "keep on keeping on" in the face of adversity (White, 1984).

FATHERNEED

In his book, *Fatherneed*, Kyle Pruett (2000), a child psychiatrist, who is a senior staff member at the Yale Child Guidance Center, uses the term *fatherneed* to describe the powerful physical, psychological, and emotional force that pulls men to children (related or not) just as it pulls children to men to shape, enrich, and expand each other's lives. According to Pruett, there is a deep need in men to provide fathering and a need in their children to experience it.

Father presence offers children the opportunity to interact with the essence of maleness: the voice rhythms and sounds, smells, texture, body size, and the difference between male and female bodies. The need for fathers in children is so strong that they may make up imaginary fathers when they don't have one or spend a lot of energy looking for a replacement (Pruett, 2000; Wade-Gayles, 1997). Some children successfully build close relationships or become "tight" with uncles, grandfathers, coaches, preachers, or good friends of mom. The urban middle-school African American boys interviewed in Thomas' (1997) doctoral dissertation, who did not have biological fathers in the home, established close relationships with surrogate fathers in their social networks. The rich relationships which the boys shared with the men fulfilled fatherneed with emotional and social support, quality time spent together, teaching and instructive talk, and guidance about sex and drugs, problem solving, and family values. Through these high-quality interpersonal relationships, boys were developing confidence and the skills they need to negotiate the transition through their adolescent to adult years. Fatherneed is central to the father's growth and happiness. A critical turning point in life occurs when a man becomes a father. Guiding and caring for children is not only developmentally and psychologically important to the child, but is central to the father's psychological growth and well being. In the father–child dyad, change is constant and complex. Children and parents go through psychological developmental stages and transitions and are constantly in a process of becoming. Fathers are changed by children as much as children are changed by parents. Ongoing reciprocal transitions between father and child fuel the development of each and power them forward in life (Pruett, 2000).

The transition into mature paternal identity can only be achieved by active and sustained emotional engagement. To become good enough fathers, men must make a conscious effort to shift their internal psychological world and external behavior to become involved in daily close interactions with children. Successful fathers need to continuously strive to develop behaviors that promote the well-being of others such as emotional openness, nurturance, patience, compassion, a willingness to love others despite their imperfections, and the ability to sacrifice personal needs for the good of others. Fathers who take responsibility for their children report that it makes them more complete people by providing them with the opportunities to develop more affectionate and feeling sides of themselves (Coltrane, 1995).

GENERATIVE FATHERING

Erik Erikson (1950) coined the term *generativity* to refer to an emergent process that accentuates parents' personal growth in relation to their children's well-being. As the primary psychological task of healthy adulthood, generative fathers have a genuine commitment to establishing and guiding the next generation. Erikson believed that in order to become fully human, a father must widen his commitment beyond the self and invest in caring deeply for others. Generative fathering includes any nurturing activity that contributes to the life of the next generation such as the development or creation of more mature persons, products, ideas, or works of art. The essence of generativity is contributing to and renewing the ongoing cycle of generations. Erikson believed that men can and want to become the kinds of fathers their children need them to be, and that the renewal of society calls for non-self-absorbed adults who are prepared to help establish the next generation of adults, products, ideas, and works of art (Dollahite, Hawkins, & Brotherson, 1997).

The Black men interviewed by sociologist Earl Hutchinson (1995) accepted generative fathering as the primary developmental task of their adult lives. Whether married, single, divorced, or remarried, they were very committed to behaving responsibly toward their children, being emotionally and physically available, and providing material support to take care of their children's needs.

Embedded in family and community networks, they taught their children the importance of being bicultural and how to survive in mainstream society with a strong sense of the power of the African American heritage with its emphasis on spirituality, extended family, resilience, and emotional vitality. Studies of inner-city African American fathers suggests that even when only marginally involved, fatherhood is a critical element in their sense of self. Many of these fathers told investigators that becoming a father was a life-changing experience leading them to drastically cut down illegal, dangerous, and high-risk activities. Fathering gave them a reason to live and the motivation to work toward personal redefinition and transformation (Coley, 2001).

There is no complete blueprint for learning how to be a generative father. Initially, behavioral psychologists emphasized that men constructed their fatherhood identities by following cultural scripts and modeling and imitating concrete male figures in fathering roles. Generative fathering in some men is, no doubt, influenced by recollections of the fathers they experienced as children as well as cultural patterns and observations of other boys' fathers in specific situations. However, more recent social constructionist theories view generative fathering as a discovery process. A man actively shapes his role as a father through improvisation, reformulation, and creatively piecing together bits and pieces of fathering behavior from personal history and social situations. Ethnographic research conducted by Daly (1995) suggests that men in modern American society regard their fathers not as role models, but as a point of reference to begin sorting out in what ways they want to be different. Rather than patterning their behavior after a specific individual or cultural script, the men in Daly's study selected particular behaviors from a wide variety of parenting behaviors around them including wives and mothers. Creating their own pattern of fatherhood by emulating desirable parental behaviors from many adults allowed the men to be more innovative and flexible with their own children in terms of discipline, guidelines for behavior, setting goals, and learning to listen to the voices and needs of their children before autocratically making decisions.

LEARNING TO BE FATHERS

Although young Black men understandably need the guidance and intimacy which generations of Black fathers can provide, many urban Black men begin the fathering process without the benefit of close bonds with men in fathering roles. Leonard Pitts (1999), an African American author and journalist, begins his journey into fatherhood as the son of an abusive, alcoholic father who dropped out of the workforce as a young adult. In the journey to discovering his fatherhood identity, Pitts followed the social constructionist model. As he struggled with doubts that he was doing it right as a father, Pitts interviewed several friends, neighbors, and acquaintances about their experiences as sons and fathers. The African American men he interviewed across the country were businessmen, teachers, coaches, playboys, students, preachers, ex-convicts, in-residence fathers, and fathers living away from their children. From the men's fathering stories and his own experiences, Pitts pieced together an integrative pattern of what he wanted to become as a generative father to his two stepchildren and three biological children. Pitts discovered that the strongest influence in his paternal style was his mother who held the family together through the years of his father's abuse, alcoholism and voluntary unemployment.

UNFULFILLED FATHERNEED: SEARCHING, UNDERSTANDING, FORGIVING, AND RECONCILIATION

When fatherneed is unfulfilled because of father abuse, alcoholism, father absence, or emotional distance between children and biological, social, or surrogate fathers, children experience an emotional void, which they carry into adulthood. In *Father Songs*, a book about African American father stories edited by Gloria Wade-Gayles (1997), many prominent male and female African American authors discussed the emotional emptiness and psychological scars they carried into adulthood as a result of unfulfilled fatherneed. The stories of unfulfilled fatherneed follow a similar sequence. As the authors move through adulthood, rage, disappointment, and feelings of rejection are supplanted by a need to understand and reconnect with fathers.

In his book, *Notes of a Native Son* (1955), prizewinning author James Baldwin wrote about his struggle to get behind the mask of his abusive, psychologically withdrawn stepfather and understand the deeper layers of the man. At his stepfather's funeral, Baldwin listened pensively as the minister described a man quite the opposite of the man Baldwin and his siblings had known. The minister presented the stepfather as the ideal generative father—a thoughtful, patient, Christian nurturing man who successfully built his life around his family and children. As Baldwin peered into the casket, he wondered if the minister had captured the true essence of the man that was hidden beneath layers of rage, poverty, and disappointment brought on by racial oppression, which psychologically destroyed many Black fathers in the first half of the 20th century. Beyond the facts of his stepfather's life, what was the real identity of the man who had lived, died, and now was being eulogized.

Several of the writers in Wade-Gayles' book (1997) actively searched for a deeper understanding of their fathers by visiting the communities where their fathers were reared and talked to relatives and friends of their fathers. Others searched their memories for happy times beneath the cloud of rage and disappointment. Some set up face-to-face meetings with their fathers or trips with fathers to weddings, funerals, and family gatherings in fathers' hometowns, which were mostly in southern states. Leonard Pitts (1999), who grew up in Los Angeles, traveled to Mississippi to conduct extensive interviews with his father's relatives and friends. John Edgar Wideman (1994), an African American college professor in Massachusetts, visits his father's boyhood home in South Carolina and later attends a family wedding–reunion with his father. As sons like Leonard Pitts and John Edgar Wideman begin to understand the oppressive racial conditions which shaped their fathers' lives as African American men in the 1920s, 1930s, and 1940s, they gradually back up from harsh criticism and bitter anger. It was not easy for their fathers to struggle with low paying, exhausting jobs (if employed at all) in factories, foundries, shining shoes, hauling trash, cleaning buildings, sharecropping, and laying railroad tracks. Police brutality, substandard housing, lack of adequate health care, long jail sentences for minor offenses, poor education, and de facto and de jure segregation, north and south, contributed to the frustration and psychological destruction of many Black fathers. James Baldwin (1955) warns us not to judge Black men too harshly who may have fallen under such heavy burdens.

Understanding their fathers allowed the authors to see fresh meaning in their fathers' lives and have faith that their fathers did the best they could to be good fathers before they were derailed and sometimes even crushed by impossible burdens. Understanding is followed by forgiveness and attempts at reconciliation and establishing new connections with father. Leonard Pitts (1999) has a heart-to-heart talk with his father before he dies. His father confesses his mistakes and asks for forgiveness. After his father's death, Pitts experiences a catharsis which leads to reconciliation and healing when he cries at his father's grave and later writes a letter to his deceased father sharing his feelings. Once free of the anger, resentment, hunger, and searching for father, Black men are psychologically liberated from the fatherneed chains of the past and free to start learning to be generative fathers.

CONCLUSION

There is little doubt that too many Black children reside in single parent, low-income homes and have limited meaningful interactions and relationships with men as fathers. However, in numerous situations, Black men are present in the lives of children, yet they are ignored and their contributions minimized. These men's roles and the importance of their interactions tend to be absent in too many discussions of fathers and fatherhood. Although the manner in which these men father may differ from notions, perceptions, and standards of "traditional" fathering, their contributions are invaluable and have impact on their children. These actions and their impact tend to be ignored, missed, discarded, and devalued. These African American men in father roles love, care for, and desire interactions with (their) children. Most tend to provide financially, as their employment circumstances dictate.

It is important to acknowledge these men and the principles, which they indicate, are important as they interact with children (i.e., the teaching of values, providing guidance, and supporting education). By so doing the actions are reinforced making them more likely to be brought to the attention of other men. Clearly children across ages, sons and daughters, want and need relationships with men in fathering capacities. Creating and perpetuating barriers to father–child relationship can only further erode the very fabric of community growth and success. Ignoring these men is short sighted and destructive.

By acknowledging the important contribution of these involved African American men, the very definition father will be expanded to more accurately depict what Black fathers are and what they do. The concepts of social fatherhood, generative fathering, and fatherneed are important in this paradigm shift. This more complete analysis of Black men will likely demonstrate that some of the men who were not involved with their children were not "deadbeat" per se, but were men bearing both psychological and physical scars—scars derived from daily interactions in an oppressive environment. The ugly remnants of these scars were passed on to their offspring in terms of an emotional distance between fathers and children. Men such as John Edgar Wideman and Leonard Pitts, aware of the rage, disappointment, and feelings of rejection, made a conscious decision to understand and reconnect with their fathers. In so doing, they discovered and began to comprehend the oppressive conditions under which their fathers lived. This awareness and insight allowed Wideman and Pitts to see their fathers in a different light, permitting a healing process to begin. Without the realization of the need to understand what these older Black men were forced to go through, it is likely impossible to let go of the anger and rage felt by Wideman and Pitts. This "letting go" allowed the healing to commence so these younger men could move on in their lives (making it more likely they would become more competent and involved fathers themselves). Knowledge and forgiveness are powerful tools for emotional healing in a spiritual people. Clearly, traditional definitions of fatherhood cannot and do not reflect cultural aspects of what Black men do as fathers. The variety of skills, activities, and interactions demonstrated by Black men are not adequately conveyed.

In summary, we note that Black men are often present in children's lives, however, they are usually ignored or their roles minimized by those outside the community. The manner in which these men parent often differs from "traditional" fathering, and thus is discarded and devalued. Data clearly suggest that African American men in fathering roles love, care for, and desire interaction with their children.

No doubt, too many African American children reside in single parent homes—yet men are present. We must find ways to acknowledge and show value for these men. Skills and behaviors which these fathers indicate are important to them as they interact with children include the teaching of values, providing guidance and supporting education. Data also suggest children—both sons and daughters—want and need relationships with men.

Thus, we must consider expanding definitions of what Black fathers are and what they do—especially social fatherhood. It is clear that traditional definitions do not reflect interactions, and activities engaged in by Black men.

REFERENCES

Allen, W., & Connor, M. (1997). An African American perspective on generative fathering. In A. J. Hawkins & D. C. Dollahite (Eds.), *Generative fathering: Beyond deficit perspectives* (pp. 52–70). Thousand Oaks, CA: Sage.

Baldwin, J. (1955). *Notes of a native son.* Boston: Beacon Press.

Billingsley, A. (1992). *Climbing Jacob's ladder: The enduring legacy of African American families.* New York: Simon & Schuster.

Coley, R. (2001). Invisible men: Emerging research on low-income, unmarried and minority fathers. *American Psychologist, 56*(9), 743–753.

Coley, R., & Chase-Lansdale, P. L. (2001). *The sting of disappointment: Father-daughter relations in low-income African American families.* Manuscript submitted for publication.

Coltrane, S. (1995). The future of fatherhood: Social demographic and economic influences on men's family involvement. In W. Marsiglio (Ed.), *Fatherhood: Contemporary theory, research and social policy* (pp. 255–274). Thousand Oaks, CA: Sage.

Daly, K. (1995). Reshaping fatherhood: Finding the models. In W. Marsiglio (Ed.), *Fatherhood: Contemporary theory, research and social policy* (pp. 21–40). Thousand Oaks, CA: Sage.

Dollahite, D., Hawkins, A., & Brotherson, S. (1997). Father work: A conceptual ethic of fathering as generative work. In A. J. Hawkins & D. C. Dollahite (Eds.), *Generative fathering: Beyond deficit perspectives* (pp. 17–35). Thousand Oaks, CA: Sage.

DuBois, W. E. B. (1903). *The souls of Black folks.* Chicago: McClurg.

Erikson, E. (1950). *Childhood and society.* New York: Norton.

Furstenberg, F. (1995). Fathering in the inner city: Paternal participation and public policy. In W. Marsiglio (Ed.), *Fatherhood: Contemporary theory, research and social policy* (pp. 119–147). Thousand Oaks, CA: Sage.

Hunter, A., & Davis, J. (1994). Hidden voices of Black men: The meaning, structure and complexity of manhood. *Journal of Black Studies, 25*(1), 20–40.

Hutchinson, E. (1995). *Black fatherhood: The guide to male parenting.* Los Angeles: Middle Passage Press.

Lamb, M. (1997). Fathers and child development: An introductory overview and guide. In M. E. Lamb (Ed.), *The role of the father in child development* (pp. 1–18). New York: Wiley.

Morrison, M. (1998). Learning through memory. In M. Perchinske (Ed.), *Commitment: Fatherhood in Black America* (pp. 5–11). Columbia: University of Missouri Press.

Perchinske, M. (Ed.). (1998). *Commitment: Fatherhood in Black America.* Columbia: University of Missouri Press.

Pitts, L., Jr. (1999). *Becoming dad: Black men and the journey to fatherhood.* Marietta, GA: Longstreet.

Pleck, E., & Pleck, J. (1997). Fatherhood ideals in the United States: Historical dimensions. In M. E. Lamb (Ed.), *The role of the father in child development* (pp. 33–48). New York: Wiley.

Pruett, K. (2000). *Fatherneed: Why father care is as essential as mother care for your child.* New York: Broadway Books.

Sondheimer, E. (2002). *Santiago's Jackson knows the drill. Los Angeles Times,* September 12, pp. B1 & B4.

Thomas, I. (1997). *The search for meaning: Exploring Black male adolescents' relationships with adult males.* Unpublished doctoral dissertation. Harvard University.

U.S. Bureau of the Census. (1996). *Statistical abstract of the United States.* Washington, DC: U.S. Government Printing Office.

Wade-Gayles, G. (Ed.). (1997). *Father songs: Testimonies by African-American sons and daughters.* Boston: Beacon Press.

White, J. L. (1984). *The psychology of Blacks: An Afro-American perspective.* Englewood Cliffs, NJ: Prentice-Hall.

Wideman, J. E. (1994). *Fatheralong: A meditation on fathers and sons, race and society.* New York: Pantheon Books.

Chapter 2

Father–Son Relationships: The Father's Voice*

Freeman A. Hrabowski
Kenneth I. Maton
Geoffrey L. Grief
University of Maryland, Baltimore County

> *I grew up on a farm in Mississippi [just after World War II], and my parents were very religious, very hardworking. I think education was the thing that was stressed most. "You want to get away from the farm, you don't want to do this hard work, son, you'd better get an education," they told me. So education was always foremost. The thing I learned was you have to work hard, and you have to be focused. Those are the things I have tried to pass on to my son. You have to know what you want, you have to work for it, nothing is free. Unless you are willing to pay the price, you're not going to make it.*

To understand how this high-achieving group of African American college-age men are succeeding, we interviewed the fathers who raised them. Most of these men were the biological fathers and were living with the sons' mothers. In a few cases, the father was a stepfather or a single father who had raised his son alone. Through our information gathering, we often felt we were weaving together threads that would result in a magnificent tapestry of family culture, history, and life. Part of that construction meant learning from these fathers about their own early experiences and how those experiences influenced how they raised, and are still raising, their sons.

Here we focus on the fathers' stories. We asked them about their upbringing. How important was education to their parents? Did the fathers re-

---

*From *Overcoming the Odds: Raising Academically Successful African American Males* by Freeman A. Hrabowski III & K. Maton & Geoffrey Grief, copyright © 1998 by Oxford University Press, Inc. Used by permission of Oxford University Press, Inc.

ceive special messages about being Black and about being male? How did the fathers' mothers and fathers work as a team? We also ask how they raised their sons and how they help them to succeed when so many young African American males do not. Through this process, we assume an intergenerational perspective.

We gained a view of life in the African American family that, in some cases, has its roots in the beginning of the twentieth century (as with the father whose quote begins this chapter) and takes form in the United States of the 1940s and 1950s, when opportunities for Blacks were greatly limited. Although all the fathers talk about their families' influence, they also describe how their approach to child-rearing is shaped by current events as they attempt to prepare their sons for a life few could have predicted. The pressures on young African American men today not to achieve and the dangers they face in the streets from drugs, violence, and AIDS are markedly more extreme than what the fathers experienced when they were growing up. Other pressures are the same. African Americans have always felt at risk when traveling through certain areas. The economic situations of many remain tenuous, and a growing global and high-tech marketplace is heightening the need for advanced training in order to find employment. At the same time, the opportunities are also greater than before if a young African American man is succeeding academically. More doors are open.

Weaving the Tapestry

The fathers provide a rich diversity of experience, from the sons of sharecroppers and military personnel to the sons of the unschooled and teachers. As they tell their stories we can see commonality both among these African American families and with families of other races who have been successful. Though they are from many different backgrounds, these fathers all have sons who placed in the top 2 percent of all African American students in terms of math SAT scores and high-school grades (and all the sons have enrolled at the same university). After listening to the fathers' voices for hours, hearing them both individually and in groups, we have discovered several emerging themes that characterize their varied approaches to guiding their sons to academic success. In some cases, these themes have been mentioned by others studying the African American family. Other themes, though, we believe, are new or require renewed emphasis.

It is important to note that not all fathers we interviewed provide descriptions that fit neatly into a theme. People's lives are complex, often unchartable. We have tried to accommodate those stories where possible. What we are left with is a tapestry of three generations of African American life—the fathers we interview here, and their parents and sons.

Unfortunately, it is becoming increasingly rare for fathers in the African American community to live with their children. Recent data reveal that only 33 percent of all Black children under the age of eighteen are living with both parents—a marked decrease over the previous generation when 59 percent were living with both mother and father.[1] In this chapter we hear from fathers who, with few exceptions, are living with their sons' mother. For these fathers even to be in the home throughout a son's childhood, as they are for slightly more than half of the sons we interviewed, has been important in the sons' success. In some predominantly African American neighborhoods, fathers are believed to be present in fewer than 10 percent of the families, though the issue of presence in the home versus presence in the children's lives is not addressed here.[2] A number of young men in the Meyerhoff Program do not have fathers in the home. Nonetheless, they found male role models in other relatives, teachers, friends, or fathers living outside of the home. We wish to make the point that while the presence of two parents in the home, especially when they are working together as a team, can be very beneficial to a young man both academically and emotionally, a two-parent family is not a necessary condition for success. Legion are the people who succeed without two parents in the home.

This chapter is divided into two parts. First, the fathers describe their own upbringing; second, they reveal how they raised (and are raising) their children. In many cases, we find that the acorn does not fall far from the tree—those values a father's parents (or extended family) stressed, he in turn stressed when assuming the responsibility of fatherhood. This also proved to be true in the lives of the mothers we interviewed.

The twenty-nine fathers bring a range of backgrounds to their childrearing. Many come from homes where parents did not attend or graduate from college. In fact, only about one quarter of their parents finished high school, and a few fathers have parents who never finished elementary school. Most had two parents in the home, a statistic that is not surprising for Black families of that era, considering that in 1960 approximately two of every three Black adults were married.[3] By the mid-1990s, that figure has fallen to less than half (43 percent), and one-parent families are almost twice as numerous as two-parent families.[4]

The fathers, with an average age of fifty, are better educated than their parents.[5] One father does not have a high school diploma, and nine others finished high school only and do not have college degrees. Nine possess college degrees only, and the remaining ten have completed at least some graduate training. Overall, they are a much more educated group than the general African American population, among whom one in eight is a college graduate.[6] Three of every four fathers are married, a similar percentage to what would be found among African American fathers in this middle-age group.[7] (In contrast, three of every four African American fathers under the age of thirty have never been married.)

In terms of employment, the fathers' occupations range from construction workers and military and government personnel to salesmen and businessmen. Several are high-level administrators, one is a professor, another a practicing physician, and another is an engineer. This last group, of course, is more highly educated than African American men in general and other men we studied in this book.

We need to emphasize again here that over half the sons interviewed lived a large part of their childhood in single-parent homes. Many of their fathers either were unavailable for interviews or refused our invitations. As a result, we gained a sample of highly involved fathers who were willing to be interviewed and were likely to be more residentially stable than other fathers. At the same time, if part of our purpose was to team about what has worked for these sons, we believe this group of fathers can provide an enormous amount of beneficial information.

Gaining a Perspective on African American Fathers

When looking historically at African American fathers, we see immediately that their role in the family has shifted considerably over time as the result of a combination of factors.[8] Before slavery, while still in Africa, fathers were intimately involved in the community and their children's upbringing, particularly that of their sons.[9] After being brought to America, and during slavery, Black fathers continued to play a significant role unless they were separated from their families by sale to a different landowner. In the years immediately following the abolition of slavery, the vast majority of Black children lived with both parents.[10] But with industrialization of the North and its promise of jobs and a better life than the rural South offered, came great population shifts. Chicago's population, for example, grew sixteen-fold from 1860 to 1900, to almost two million people.[11] With migration, which continued into the twentieth century, came family breakdown as the bonds of the smaller community were erased. E. Franklin Frazier wrote in the 1940s, "If these families have managed to preserve their integrity until they reach the northern city, poverty, ignorance, and color force thetas to seek homes in deteriorated slum areas from which practically all institutional life has disappeared."[12] These stressors tore at the family fabric. With the difficulty many men had in finding work, the balance of economic power in the family slowly shifted over generations to the women, who were able to find domestic and other low-paying work.[13]

Despite the sea change occurring in Black families, gaining an education remained a primary goal. According to Griswold, research undertaken in

Pittsburgh on Black, Italian, and Polish fathers between 1900 and 1960 reveals that Black fathers, more than the others, encouraged personal resourcefulness with an emphasis on education. The other immigrant groups were much more likely to remove children from school to aid the family's economic resources. Black fathers, however, were aware of the limited work options open to them because of race and viewed education as the only road to success.[14]

Continued economic shifts in the 1960s away from unskilled labor, Great Society programs that were often seen as encouraging the single-parent structure, and discrimination further eroded the two-parent family.[15] A correlation has been found between rising unemployment rates among African American men in the late 1960s and a rising rate of single-mother-headed families.[16]

What, then, is the modern-day role of the father in the family? Different theorists have considered this question. According to John McAdoo, a researcher who has focused on African American fathers, the role of provider is usually seen as primary.[17] As provider, the father sustains the growth and well-being of the family economically. Because our society tends to define men by their financial contribution to the family, the father who is underemployed or unemployed is at a significant disadvantage. An African American father often shares this provider role with his wife. If his ability to provide wanes, so might his influence on the family as well as his presence. It is difficult for men to stay involved when they feel they are not providing what they should. If they have little (economic) power in the community, it is difficult to wield influence within the family.

Closely linked with this role is that of decision maker in the family. This rule involves making decisions about discipline, shopping, insurance, medical care, and residence, among other matters. This role diminishes if the provider role fades.

Fathers are also significantly involved in the child-socializer role (though to a less extent than mothers, McAdoo notes). The father functions here as a nurturer and reinforces family values. McAdoo believes that this is often an underrecognized function of the African American father, as the mother's participation has received the most attention. His own observations of middle-class fathers found them to be warm and loving with their children, yet strict. Charles Willie has noted the sharing of roles that occurs between mothers and fathers in the family, with both pitching in to maintain the family in ways that White families, with a more traditional splitting of roles, do not experience.[18]

Finally, the importance of the father's marital role is noted. When fathers nurture their wives, their children benefit.[19] In fact, marriage benefits fathers, too. Married African American males have been found to be happier than unmarried African American males.[20]

These roles—the provider, the decisionmaker, the socializer of children, and the husband—come through loud and clear as we hear the fathers in this chapter describe how they rear their children. We learn here how these family roles relate to education and how family structure and behaviors within the home can positively influence achievement. We must emphasize, however, that these are not simply roles identified by social scientists and educators. Religious and political leaders, community activists, mothers, and fathers themselves are calling upon fathers to become more involved with their children. One cannot pick up the newspaper, turn on the news, or go to a religious or social gathering without hearing about the role of the father in the family. Many fathers are struggling with this role, and they need to learn, or relearn, how to help their children survive and succeed in difficult neighborhoods, school systems, and work environments.

We also note that fathering, like parenting, is a dynamic process, not a static one. Children's developmental needs change as they age. Older children need different types of guidance than do younger children. Children within the same family differ by virtue of their personalities and the way they interact with the parent or parents. A parent may need to be more authoritarian with one child than with the next, based on the nature of the child or the "crowd" with which the child is spending time.[21]

The fathers that we interviewed describe a special relationship with their sons, one in which they are clearly in charge. This unique bond is consistent with at least one theory of healthy family functioning.[22] To appreciate these men, one need only remember how difficult it is to be a parent today, how tenuous the African American father's role has become, and that not all children have the benefit of a (biological) father successfully playing these multiple roles. To learn about these fathers, we first asked them to describe their own upbringing.

When the Fathers Were Young

I grew up on a farm in Mississippi [just after World War II], and my parents were very religious, very hardworking. I think education was the thing that was stressed most. "You want to get away from the farm, you don't want to do this hard work, son, you'd better get an education," they told me. So education was always foremost. The thing I learned was you have to work hard, and you have to be focused. Those are the things I have tried to pass on to my son. You have to know what you want, you have to work for it, nothing is free. Unless you are willing to pay the price, you're not going to make it.

The education system in Mississippi was very poor, so they worked hard to get me into a private school. When they were about to close that school down, the parents worked hard to keep it open. I had to walk four miles to school every day, and my fa-

ther would cut the grass along the field so we could walk there. That's how it was for my parents. Discipline, religion, education.

Now a medical technician, this father completed one year of specialized training after he graduated from college. When he was growing up, he did not feel poor compared to the families around him, although when he moved away, he realized how impoverished he had been as a child. Even more important, he clearly appreciated the values he learned from his parents.

A second father received a similar message. A college graduate who works for the government, he told us:

My parents had a strong sense of discipline and a strong belief in God, so I had to go to church, even if I didn't want to. As long as I was in their house, if I went out Saturday, I had to go to church on Sunday. School was always very important. I had to do homework before I went outside. They did not freely give me things that they didn't think I needed, in part because they didn't have a lot of money even though they weren't poor.[23] I think my parents did a good job of raising me.

When asked about the role that being an African American played in his getting ahead, he responded, "Integration was just coming into being. People would tell us you have to outdo the White guy. Whatever he'd do, you have to do one better. Good is not good enough."

The father whose quote begins the chapter was also poor as a child. Contrary to most of the other fathers we interviewed, his parents emphasized work over education because of its utility in the South's agrarian society. "In my home, you would take a person out of school to work in the fields. That was more important work than getting an education." With a high-school diploma in hand, his commitment to work followed him into his lifelong career in the armed forces.

A fourth father, who now heads an elementary school, had to make it on his own. "I lived in the Baltimore projects. My father died before I started school, and my mother only finished sixth grade. Even though she worked long hours, she always showed an interest in education. My biggest motivation, and she died when I was in junior high school, was that she felt you could be whatever you wanted to be, and education was the key."

The themes in these four fathers' stories are repeated with minor variation through the words of a number of other fathers we interviewed. We see in their upbringing a dedication to work, education where possible, and the church. For many of the families in which these fathers were raised, we also see a strong drive to overcome great hardships, including poverty, limited access to employment and education, and racism. Having a closely knit family existence is another theme that becomes clear, with grandparents and children often pitching in to help each other.

Not all of the fathers are American-born. Here we learn about the role of the village in the rearing of this father.

I grew up in a totally different environment, being raised back home in Africa. The family unit is closer together, and it is not just a mother and father, it is an extended family with aunts, cousins, and even distant relatives. If you did something wrong in a small village, anyone can discipline you. Right from the beginning, you have to do right. School and religion were important, and if you didn't go to church Sunday, they had a list with your name on it in school on Monday.

Several of the fathers spent significant periods of their youth in single-parent families. This father, for example, shared time with each parent after their divorce and, before eventually becoming a school administrator, experienced a few detours along the way.

Both my parents completed high school. They separated when I was young, but I was lucky in that I spent time with both of them. My mother was a housewife and raised me, my five brothers and sisters, and her own brother and sister, who were only a few years older than me. I dropped out of high school, and that brought a lesson home that you have to complete your education. My father was a truck driver and then a foreman. I would travel with him, and we'd see all kinds of traits in people, and he'd ask me, "Do you want to do that?" And I'd say, "No." He'd say, "You've got to get an education." I was working when I was fourteen as a laborer, and as I got older I was doing the billing. I realized that to get a good job, I'd have to have an education, especially being a Black man in the 1950s.

Another father's experience exemplifies the nature of parental teamwork, of parents pulling together and working hard for the benefit of the children. He also showed what a positive influence a father can be regardless of educational level.

My father was a truck driver and my mother a midwife. He lost his leg in 1940 and was a huge role model for his perseverance to carry on as he did. My mother supported him along the way. My mother only made the fifth grade and my father the eighth, so their push was to have us graduate, which we all did. That was a great achievement for them.

My father was a strict disciplinarian, especially for the boys. We were like Cinderellas growing up—we had to be in by midnight. He made sure we were home safe. He was from Jamaica, a proud man who wanted to keep his sons and daughters intact. I think that had a great influence on how I raised my children!

We should caution that not every father necessarily heard what his parents were telling him about the importance of education. At least one father who has a high-school education has regrets about his misspent youth.

I wish I had listened better to my parents when they were talking to me because it took me a while to understand the impact of education and being able to acquire the things you want in life. You understand that people who are well educated rim the company. I wish I had done more.

We can see from these fathers that a premium was placed on certain values—hard work, discipline, and education. Often, with a foundation of religion and family togetherness, these tenets were the cornerstones of their early experiences.

GENDER ROLES

We asked the fathers about the role that gender played in their upbringing. We were interested in the gender issue because of the particularly precarious position of Black males in the United States today. Current research on the Black family indicates that, out of economic necessity, there is a great sharing of roles in the family unit. We wondered if this was the case and if boys in the home were treated differently than were girls.

Without exception, it seems that these fathers carne from families in which the father was, in the words of one of the fathers we interviewed, the "enforcer," while the mother was the more nurturing, hands-on parent. If the father was not a presence in the home, either the mother fulfilled both roles or relatives were actively involved. From the next two fathers we hear about the roles of fathers.

On the farm, there was a strict division of labor. The mother was in charge of the household—cooking, milking cows, and things like that. The dad saw to the finances and served as sort of the disciplinarian. If my mother said to do something, behind it was that if you did not do it, your father would take care of you.

My father played the role as the person who basically set the standard, the foundation. My mother was the implementer, or the nurturer. Whatever values existed in the family centered around the expectations of my father. The way we went about implementing that was more or less orchestrated by my mother. Obviously she was the one who had the contact with us. My father, being a man of the world and a Black male, understood the importance of being the very best that you could be. He understood the significance of being able to work against the odds.

Even when a mother was described as being a jack-of-all-trades (as many were), the father still played a significant role.

I think my mother was probably the dominant one. She was a very multifaceted person and did a lot of things in the community. She'd take care of other kids, and our house would be a meeting place for a lot of the people in the neighborhood whenever different things would arise. My father was a disciplinarian also. When he came home, my mother would tell him that one of the children did not do something, and he would be, in my term, the enforcer. As I look back on it, they were a good combination—the good-guy-bad-guy team.

Sisters and Brothers

If sisters were present in the homes when these fathers were growing up, there appears to have been a diversity of approaches. Some fathers describe differential treatment, while others say everyone was treated equally. The messages given about how members of the opposite sex should be treated also varied, as these next examples show.

I know my father treated my sisters differently. He never spanked them. They could blow the roof off the house, but he wouldn't put a hand on them. It was a whole new story when it came to my brothers and me. As far as respecting them and pushing them the same way, he pushed us all in school. I think his treatment is related to the notion of a proud heritage where the sons were to be dominant in all relationships in the family, and we were to go on to do great things. Daughters were to go on to marry great men.

My father made it clear he was the authoritarian in the family and that the man ran the household. But my brothers and I have the utmost respect for women. I think we got that from my mother even though I had thought until now that my father's influence and his being domineering would have the effect of the male children growing up to be disrespectful of their spouses. In fact, it's the opposite—the male children are unusually respectful.

My family was raised to respect women. My sisters were tomboyish, and that was accepted. If they wanted to try something out that was not considered female, they were encouraged. I think that has given me more respect for women. But if the sisters or the brothers did something wrong, you got spanked.

The same discipline was for both boys and girls, but there was a higher expectation for boys in terms of education because it was felt they were going to be the family leaders. Even though the girls were in school, my parents did not expect as much from them.

Here we observe that within these traditional families, the males received the message that the mother's role is important and commands respect. In this way, the woman's role is upheld. At the same time, some sisters were protected while others, as in the last example, were not encouraged to get an education. Rather, through motherhood they would find their niche.

These fathers' stories offer a number of insights into what influenced them to become the kinds of fathers they were with their academically successful sons. Seven primary messages emerge. Six components of parenting are reflected here and are shown in parentheses:

1. Families placed the highest value on education and succeeding academically. Almost all of the parents of these fathers stressed the importance of getting an education and doing well in school. The message given was that in order to get ahead and avoid the poverty that so many experienced, one had to have an education. Mothers, in particular, checked over homework and were involved in school-related activities, such as the PTA. A few fathers mentioned being primed for the first grade with the preschool study of reading and math. (This is the strategy of continually setting high expectations.)

2. Fathers were raised by parents who worked hard. Regardless of the level of the parents' education and the type of work they were performing, being vigorously engaged in work was the standard. Fathers were specifically encouraged to do their best and received the message that if they

could not succeed academically, they should develop a skill and work hard at that. (These are the strategies of strong limit setting and consequences, and continually setting high expectations.)

3. The fathers were raised strictly. Discipline was doled out to sons who stepped out of line and also frequently to daughters. The fathers appeared to have a clear sense of right and wrong, taught to them by their parents and, often, by the extended family. This was manifested by having strict rules about dinner, bedtime, household behavior, and schoolwork. (This is the strategy of strong limit setting.)

4. Religion was emphasized. Many of the fathers describe church attendance as a family requirement and religion as a theme in family life. This underpinned their strict upbringing. (The strategy of making effective use of available community resources is captured here.)

5. The fathers' parents, regardless of how many children were in the family, were actively involved in their children's lives. The fathers sensed that they were individuals, even in large families. One manifestation of this was that the fathers' friends were closely scrutinized. Contact with friends who had inappropriate values was discouraged, while friendships with others involved in positive activities were praised. (This is the strategy of child-focused love.)

6. Families usually had a traditional division of roles. Fathers in the families tended to be the disciplinarians, and mothers were the nurturers. Fathers set the tone, while mothers implemented family policy. The fathers were strong and often silent, and their presence was felt when they were in the home.

Related to this is the sense that parents worked together as a team. This bred in many of the men we interviewed a keen respect for women. (This is the strategy of emphasizing appropriate positive identity.)

7. Families encouraged overcoming adversity. Whether facing poverty or racism, they emphasized trying to get ahead. Education was viewed as one way to try to reach a level playing field, a theme that Blacks have historically honored. The message, as is seen more clearly in the stories that follow, was that African Americans have to work harder to get ahead because they are Black.

The parents' upbringing had a profound influence on how they chose to raise their sons. To digress slightly, we now ask what the message is for today's parent who was not raised so well, who did not receive the attention or messages about the value of education or getting ahead. As will be discussed at the end of this chapter and in the conclusion of the book, one can overcome the obstacles of the past. We believe upbringing sets the course (and the more impoverished the past, the more harshly the course is set), but the course can be changed. Past oversights, neglect, or mistakes can be undone. A parent raising a child today, who himself received inadequate parenting, may start with a deficit, but the deficit need not remain a permanent impediment. Rather, it provides one more challenge for the parent. The parent who was inadequately raised need not always repeat the mistakes of his parents. Parental education, new role models, and significant relationships can help to steer the parent anew.

Having gained an understanding of the fathers' family backgrounds, we can now turn to their own child-rearing approaches. In many instances we see consistent themes passed on from one generation to the next, a continuation of the tapestry.

How Fathers Raise Their Sons: The Weaving Continues

The fathers provide a clear portrait of hands-on child-rearing. For example, seven of eight fathers monitored, to at least some degree, the amount of time their sons spent studying in high school.[24] They monitored their sons' studying during the elementary- and middle-school years to an even greater degree. Throughout their sons' twelve years of school prior to college, all the fathers encouraged them to achieve academically and to participate in extracurricular activities.

Other aspects of their sons' lives were also followed closely. Two thirds of the fathers kept tabs on the amount of time their sons spent with their friends in high school, about the same as when they were in middle school. Two thirds kept a close watch on television viewing and video game playing throughout the school years.

Perhaps most interesting is the fathers' perception of themselves compared with other parents in the neighborhood. Seven of eight fathers believed they had been stricter than other parents, and five of six thought they monitored their sons' homework more closely than other parents.

The fathers were also asked to indicate their level of concern about their sons. We learned they had little concern about their sons' finding a job after graduation or succeeding in graduate school. Given their sons' record of success so far, it is not surprising they would have such confidence. One third, though, had at least some trepidation that their sons would associate with the "wrong crowd." The very real distractions that parents fear their children will find in high school clearly continue to haunt some fathers when their sons enter college. Most significant, almost two thirds indicated they had at least some worry that their sons would not be treated fairly at a job because of race.

The fathers' responses show the enormous investment they have made for years in their sons' lives. They also show that the fathers see themselves as exceptional within their own community. Their hopes, though, are tempered by their awareness that the job market may not be a friendly environment. How do these fathers prepare their sons for this? We will return to this question, but the answer, we believe, is found in the fathers' own upbringing.

We also wanted to know how the fathers helped their sons succeed academically, how early the fathers realized their sons were academically gifted, and what problems they encountered in terms of educating and raising an African American male. We immediately begin to see common threads repeated from one story to the next. We also see that the fathers carried with them the lessons learned from their parents. Sometimes the mother was the leader; sometimes it was the father; and often the parents worked as a team to guide their sons in their endeavors.

SUCCEEDING ACADEMICALLY

We know that the fathers, almost to a man, were involved with their sons. But what was the nature of the involvement? What do the fathers say worked? What was the atmosphere in the home and the view of education?

Regardless of the father's educational level, each contributed significantly to his son's development. For example, a father whose formal education stopped with high school told us:

I gave my son my time. I like the term "quality time." After a certain point I could no longer help him with his studies, as it was beyond my capability, but I always made sure he knew I was there if he needed me.

Another father followed the advice of his wife rather than his own early experiences.

My wife is an educator and insisted on putting the children in school as early as possible. I was resistant because I didn't start that young. But she won out, and it turned out well. He was in the wrong school at one point, and we put him in a private one where there was a lot of structure. We explained, just as we explained our jobs to them, that their jobs were to be good students. The teacher's job is to help you learn and you should ask questions if you don't know the answer. There were rewards for achievement, like going to McDonald's. Because he was not in school with kids in the neighborhood, we got him enrolled in community sports. We got involved in the school, too.

Communication is often mentioned as the key.

Maybe the most important thing is just talking to my sons, right from the beginning. Let them know that they have to achieve something. Set sights high from the beginning. Put them in school early. Maybe the best thing I did for them was to put into their head they have to be good academically.

Challenging their sons intellectually, advocating for them within the educational system, being supportive, and providing stability at home were other themes mentioned by fathers.

We insisted he be in the most challenging courses. In our county, they have a gifted and talented program, and there were very few African Americans and other minori-

ties in it. I was one who would question why there weren't more Black students, and I got the usual: "We couldn't find enough who were qualified." I knew my son could do the work, and I insisted they put him in. We always insisted on advanced placement and told the teachers to get back to us if there was a problem, and we'd make sure he gets the help he needs. If things got tough, we would be there to say "This is going to help you in college, and to solve problems and face challenges."

We tried to allow our boys to grow in a natural way, not be overbearing, but be vigilant for those critical moments when they needed support. My son had three or four junctures in his life when he could have given up. In every stage we were there. I remember personally insisting that he not quit. It's a thin line between success and failure. We made the critical decisions when he was indecisive in terms of the courses he would take. Whenever he thought a course might be too tough, we were there to balance the focus and to get him in the frame of reference that he could do it, and we wanted him to stick with it. We were always there saying, "you can't afford to give up on yourself." I've always been there on the sidelines. We can't run our children's lives, but we can certainly be there to reinforce the values.

When he was young we tried to set some goals—we told him he was going to go to college, that he was going to get an education. I stressed to him to pick courses that would help him get into college. If you take the challenging courses, you will be better prepared for college. I also always tried to give him respect as a young man and that trying your best is all I can ask.

We paid close attention to what they were doing. They did not go out to play until their work was done. We had a set time for bed and did not bend very much on that unless there was a special on TV or something. We played a big role in encouraging them to do well in school and to help them when they needed help. He was very interested in sports, and we went to sports activities but stressed academics. We didn't care if he dribbled the ball. Our goals for him were to get an education first.

Not all fathers took credit or felt they personally had been instrumental in the success of their sons. In one remarried family situation, for example, the stepfather backed away and let the mother take charge because of interpersonal conflict:

I have known my stepson since he was five, and we have not had the best of relationships, to be honest. We only tangle with each other. When I married his mother, he probably felt the need to be loyal to his [biological] father. That never got resolved in our relationship. It might have been my fault for not trying harder. So as it relates to education, my wife has been the prime mover. I have accused her of being a stage-door mom. He has that drive from her to produce the first college graduate in her family.

Recognizing Sons' Talent: Fathers and Schools

The fathers recognized their sons' academic abilities at various times. Some recognized abilities immediately when the children were very young. Others thought their sons had only a modest amount of talent until they reached their high-school years.

Recognizing talent was a central issue because it affected the advocacy role that parents played. (Not all the sons described here are naturally gifted. All are high-achieving, but some are academically more gifted than others, and some worked harder than others.) Many fathers believed, regardless of their sons' talent, that they were being underestimated by the educational system. This often spurred them to work (and, in some cases, fight) with the school to provide a challenging educational environment for their sons. The fathers saw racism as the reason many of the schools did not initially place their children in gifted and talented programs. Once parents fought for and got their children enrolled, the boys were usually able to maintain their position in class. Other parents reacted to an unresponsive school system by removing their children and placing them in other schools, sometimes public and other times private (often parochial schools).

First, five fathers describe their realizations about their sons' talent, and then we hear from other fathers who report less impressive academic beginnings.

He participated in science fairs in middle school, and he had an engineering project and won first place for his school and for the county in eighth, ninth, and tenth grades. For one of his projects, I took him over to a friend's house who was an engineer, and they were just talking, and I had no idea what they were talking about. So that was something of an indication to me about his talent.

Early on I used to take him to work. In order to keep him interested, I put him in front of a computer, and he was very good at that. Then his high-school grades starting coming in and were very high.

Our son was always a show-off. Even as a toddler, he liked to get praise for knowing how to spell. I think we realized early on that he was academically inclined. It seemed he didn't have any trouble learning that type of thing. He really got into science in the ninth grade and it has been his main focus ever since.

The first thing that got my attention were the SAT scores. I thought he was just a typical high-school student with As and Bs before that.

I think he picked up mathematical concepts very quickly. But sometimes the teachers just put the kids in lower classes, classified them, and they never get out. He was in the lower class, and he was never going to do well, so I moved him to a private school. In high school he got on the honor roll. But if you belong to a certain class or group of skin, they just bring you down, they don't expect you to do well.

Despite the sons' success in high school, it was not always smooth sailing. Many had periods in their lives when they had academic problems, and their parents became involved, as indicated in the following three examples.

We moved a lot, and when he moved back into the second grade, he experienced some problems. He was always good in math and always asked people to give him math problems. But at one point, his teacher graded him down to a C because he wasn't motivated. So we talked with him about his attitude, and that helped his motivation.

Somewhere in the middle grades, his marks started to fall. We asked him if he was trying, and he would say he was, but I felt he wasn't. My wife would scold him. We threatened to hold him out of activities he enjoyed, and that helped straighten him out.

My son only had problems two times. In the eighth grade he really got into video games. It was new to us at the time and we didn't realize how addictive it was. He was hitting it in the afternoon when he got home from school. We talked about it, and he was really giving me lip about how he was going to hide them from me so I couldn't take them away. I actually cut the plug off the power cord because I knew at that point he didn't know how to wire the plug. That got his attention. I told him when he got his grades back up, we'd give it back to him but monitor it like we do TV. I told him he was not going to end up fouling up his academic career. That worked.

In the ninth grade there was a minor dip with moving to a new school and he realized on his own that he was going to have to become more serious.

Sometimes a teacher was the prime influence in the son's getting on track emotionally and academically.

He had problems at various times at his schools, mostly behavioral, but also with his grades. He ran into a prejudicial situation at one school because he was Black, and he fell behind. When he got to middle school he recovered. He worked hard and finally got into the honor society. A Black teacher came up to us and said, pointing to a White teacher, "That man is responsible for your son getting into the honor society." They had wanted to keep him out because of his behavior, but that particular teacher said that behavior didn't have anything to do with it, it is scholastics. And my son, incidentally, couldn't stand this man. I credit that excellent teacher for being significant and taking my son over the barrier.

From listening to these fathers, we found ten specific education-related actions that were mentioned by at least one of every five fathers. Included are both general and specific actions, and the strategies most frequently cited are listed first: (1) talking to teachers if there was a problem with their sons' school situation; (2) paying close attention to schoolwork; (3) teaching their children at home to prepare them for school at an early age, and providing academic challenges at home; (4) making sure their sons were placed in the proper classes and advocating for them if they were placed below their ability; (5) encouraging extracurricular activities; (6) helping with homework; (7) getting to know their sons' teachers by being a presence in the school; (8) setting high standards and encouraging their sons to do the best they could in school; (9) setting limits on their behavior and not allowing playtime until after homework was completed; and (10) moving their sons to different schools when they felt the public school system or a particular school had failed them.

GENERAL CHILD-REARING ISSUES:
THE OTHER SIDE OF THE TAPESTRY

While the primary focus here is on academics, all parents are concerned also about other aspects of their children's lives. This is what makes the tapestry of life so rich. If all that was needed for children to be academically successful was for parents to drill them on math tables and spelling, that could be accomplished relatively easily. But the fabric of the family and how that fabric is woven are also crucial factors. To learn about child-rearing challenges and how they were overcome, we asked the following questions: What issues do parents face raising a Black male? For what types of behavior were they most apt to discipline their child, and what serious discipline problems have they faced? How did they talk with their sons about sex and drugs? Were there family rituals that were followed at home?

Race and Being Male

This was one area where the fathers seemed to hold particularly strong feelings. Preparing their children to deal with the world is always on their minds and provides the most difficult challenge of all given the "at risk" state of African American males. One consistent message they give their sons is to always be on guard for mistreatment. We have chosen to include a variety of quotes here because we believe this is such an important issue for these fathers and sons.

I think this is a major problem because from the beginning, society thinks the Black male should achieve less. They put my child in a lower class, and then they have some idea that since you are Black all you can do is run or do sports. This is nonsense. It has come to the point, though, that even some Black kids have low self-esteem, and in some schools if the Black child is doing well, the other Black children make fun of him. These are all problems we have to deal with in the Black community. Maybe we have to organize the Black children who excel to go into the schools very early and talk to the children.

My son went to Colorado last summer to do a science project and one of the ladies asked him what he was doing there. He said he was in college, and the next thing she asks is if he plays basketball because he's tall.

I have concerns [about raising an African American male]. I've had experiences I would hope my children wouldn't have. I've made sure I've told them about them. I still tell them, "You can't be as good as, you have to be better than." I try to prepare them to keep a strong faith in God. I also taught them that I work in situations where in some cases I'm the only person from my office at many conferences I go to and there are few African Americans. So I have to say a little prayer before going to a meeting to give me strength. We've taught them there are going to be challenges in life and to put their faith in God.

I think it is always something that's in one corner of my brain, and I think it is the seed that is constantly germinating in terms of this notion of family values and learning to stick with a task against the odds. When my son was small, he was the only Black in the classroom, and he was fine as long as he was quiet and behaved. We ended up transferring him because there were subtle things that have impacted on Black males. Since integration, if there is a Black who is highly skilled, confident, and intelligent, there is some comment made to try and discredit his competence to make it seem it is not as significant as a European.

As far as the job market and getting along in the world's multicultural society, there's a little fear in every one of us I guess. Especially the thing that happened in South Carolina. [This is a reference to Susan Smith, a White mother, who drowned her young children in her car and initially fueled racial tensions by saying a Black man had carjacked them.] Her description could fit any Black male. If there were any Black males walking down the street, they would get arrested. Our county, until ten years ago, was pretty bad. I was in New York, and a policeman walked alongside a young Black guy, put a gun to his head, and blew his head off. And he gave no reason except that the guy he killed had recurring seizures.

I tell my sons, "Don't ever forget you're an African American, regardless of how you're accepted. If the alarm goes out that a Black person committed a crime, it could fit you. You're going to be a suspect."

There's a perception among Whites that Blacks get everything and among Blacks that Blacks don't have anything. Neither is correct. I have seen the perception talked about earlier about Black kids being ashamed of their accomplishments. Overall, I would say the Black male is at a disadvantage. We have to get more Black people into college to change this trend.

Race did play a role. I've read a lot about Egyptology and going back to the history of African Americans, and I know it's important to instill those qualities in African American boys. They have to be aware of their culture and to know history in order to achieve. A lot of Black males don't know how rich a history of math and science we come from and how others have piggybacked on us. That's important for them to know, especially with all the negative things that are happening on the streets now. They could look at another person that looks like them and see more to appreciate in them other than this self-hate.

It was very important for us that our son not have any confusion about who he is because he is biracial.[25] *Before we got married we knew that because of society, our child would be raised believing he's Black. So, from the start, we raised him as a Black male. That presented a challenge for me because I'm White, so I had to learn from my father- and brother-in-law or from what I read. I always made it clear that he can be proud of what he is. He's a Black male who happens to have a White father. I encouraged him that being proud of the Black culture was no insult to me as a White father. When he has cared to, he has talked to other Black relatives. Because he was confident in his identity, he never had any problem in school.*

Because both my wife and I grew up in an environment that was more polarized than now, we have always been cautious about racial issues and the potential for discrimination. We have instilled in our children the need for being careful and aware that this is still the case, and that they have to be prepared to deal with that aspect of life. Our son has a lot of friends from different backgrounds, and we refer to him as an international person.

What we have to worry about, though, is educating him that a nice environment in any one school or neighborhood is not the world. There's still discrimination in the workplace based on race or religion and just driving around the country. When we go down south to visit relatives we make a point of saying, "You're a Black male. You don't want to get off on every dirt road in the back country of Georgia or Alabama or Mississippi, especially if it's a place where there are Klan lodges identified with their Aryan Nations." You have to stop and think about this stuff.

My biggest concerns are regarding drugs and AIDS. I think this society is really racist, but that's a reality that he has to deal with. We taught him that he's an individual, he is not a group, and he has to have self-esteem and self-respect to make others see hire as an individual. The concept that he is an endangered species is a reality, and it is because of crack and AIDS. When I was a teenager it was heroin and liquor. They were the drugs of choice. I went away to college with ten friends from the neighborhood. Two of us graduated, and the rest are either dead or in jail. So I try to stress to him to associate with whom he wants, but if there is something he doesn't want to do, he doesn't have to.

What comes through in these fathers' messages to their sons is that society will treat them differently because of their race, but that they cannot let that fact keep them down. The fathers advise their sons to try harder, to take pride in themselves, and to be careful.

Another aspect of child-rearing needs mentioning here—the role of a male with a son. To varying degrees, all of the fathers endorsed the importance of fatherhood and of having a male involved with sons. This issue is at the forefront of current considerations about the importance of the father's role in families, whether fathers are absent or present. The involvement of the father in the two-parent and single-parent family is a significant factor in shaping work- and family-related policy, and important questions arise: How much time should a father be allowed to take off from work for child-care responsibilities? How should a single father who visits his child be kept involved in child-rearing decisions?

The next father speaks directly to this issue, arguing a point that many other fathers have made. His words are echoed in one of the in-depth case studies that conclude this chapter. (We see it in the next chapter, too, when mothers talk about letting a father be the most involved parent when he is available.) When he was asked about male role models for sons being raised alone by mothers, he said,

I think it is important, either through a minister, a coach, or a brother, to find some male who could be part of these men's lives if possible, someone who will be there consistently. There are certain things that males can do with boys. Mothers raise daughters and love sons, and they need to discipline them. Some mothers dote too much on their sons.

Limit-Setting: How Did Fathers Discipline?

The common point of agreement among the fathers is the necessity to prepare their sons for the "real world." Yet this is difficult for all parents of adolescents. To what extent should parents provide a cocoon rather than encourage their sons to be autonomous? What messages should parents give that will sufficiently warn their children about the dangers that exist, without causing them to be tempted by those dangers? For the most part, according to the fathers, the sons did not pose serious disciplinary problems (a less rosy picture emerges from the interviews with the sons). Most fathers emphasized talking to their children rather than resorting to physical punishment. Fathers attempted to set clear rules and would not tolerate behavior that would reflect badly on the family.

In these first two examples, we see the fathers' wariness about involvement in the drug culture and hanging out with the "wrong crowd." In each example the father dealt with it directly.

One incident I will forever cherish because I know I did the right thing and kept him on course. A friend of his, a girl, had a boyfriend who always had a lot of money. He had this nice coat, and my son didn't have a coat. This guy was trying to impress my son and told him he could have a coat just like it. That's how you get sucked into the drug culture. I saw my son in it, and I asked him where it came from. I knew he didn't have the money for it. So he told me he got it from this friend, and when I asked him whose it was he said, "It's mine." I told him to give the coat back.

As men, we all face personal dangers and deal with them. But when you see the potential danger for your child, it becomes indescribable, I was in a state of panic and fear. That's why I insisted he give the coat back. I understood enough about the culture in terms of how they prey on innocent, naive, unsuspecting youngsters and suck them in. Once my son began to see the bigger picture, he understood exactly why I made the decision.

I got a call from the teacher one day saying, "You'd better watch your son. He's hanging with the wrong people and fooling around." I told the teacher I appreciated that, because it went beyond the call of duty. I went up to the school and told my son if he wanted to be a clown to do it right then and there in front of the class. I really didn't know what I was doing. I was trying to figure it out at the time.

Some fathers placed a high premium on telling the truth as a foundation for building trust and being respected, important values in these families.

I was most apt to discipline him for lying and being disrespectful. If he lied to me, it really bothered me, and I tried to teach him to come to me even if he had done something wrong.

I'm very stern, but at some point, I guess when they were around ten, I didn't spank the children anymore and would talk to them instead. If something was broken and all three of them said they didn't do it, I would let them all go but tell them that if I found out who did it, he would get a double spanking for lying. I will not tolerate a liar. We also sent them to their room as punishment. I think punishment is the key to a lot of the bad things that happen today. I was raised that way, and all my brothers and sisters and I are doing well today.

I know families who lived in the same town as us—half of them are dead and the other half are in jail. And yet my family is not. There has to be some reason for that.

Punishments were swiftly delivered and were often fairly severe.

I can remember one incident when my son was in middle school. He was responsible for doing his homework when he got home, and then he could go out and play. One time he went out to play without doing his homework. I went out and found him, and his mother and I decided that for the rest of the school year he couldn't go out and play during the week. He had to wait until the weekend. That had a profound effect on him. I explained I had a job I had to go to, and he had to do his work. "Take care of business and then BS" was our saying.

From an early age, we decided if there was anything that needed discipline, it was administered immediately. If you're out somewhere, even church, and you do something wrong, you got it. I recall giving the belt to my son on only one occasion. He was five or six and he lied. That was not going to be tolerated. I never had to do it again. If they stayed out longer than they should have, they were given a stern lecture.

Talking About Sex and Drugs

These fathers do not believe in protecting children by being evasive or avoiding troublesome issues (though they do encourage avoidance of certain situations). Rather, they tend to explain and discuss sensitive questions at length as accurately as possible to prepare the sons. Using verbal persuasion is characteristic of well-educated parents.

You have an ongoing conversation with your children about these things. My wife taught at the same high school that my son attended. She knew about students who were rumored to be dealing drugs, so she would ask my son about it. That helped us stay in tune with what was happening and to talk about it.

I always tried to be as realistic as possible. I told him the truth as I knew it. Sex or crime or bad influences out there—I told him of some of my experiences and some of the people in the family and friends and some of the errors they made. When someone was in the news for something he did, I pointed out to him that he wouldn't be in trouble if he had avoided the situation. If you get into a situation you shouldn't be in, get away. Leave the environment. We always tried to be as real with him as we could be.

We try to keep constant communication open. Drugs or crime were never problems per se. We had a general philosophy, a religious upbringing, and he went to school where there were classes on sexuality. We were always vigilant because we heard that parents were the last ones to know.

As soon as they asked questions about sex when they were little, we used the right words for all the body parts. We tried to answer questions as simply as we could. On the drug thing, I made myself available to my kid as an excuse. If he gets to a party where they are doing drugs, I gave him the freedom to say, even if it's not true, "My dad's an ornery SOB, and he'll kill me if he knows what's going on, and I have to get out of here." Also, make a contract with your kid that you'll come and get him at any time, no questions asked, if they want to get out of a situation.

We taught our children everything about sex, and one time a neighbor told me my seven-year-old daughter was fresh because she knew where babies came from, and I said, "What's wrong with that?" We try and control our language and don't swear in front of them and don't expect them to swear either. One time they were singing a song, a jingle, "Bang-bang, you're dead, bullets in the head." I told them they didn't talk about things like that. I took the tape and wrecked it and told them to listen to something else.

Fighting

Instruction concerning fighting has traditionally been a father-son rite of passage. Most fathers had the philosophy that their sons should avoid fighting. At the same time, they inculcated in their sons the feeling that they had to be prepared to fight as a way to defend themselves and avoid further harassment. Variations in approach occurred by neighborhood, with fathers raising sons in tougher neighborhoods being more likely to teach them how physically to handle such difficult encounters. Perhaps uniquely for fathers and sons, as is the explicit situation with the first two fathers, their own experiences with fighting affect their advice.

My father instilled in us a sense of survival. I was taught if you see something brewing to walk away. I think that rubbed off on my son. He's big and he didn't get into fights because people don't pick on him.

My son didn't face growing up in his neighborhood like I did. I had to fight the first day I moved in when I was young. My son got pushed one day in the chest and came home mad. He didn't fight, I think, because I didn't teach him how to. It just didn't occur to me that he's going to be intimidated. He's mad at me because I didn't teach him. I taught him if you see anything like gunplay or drugs, walk away.

He was worried when he went to a tough high school and did not know anyone. But we wanted him there because of the gifted program, and we thought it would be good training about what the world is about. He loved it from the beginning, and I think that helped him learn there's an element in school that likes to fight and another that does not.

I moved a lot because of the military. Whenever my son would be new to a neighborhood, they'd try him. There were a lot of times I had to teach him to defend himself. If you're going to go out there and play, you have to deal with the fellows out there. If someone hits you, you hit him back. He did learn to protect himself, but he also learned as he got older that you can prevent a lot by evaluating the situation.

I taught him how to fight because he was getting in little scrapes. You have to stand up for yourself. If you're a weakling, they'll pick on you. In middle school, a couple of guys began picking on him. It was a racial thing, and he settled them down but I had to bail him out of the principal's office. We taught him to avoid fights, but there's a time, especially if you are male, that you're going to face a bad situation, and you've got to decide. We taught him it is better to stand up and get knocked down than to crawl away.

It is difficult to conclude that one approach is right or wrong when it comes to helping a son cope with self-protection as a rite of passage. We do know that if children fight in school, the result is often punishment and expulsion. African American males are often caught between the two worlds of having to act a certain way in one environment and a different way in another. For example, a self-protective. Posture assumed in the neighborhood may cause anxiety among authorities in a school environment. It is important that parents be able to evaluate situations with their sons in such a way that they can offer advice about how to cope with these contradictory contexts.

Family Rituals

Finally, we looked at the family unit as a protective factor. Research on successful family functioning shows that families that spend time together at holidays, for example, tend to cope better with life's ups and downs.[26] Family interactions that are rewarding can build a sense of comfort and stability. Rituals, such as going on vacation together, attending church together, reading together, and eating meals together, help to build cohesion and a nurturing environment. They provide a vehicle for talking about daily life and conveying family values. They also provide a buffer against stress. We asked these fathers about rituals in their families that may have helped to build this sense of comfort, stability, and ability to cope.

We felt the way to help academically was to have a stable family life. We both grew up in families where the family ate breakfast and dinner together most days. It was a regular routine, and we did the same thing with ours. There was always the emphasis on going to bed and getting your rest.

My wife and I put into perspective that we're a family now. It became a yearly thing that the kids would see their grandparents during holidays, especially Christmas. We didn't force it, like Ozzie and Harriet, when it came to sitting around the table, but we are together on holidays.

When we became a middle-class family, we could afford to do things outside of the community, so we would take them on business trips, try to make those a family affair. Though the children are independent now, I can guarantee you they will be there on Christmas.

I think it's important for families to do things together. Maybe I have a tendency to put too much emphasis on it because my family never did anything together. Every opportunity now, because we don't have much time together, I'll have food on the table if I know they are coming home, so I know they'll eat.

We did go to all of the children's dancing classes and meets when they were young. My wife came from a family where she always had dinner with her parents, and without making a big deal of it, we have tried to do the same thing.

We cannot overemphasize this sense of togetherness. The bond that is formed serves to strengthen whatever messages the fathers convey. As the family tapestry is completed, the traditions that are so fundamental to Black families are continued from one generation to the next.

AN IN-DEPTH LOOK AT TWO FATHERS

Two case studies provide further understanding of these fathers' experiences. The first is a single parent who raised his son alone during much of his son's formative years. We chose him as one example because, while great attention has been placed on Black females as single parents, we rarely think about Black males in this role. In fact, only 5 percent of Black children in the United States being raised by a single parent are currently living with their father.[27]

A Clear Case of Identity: A Single Father

For two years, the son of our first father was the object of an intense custody battle and lived with his mother. Being involved in a custody dispute could have possibly had a profoundly negative impact on the son, but that does not seem to be the case. The father, who has earned a master's degree, is an administrator in a large organization. A highly religious man, his faith offered clear guidelines for family values.

My father was an extreme disciplinarian and there was little affection shown. There were many times when my father would take me along on trips. I used to hate them, but it was a time he could dream. He would show me other people's homes and talk about the things he wanted for my mother. He told me about the mistakes he had made when he was young. Even though I hated the trips, I find myself doing the same thing now with my son. I've shared what my dreams are, and I'm sure he hates them as well. [He laughs.] Many of the things my father did not accomplish, I have been able to do.

In terms of education, it did not happen much in my family. My parents never talked about it. I'm not sure my mother graduated from high school, and I didn't know my father went to college until I finished graduate school. I had to pay for my own college education even though he had promised me when I was in the first grade he would pay.

Two important messages came through when I was young—we had to attend school, which was more important than what grades we received. Second, don't accept labels. I used to fight a lot in junior high school, so the school sent me to a psychologist. I was in an integrated school, and the staff was all White. They did some testing and determined I was mildly retarded. In high school I got into more fights, and they again sent me for an evaluation, this time right after one of the fights, and I didn't answer any of the questions. And again I was labeled retarded. They wanted to transfer me out of the school. My father was going to get a gun and go up there and clean out the school when he heard that, but after some coaching from my mother, he went up there and used some curse words and insisted I stay in school. That was one of the few times he was ever in the school. Then he told me I better get my grades up.

So I became the "mildly retarded" person who became student government president of a White school, the first one in history. I graduated with honors. Then I graduated with honors from college. I just never accepted their labels. There were clearly cultural issues related to all their test findings.

My father was always supportive of my mother. I remember him saying to us, "I know there's a God because he made your mother." He also said that Black women were the most beautiful women in the world.

Raising His Son

Unlike many of the families here [in the Meyerhoff Program], I was a teenage parent, and I was single and raised my son alone. I didn't have much, so I used to play games with him with a deck of cards. Even before the first grade, we'd match colors and play memory games. He was not allowed to accept a gift unless it had an educational nature to it. He was never allowed to have a toy gun. I had him memorize little prayers like "My mind is the most important thing I have," and I think that helped him. I always spent a lot of time with him. I took him to my meetings at work and in the community.

I always talked to every one of his teachers and made him understand that I knew them and the principal. If he got a low grade, I would ask him for an explanation and then write a letter to the school asking for their version, because sometimes my son could be a little creative with his reasons. I wanted him to know that he was responsible for everything he said. Even now, in college, when he gets his report card, I want an explanation for everything on it.

We never had any behavioral problems with him. His problems always had to do with external factors interfering with his grades.

There was a time in his life, though, when his mother and I were living apart, and she wanted him with her. There was a custody battle, and she won only because she was a woman. But after living with her for a while, they had relocated out of the country, he wanted to come back and live with me.

One particular hard time I had with him was in his junior year, when we were going over his report card like we always did, and he blew up. He said, "Look, Dad, get off of it! Leave me alone. I just want to be like everyone else." That was the first time I experienced that he was not going along with me. I stood back and thought a minute and told him, "But you're not average. You were never average and never will be. Even if you try to be average, you won't be." And he said he just wanted to be like so and so and named some of his friends. And I said to him, "You know those people whose pictures are on your walls? Michael Jordan and those musicians? Those people are not average. They tell you they are average but they are not. If they were, they would not be making millions of dollars." When I was done talking to him I was pleased and I said "Whew" to myself.

I kept telling him one thing when he was young—I would ask him, "Who am I?" And I would say, "I am your father first and your friend second. And when you become wise enough, I'll become your friend first and your father second. And I'll decide when that time comes."

Educating About Gender and Race

In terms of gender and race, my son is the third-generation Muslim in our family, Nation of Islam. We have strong feelings about gender and race. In terms of gender, I've taught my son that he should be very protective of women, the African American woman. Times when he was not treating a woman with respect, I talked to him about it. Given my situation, I believe more in the concept of parenthood than motherhood or fatherhood. If you only have one parent, roles have to be relegated to one gender, and you have to wear both pairs of shoes. I taught him he has to survive himself, take care of himself, cook, and the whole nine yards. When he has the responsibility to cook dinner, he has to have a complete meal. There is no excuse for not being home for dinner.

The only other thing I'd say is that in the United States, there is a war on for African American males. I'm not saying there is a conspiracy. When I drive a car and I'm stopped, whether it be in a northern or a southern state, I'm a little concerned. When I can't get a taxicab downtown in any city, I'm concerned. And I've taught him that he needs to be aware that he is a target and to use that and grow from that point.

I don't consider my religion racist, anti-Semitic, or any of those things. I'm vice president to a CEO who is Jewish and very religious himself. I'm his most trusted person, and we work extremely well together. I taught my son the same thing—the virtue of working together in a world that is not perfect.

I helped to create this in him by always teaching about African American history, about how we came to the United States, and the many obstacles that we had as a race. The laws against us reading and writing and getting together and how that has all changed. And to just imagine, with all those obstacles that were there, where we will be in the very near future. His role, as the one who came after me, is to take on the challenge and create a better world for us all!

This father did not come from a home with highly educated parents, yet they saw the value of education. Despite their own insecurities, they were his staunchest defenders as he fought against being considered retarded in school. He became a teen father, and as he grew into adulthood he became a vociferous defender of his own identity as an African American and a father. His standards for himself and his son are very clear. We can see that the support he received from his parents encouraged him to set high standards for himself and his son. We also see how, returning to McAdoo's conceptualization, he was the provider, the decision maker, and responsible for socializing his son. Although he did not fulfill the marital role, he did provide strong messages about how women should be treated.

Responsible Parenting: The Father in a Two-Parent Household

The second father is married and possesses a high-school education. A career serviceman, he became a construction worker when he retired from the army. His story was selected to be presented in depth because, though less well educated than some of the fathers in this chapter, he more closely resembled the educational level of many fathers of the sons we interviewed, and he provides an excellent example of responsible parenting.

I come from a nuclear family where my father was a longshoreman, and my mother was a homemaker. He was the disciplinarian without being physical. My mother handled everything—the love, the discipline, the morality. She made sure we went to church and she was always in our lives. Things can work with a single parent but it is easier if both parents are there.

I was raised in a home with three other brothers. My mother was the lady of the house. She taught us that boys do not cry. She also showed us how to wash, iron, sew, cook, and scrub floors, because there weren't any girls around. She said that in case we didn't marry, we'd be able to take care of ourselves. [He laughs.] But she also said that men have certain responsibilities, and if you did not take care of your family and your children, you were not a man.

Education and Discipline

When my son was born, my wife and I were avid readers. The big thing for him was getting his own library card when he was five. He had his name on the card and felt like a big shot. We read to him all the time, so he knew his ABC's by the time he started school. Parents must do this before school because teachers cannot do everything.

When he got to the first grade they skipped him to the second and then the next year wanted to skip him again. I stopped it. They were putting too much pressure on him, and he was too young to be that far from his peers. It was not to hold him back, but I know what he can and cannot handle. I also did not accept any failing grades because I knew he could do it. He appreciates it today.

I used to tell him if he had a problem with a teacher to let me know. He did have a problem with ethnicity because he didn't understand. One day I was called down to the school because he used an ethnic slur. He called a White boy a "nigger." He thought that was the nastiest thing he could call someone. So we had a talk with him. One of us—I worked days and my wife worked nights—was always there for him. Even as he got older, sixteen, seventeen, and eighteen, we were always watching him. I wanted to know where he was all the time and why he was sleeping late the next morning. We set boundaries for him.

We had little discipline problems. One time when he was ten, he had a BB gun and it was a responsibility he couldn't handle. We had a dog who was pretty vicious, and I caught him shooting at the dog. He tried to tell me he was shooting at the tree the dog was tied to, but I saw the truth. He lied to me, so I got physical with him and spanked him. That was the first and only time I ever spanked him. And, as far as I know, he has never lied to me since.

We cracked down on his homework. One time he brought home a report card of all As and one C in business, so we began to monitor his homework in that area. We told him he could do it, and he had to take control. He used to find mistakes in his text-books. When he was in the ninth grade and was taking physics and calculus, he found a mistake in a new book. The teacher insisted that he had gotten the problem wrong and that the book was right. So I took the question down to the Naval Academy, to a friend who ended up agreeing with my son. So I taught him to go back to his teacher and say politely what we had learned. Not to go in and say that the teacher was wrong, wrong, wrong.

Raising a Black Man to Be Successful

One incident illustrates what it took to raise him to be a man. One time, he came home without his football after playing with some boys. He was about ten. He was crying, and his mother was upset. After she found out who took his ball, she was going to get on her coat and go down and get it back. I told her, "No, no, no. Leave him alone." So he sat there for awhile, got himself together, and then went down there himself and got his ball.

There are certain things that women can't teach a Black man—and that is how to be a Black man. [Here again we see the role of child-socializer, according to McAdoo.] I know that sounds antiquated, but certain things cannot be taught. Things like, if you are driving a nice car and are stopped at night by a policeman, you don't make any fast moves toward the glove compartment because you are going to get shot, if for no other reason than you're Black.

One time, when he was seventeen, he came home with some kind of haircut, and I asked him about it, and he said it was his Black identity. And I said, "Go look in the mirror. What do you see?" And he said he saw a man, and I asked, "What kind of man?" and he said a Black man and I said, "Thank you. Now go get it cut." [In this example, the decision-maker role is being fulfilled.]

I tried to instill in him that he had to be good. You have to be around money to make money. Learn how to play golf. If you want to be successful, get out on the golf course, where deals are made. I'm sorry, that's the way it is. If you hang around the cesspool, only one thing will come off on you. Use money as a tool. After money, then you've got power and you can make changes. [The message of providing is being delivered.] You've got to get within the system to change it. And the only way is through education. No hostility, no militant stuff. You have to be exposed to a cultural environment. It is not a Black world. We would like it to be sometimes, but it is not.

I taught him about sex and to take responsibility for himself. He can't take the girl's word for it—you protect yourself. When his hormones were causing him to bump off the walls, I sat down and told him honestly what the deal was. I taught him control, and if he couldn't control the situation, to get out of it. We didn't need to create another problem. His priorities are to finish school, get his master's degree, a job, a car, an apartment, a wife, and then children. [The marital role is emphasized.]

There are certain things you don't do around your children. You don't party and drink with them because eventually they will lose respect for you. I've always been honest with him and told him he can tell me when I'm wrong, that I will listen. The emphasis is on loving and respecting each other.

Within a two-parent family, this father shows the value of the father's restraining the overprotective tendencies of the mother. The son had to deal with the football situation himself, something the father clearly understood. The father was present when other crucial events took place, from mediocre grades on his son's report card to a new haircut. His presence, firm hand, and clear values helped his son to succeed.

SUMMARY

A number of specific points can be drawn from how the fathers handled the nonacademic aspects of their sons' lives.

1. Fathers need to prepare their sons for being an African American male. The message here is never to forget that they are Black and that Black males are often placed in difficult situations. This is conveyed through statements related to their sons' always being suspects whenever a crime is committed, and the need for their sons to avoid areas that might be dangerous to them because of their race.

2. Children need to learn African American history. Fathers emphasize the need for appreciating culture so that their sons will have even greater pride in their own accomplishments. The sense of pride in their heritage is related to combating the problems of being an African American male, as presented in the first point.

3. Do not expect life to be fair. The notion conveyed here is that their sons will be hindered if they enter situations believing everyone is playing on a level playing field. Their sons, because they are Black, have to be on guard and will have to work harder to achieve parity.

4. Do not expect all neighborhoods to be the same. The sons who were raised in advantaged neighborhoods or home environments need to be aware that the rest of the world may not be as nice a place. Related to the first point, the fathers wish to prepare their sons for every eventuality and are keenly aware that the environment their sons grew up in may give them a false sense of security.

5. African Americans need as much education as possible in order to help others. If Blacks achieve more academically, they will be able to combat the insidious message that achievement in school is not to be valued.

6. Appropriate discipline is needed. With disciplining their sons, the fathers emphasize setting high expectations early, discussing the punishment with their children when they misbehave, and reacting on the spot. Lying, in particular, is offensive to the fathers. Mirroring this is the repeated message of the need for trust and communication between father and son. Showing a lack of respect is also mentioned as something that needs to be addressed. A few fathers cited specifically the need for a parent to be a good role model in order to be an effective disciplinarian. This is achieved most easily when the father and son have a strong bond between them.

7. Fathers must teach their sons about the dangers of sex and drugs. Fathers engaged their children in ongoing conversations about sexual relations and the drug environment. The facts should be handled honestly. The message to the sons is that they need to act responsibly about both.

8. Fathers and sons must deal with fighting. Two slightly different messages were given about fighting. Some fathers mentioned teaching their children to walk away from situations where fights were occurring or about to occur. Other fathers described the need to teach their children how to defend themselves if they had to. No one discussed the need to instigate a fight to establish a reputation, but it was mentioned that unless a young man defended himself adequately, he would be victimized.

9. Family rituals are important. Family rituals, in the form of vacationing, eating meals, attending church, and reading together, as well as supporting family members at sporting events or art performances, were mentioned frequently. Yet it was also cautioned that busy schedules and

encouraging children to be involved in community activities often militated against family togetherness.

10. Fathers have an important role in raising a son. As illustrated most succinctly by the second extended case example, fathers play a unique role in their sons' lives. They feel they prevent the mother's overprotection, while teaching about manhood. Given the dearth of men in many African American families, they take particular pride in the positive role they play and see themselves as good fathers. Respect for women was also conveyed as integral to mature manhood, as was sharing parental responsibilities with the mother and supporting her in her parenting. The fathers provide living examples of fathers and mothers working together to raise sons.

THE SIX STRATEGIES OF SUCCESSFUL PARENTING: WHAT'S A FATHER TO DO?

We found that the six components of successful parenting take on greater meaning when placed within the context of these fathers' stories.

Child-Focused Love

Fathers constantly encourage their sons to try hard. At the same time, there is an emphasis on accepting results if the attempts fail. Thus the children are raised knowing there is a keen interest in their accomplishments, that they will receive praise for them, that they will be accepted if their accomplishments fall short, and that they can bounce back from failure.

Strong Limit-Setting and Discipline

The fathers clearly set rules in these homes. They hold their sons to a focus on work, respect, and telling the truth. When there is variation from this, the retribution is usually swift.

Continually High Expectations

The fathers present a picture of setting high expectations (the sons will say, in some cases, they were too high). Homework came first, and children were pushed, sometimes with great effort, into gifted and talented programs, even though the school inappropriately thought they should not be there. When a parent goes that route for a child, it sets the goal for the child that he must achieve or else he is letting down not only himself but also his parents.

Open, Consistent, and Strong Communication

The fathers emphasize having conversations with their sons and using those conversations as a springboard for handling problems that arise. The basis for the conversation is to prepare their son for life, to teach about "the real world." Disciplining, for example, is used by some fathers as a way to teach. It is difficult to know to what extent the mother may also have been a force here, at times helping when the father felt uncomfortable.

Positive Racial Identification and Positive Male Identification

Taking account of the unique status of the African American male, we have combined these two components. In the United States, given their endangered position, it is difficult to consider race and gender separately. Although fathers spend considerable time preparing their sons for life as Black males who must be on guard, they also emphasize both the need for taking pride in the history of African Americans and the sons' abilities to compete in a variety of arenas. It is a significant challenge for some fathers to prepare their sons for negative treatment while teaching them simultaneously that their skills are equal to or better than the people who may treat them negatively. The fathers, strong positive role models in their own right, convey this message within the context of the other components cited above.

Drawing Upon Community Resources

Throughout, we hear of the influence of the church as an organizing factor in the lives of these families. We also hear about friends, family members, and teachers who recognized talent in the sons or helped out with school projects. Schools are often mentioned as breeding grounds of success, though some schools are identified as potential stumbling blocks.

These components undergird, along with specific examples of parenting techniques, the support that fathers provide. They also serve to guide future fathers. It is prescriptive and reassuring to see how others have succeeded in what is often a difficult task. Many of these fathers came from impoverished beginnings but were able to succeed through perseverance. In turn, they have helped their sons to achieve. As the fathers demonstrate, the die is not cast immutably when one does not have a privileged background. Many African American males are prospering at the highest levels, despite frequent portrayals to the contrary.

Perhaps most important is the overall message that many fathers have given their sons: "Yes, there is bias in society. But no, do not let it hold you back. Push yourself to become the best that you can be." With that message drilled into them by their fathers (as it is by the mothers, too), these sons have made it.

NOTES

1. U.S. Bureau of the Census 1996.
2. Blankenhorn 1995.
3. U.S. Department of Commerce 1984.
4. U.S. Bureau of the Census 1994; U.S. Bureau of the Census 1995.
5. One father in this group is White and holds a bachelor's degree.
6. U.S. Bureau of the Census 1993.
7. Solid data do not exist on the percentage of African American single parents of children eighteen and over who were married at least once. For purposes of comparison, it is known that in 1993, 79.6 percent of African American men ages forty to forty-four and 85.6 percent of the men ages forty-four to fifty-four had been married at least once (U.S. Bureau of the Census 1994). Here, though, we are speaking about current marital status.
8. See, for example, Wade 1994.
9. Boyd-Franklin 1989.
10. Griswold 1993.
11. Wilensky and Lebeaux 1965.
12. Frazier 1948.
13. McAdoo 1993.
14. Griswold 1993.
15. Bryan and Ajo 1992; Wade 1994.
16. Garfinkel and McClanahan 1986.
17. McAdoo 1993.
18. Willie 1988. Both Black fathers and mothers agree that men tend to spend less time on child care than Black women (Ahmeduzzaman and Roopnarine, 1992).
19. McAdoo 1993.
20. Zollar and Williams 1987. A recent study conducted by Bryan and Ajo (1992) of fifty African American fathers from two professional organizations and two homeless shelters attempted to learn more about father role perceptions. The role of father was conceptualized to include economic provider, advice giver, disciplinarian, companion to children in leisure activities, ensurer of children's safety, and child-care provider. It was hypothesized that the respondents' perception of the importance of fathering would increase with the father's educational level, work hours, income, and age. Half the fathers were living with their children. Higher income and employment did show a positive relationship with the fathers' perceptions of fathering. This reinforced the previous points concerning the significance of the provider role to a father's self-concept.
21. The literature on parenting has various definitions on what "authoritative" or "authoritarian" parenting means and how "autonomy" and "nurturing" are defined. Mosley and Thomson (1995), in reviewing some of the literature, make the following relevant points: Black parents were found in one study, when compared with White parents, to emphasize obedience over autonomy, and, in another study of middle-income Black parents, to be

more involved and nurturing when compared with White parents. Mosley and Thomson's own findings supported earlier research findings that Black fathers were less actively involved than mothers and that fathers' involvement was beneficial for sons. These findings about the authoritarian and involved nature of parents, as well as about the different levels of involvement and the positive outcomes of that involvement, area consistent with our observations. We also are aware that the whole notion of what authoritarian parenting means may be culture-specific. For example, Chao (1994), in studying immigrant Chinese parents' apparently authoritarian parenting style and school outcomes among children, concludes that the concept of "training" is more culturally relevant and positively connotated. This is consistent with the classic work of Baumrind (1972) which concluded that when Black families were viewed by White standards, they appeared more authoritarian. Those Black families who were viewed as authoritarian also produced the most assertive and independent girls.

22. See Minuchin and Fishman 1981.

23. A few fathers stated they did not know they were "poor" until they grew up, left home and both saw how others lived in poverty and heard descriptions of it. This is also a point made by Henry Louis Gates, Jr. about his own upbringing (Gates and West 1996).

24. The fathers were asked to describe the accuracy of a series of statements using a scale ranging from 1 to 5, where 1 indicated that the statement was not at all accurate, 3 that the statement was somewhat accurate, and 5 that the statement was completely accurate. The first statement was "In high-school, I monitored the amount of time my son spent studying." If a father gave a response equal to 3, 4, or 5, he was judged to be at least somewhat involved in monitoring his son's studying.

25. This is one of three biracial families in the book for which at least one member was interviewed.

26. See, for example, Imber-Black 1988.

27. By comparison, 17 percent of White children being raised by one parent are living with their father (U.S. Bureau of the Census 1994).

REFERENCES

Blankenhorn, D. 1995. *Fatherless America.* New York: Basic Books.

Bryan, D.L. and A.A. Ajo. 1992. The role perception of African American fathers. *Social Work Research and Abstracts* 28 3, 17–21.

Chao, R. 1994. Beyond parental control and authoritarian parenting style: Understanding Chinese parenting through the cultural notion of training. *Child Development* 65, 1111–19.

Frazier, E.F. 1948. *The Negro family in the United States.* New York: Dryden Press.

Garfinkel, I. and S.S. McClanahan. 1986. *Single mothers and their children: A new American dilemma.* Washington, D.C. Urban Institute Press.

Gates, H.L. Jr., and C. West. 1996. *The future of the race.* New York: Alfred A. Knopf.

Griswold, R.L. 1993. *Fatherhood in America: A history.* New York: Basic Books.

Imber-Black, E. 1988. Families and larger systems: A family therapist's guide through the system. New York: Guilford.

McAdoo, J.L. 1993. The roles of African American fathers: An ecological perspective. *Families in Society* 74, 29–35.

Minuchin, S. and C. Fishman, 1981. *Family therapy techniques.* Cambridge: Harvard University Press.

Mosley, J. and E. Thomson, 1995. Fathering behavior and child outcomes: The role of race and poverty. *In Fatherhood: Contemporary theory, research and social policy*, ed. W. Marsiglio, 148–65. Thousand Oaks, Calif.: Sage.

U.S. Bureau of the Census. 1991. Marital status and living arrangements: 1990. Series P-20, No. 450. Washington, D.C.: Government Printing Office.

——. 1993. *The black population in the United States: March 1992*. Series P20, no 471. Washington, D.C.: Government Printing Office.

——. 1995. *Household and family characteristics: March 1994*. Series P20, no. 483. Washington, D.C.: Government Printing Office.

——. 1996. *Marital status and living arrangements: March 1994*. Current Population Reports. P20-484. Washington, D.C.: Government Printing Office.

U.S. Department of Commerce. 1973. *Statistical abstract of the United States: 1973*. Washington, D.C.: Government Printing Office.

——. 1984. *Statistical abstract of the United States: 1985*. Washington, D.C.: Government Printing Office.

Wade, J.C. 1994. African American fathers and sons: Social, historical, and psychological considerations. *Families in Society* 75, 561–70.

Wilensky, H.L. and C.N. LeBeaux. 1965. *Industrial society and social welfare*. New York: Free Press.

Willie, C.V. 1988. *A new look at black families*. Dix Hills, N.Y.: General Hall.

Zollar, A.C. and J.S. Williams. 1987. The contribution of marriage to the life satisfaction of black adults. *Journal of Marriage and the Family* 49, 87–92.

Chapter 3

Generative Fathering: Challenges to Black Masculinity and Identity

Leon D. Caldwell
University of Nebraska–Lincoln

Joseph L. White
Emeritus, University of California, Irvine

> *This chapter is dedicated to the memory of Kenneth M. Caldwell: We loved you as a son, a brother, a fiancé, and a friend. You were prepared to become an ideal African American father when the Creator called you home from the Twin Towers on 9-11-01. We know your spirit is living in peace with the ancestors. We will all meet again someday.*

Generative Fathering is very much consistent with the identity of African American men. Evidenced by the hierarchy of masculinity found even in the names we call each other like "old head," "OG," and "Ole School," following generations revere those who have gone before them and can relate their life's triumphs and struggles in a manner appealing to the current generation. Generative fathering is not only necessary for transgenerational continuity of African American masculinity but we suggest that it is necessary for the health of elder African American men. African American men who take on the role of fathering, biological and nonbiological, children gain to benefit in their development into later adulthood. The benefits to the community are inarguable. African American men secure in their masculinity and conscious of their identity can revolutionize a community by preparing the next generation of African American men (Lee, 2003; Madhubuti, 2002; Winbush, 2001).

Generative fathering recognizes the dynamic nature of parenting. It requires that adult African American men commit to participating in the lifespan of children as an obligation for cultural and community continuity. It also requires that adult African American men redefine masculinity and re-affirm an identity that allows them to see their importance to the extended network of an African American family. Ultimately, adult African American men must reclaim the next generation as their responsibility despite the ab-sence of a few. We must acknowledge that in the absence of systemic proc-esses to provide continuity of social standards, community expectations, and definitions of masculinity and identity they must be recreated. In this chapter we discuss generative fathering as both a concept and practice to maintaining healthy definitions of African American masculinity and iden-tity intergenerationally.

GENERATIVE FATHERING IN THE AFRICAN AMERICAN COMMUNITY

Generative fathering is a major dimension of the psychological, social, and interpersonal roles Black men are expected to fulfill as they move through the adult life cycle. The idea of generative fathering is derived from Erik Erikson's (1950) concept of generativity, which as a fundamental task of adult psychosocial development, is to care for and contribute to the life of the next generation (Dollahite, Hawkins, & Brotherson, 1997) as part of healthy adult development. The role of the generative African American fa-ther involves carrying out child-rearing activities that promote children's abilities to develop to their full potential. Generative African American fa-thers are expected to expand their life's commitment beyond themselves to care for the next generation (Allen & Connor, 1997). Generative fathering includes any nurturing activity that contributes to the spirit of generations to come such as being responsible creating new or more mature persons, ideas, or works of art. African centered scholars assert that principles of MAAT[1] provided the natural order of the human spirit to procreate and progress (Akbar, 1998; Kambon, 1998) thus creating a generative process that is rooted in spiritual obligations.

African American generative fathers not only care for biological chil-dren, but also other young people in the African American community. Ac-cording to Erikson (1950), the larger society needs mature adults who are prepared to commit themselves to help establish the next generation of persons, ideas, works, and products. The underlying assumption is that men have the potential and motivation to become the kinds of fathers their

---

[1]In ancient Kemetic (Egyptian) society, life-affirming principles were reflected in the spirit of maat. Maat represented the fundamental set of rules that define the natural order of social interaction and it represented all that was good and proper in life as expressed through seven cardinal virtues. These virtues included: truth, justice, righteousness, harmony, order, balance and propriety (Parham, 2002, p. 41).

children need them to be. To become fully human is to invest in the care and development of others. In order to enhance generative fathering in the African American community, the positive characteristics inherent in Black men must be appreciated and encouraged (Dollahite et al., 1997).

THE ROLE OF THE EXTENDED FAMILY

In the African American community, the extended family has always shared the responsibility for raising young children and educating young men to function as productive citizens, family members, mentors, and generative fathers. The extended family in the African American community is a complex web of intergenerational kinship and quasi-kinship networks that extends across households and involves community groups (White, 1984). Extended families involve parents, grandparents, aunts, uncles, cousins, children, stepparents, preachers, teachers, coaches, and respected community elders. African American fathers and children are part of a family social system in which each person affects the other reciprocally, directly and indirectly (Lamb, 1997).

Because of its emphasis on unity, flexibility, and collective survival of its members, the Black extended family has been able to survive through changing historical periods beginning with slavery and continuing through de facto and de jure segregation after the Civil War and the migration to urban America from rural areas of southern states in the 20th century (Billingsley, 1992).

In an optimally functioning extended family where adults and children work together in cooperative relationships, African American fathers are expected to take a leadership role in fostering love between generations and fostering healthy relationships with family members who are important to their child's well-being (Hunter & Davis, 1994). In the Black extended family, and overlapping family social systems in the Black community, Black men have always been available as fathers, uncles, grandfathers, godfathers, preachers, and boyfriends of mothers to guide and act as role models for children to emulate and observe. These men hand down father values and survival traditions from generation to generation.

The extended family and family-oriented community networks provide opportunities for African American boys and young men to experience and learn how to become generative fathers by engaging in caring and nurturing activities with younger siblings, stepchildren, nieces, nephews, and cousins. They are also influenced by their own fathers, father figures in the extended family, cultural images of fathers in the mass media, and community values surrounding fatherhood. Through each of these experiences, African American young men and boys can learn to model generative fathering. The help or despair of extended family systems and community networks can have a direct influence on young men's commitment to nurture and provide for the next generation (Allen & Connor, 1997).

BLACK MEN AS SOCIAL FATHERS

Generally speaking, public perceptions of Black fathers are more negative than White fathers. Black fathers are more often perceived in stereotypical terms as irresponsible men who are not constructively involved in the lives of their children. Many of their children are born out of wedlock. Traditional Euro-American definitions of fatherhood as an in-residence married father may tend to underestimate the role of fatherhood in the African American community and do not adequately capture the cultural nuances of African American fathering roles. Regardless of the mother's marital status to a child's biological father, some adult male is usually involved in a fathering or mentoring role (Mott, 1990; Pitts, 1999).

The concept of social fathering is a better fit for generative fathering activities in the African American community. The term *social fathering* encompasses biological fathers as the most important group, but also extends to include men who are not biological fathers. Social fathering includes all the child-rearing roles, activities, and duties generative fathers are expected to fulfill. Social fatherhood differs from biological fatherhood in that it is a fixed status created by biological appropriation. Regardless of how paternal responsibilities are carried out, biological fatherhood is only permanently revocable through the death of a child. Social fatherhood, on the other hand, is not a fixed status; it involves a more diverse set of rules in which men can assume the fathering role for children within the extended family circle and the Black community that may or may not be tied to biological paternity (Marsiglio, 1995).

African American boys and young men with and without resident biological fathers in the home tend to seek out social fathers in the extended family and surrounding Black community to augment or fulfill the fathering role. Urban middle-school African American boys interviewed for Ira Thomas' (1998) Harvard doctoral dissertation, who did not have fathers in the home, established close relationships with surrogate fathers in their social networks. The rich relationships which boys shared with social fathers fulfilled their fathering needs with emotional and social support, quality time spent together, teaching and instructive talk and guidance about sex and drugs, problem solving, and family values. High-quality relationships with social fathers help the boys learn about generative fathering and provided experiences to develop the confidence and skills needed to make the difficult transition through adolescence into early adulthood. Steady Black male figures who work with youth as social fathers in the African American community are admired by everybody (Furstenberg, 1995). Social fathering is no longer something that happens primarily in the Black community. Because of increasing rates of divorce, out-of-wedlock births, separation, and family breakups, more men from all communities are assuming father-like roles for children who are not their biological offspring. This is evidenced by the number of mentoring programs for children of all ethnic groups.

SELF-DEFINITION OF AFRICAN AMERICAN MASCULINITY

Masculinity or defining one's self as a man is a major component of generative fathering. Psychology professors Joseph White and James Cones (1999) in their book, *Black Man Emerging: Facing the Past and Seizing a Future in America*, define African American masculinity in the context of four major challenges Black males encounter as they move through the life cycle in America: identity, establishing close connections with others, coping with racism, and finding a source of psychological and emotional strength. Research conducted by University of Michigan psychologists Andrea Hunter and James Davis (1994) supports the masculinity challenges posited by White and Cones. Using structured interviews as their primary source of information, Hunter and Davis asked a sample of 32 married and nonmarried Black men in a diverse age and occupational group to elaborate on what manhood meant to them. The men described identity, connectedness to family and community, and spirituality and world view as the central challenges of masculinity.

Identity and self-definition for the men involved having a vision of what one wanted to become and a sense of direction to pursue one's own mind. The men felt it was important to persevere in the face of obstacles, be responsible for one's actions, continue to work toward self-improvement, demonstrate the ability to bounce back from setbacks, and rectify past bad behavior. In psychology, identity is defined as a process of becoming in which a young man dreams a dream of who he wants to be, where he is going in life, and what is important. The dream provides the energy and motivation to "keep on keeping on" in the face of barriers and obstructions (White & Cones, 1999). Sadly, for many African American men the combination of poverty, inferior urban schools, and job discrimination prevent them from achieving their dreams of what they want to become in life. Psychologist A. J. Franklin (2002) refers to this as a process of "dream snuffing," which leaves a residual of anger and disappointment.

For the men in the Hunter and Davis investigation, regardless of age, marital or family status, family and connectedness to others were major centers of their lives and closely associated with what it meant to be a man. Family connectedness encompassed responsibility for others in the family network, leadership, meeting the expectations of fatherhood, being a role model for spouses and children, keeping the family together, equity in gender relationships, and being a provider. With respect to family relationships and gender equity, the men expressed a range of views from traditional to egalitarian. Both views were held by many men. The men felt that fathers must create and maintain healthy relationships between generations with family and extended family members who are important in raising their children. Other sources of close relationships for African American males are same gender peers, romantic relationships, and relationships with older males who act as mentors (White & Cones, 1999).

Being an economic provider for their families was a fundamental component of the men's values, commitments, and aspirations. Not only in the Hunter and Davis (1994) research, but in other studies, the majority of Black men endorsed the provider role as part of their responsibilities in family life (Cazenave, 1984; Pitts, 1999). With Black male unemployment consistently running at twice the national average, many Black men are unable to find validation in the traditional breadwinner role and end up going outside the mainstream work world and start hustling in the street economy.

Although blatant racism is definitely on the wane, Black men are often forced to cope with more covert residuals of structural and institutional racism in the work world that prevents them from obtaining jobs and being able to receive promotions on jobs for which they are well qualified. The bleak economic situation in the predominantly Black neighborhood of North Lawndale on Chicago's West Side is a prime example of structural economic conditions which reduce the possibility of Black men finding jobs. Two large factories that served as the employment anchor of the North Lawndale community are no longer in operation: Hawthorne's Western Electric Plant, which employed 43,000 workers, and the International Harvester Plant, which employed 14,000 workers. A 29-year-old unemployed Black man, interviewed for a story on Black employment, said there were no jobs anywhere around. He went on to say that people want to work but can't find anything. In the Black Belt of Washington Park, on Chicago's South Side, a majority of adults had jobs in 1950; by 1990, only 1 in 3 worked in a typical week (White & Cones, 1999).

Institutional racism exists where Whites restrict equal access to jobs and promotions to business and housing loans and the like. The case involving Texaco is a textbook example of institutional racism at work in America's corporate system. In its public posture, Texaco was a model of equal opportunity and racial equity. Written antidiscrimination policies and channels for discrimination complaints were in place. Glossy brochures with pictures of cheerful groups of multiethnic employees proclaimed the company's commitment to diversity and its promise of a work environment that would provide respect and dignity regardless of one's race or gender (Roberts, 1998).

It was demonstrated in court that behind the scenes, however, Texaco was a hornet's nest of covert bigotry and blocked pathways for Black employees. It was a company that said all the right things but did little to ensure that its words were carried out in reality. In June 1994, six Black employees filed a racial discrimination lawsuit on behalf of themselves and at least 1,500 African Americans who had worked for the company from 1991 to 1994. The lawsuit charged that Black employees were systematically denied chances for advancement and opportunities to attend seminars and to travel abroad, while less qualified Whites (sometimes trained by Blacks) moved ahead. Secret lists from which Blacks were excluded were used to fast-track White employees who were thought to have the potential for senior management. Statistical evidence presented as part of the lawsuit indicated that at Texaco fewer than 1% of 873 executives making more than $106,000 a year were Black, and not one of the highest paid executives was Black. While the number of Texaco executives in the highest paid echelon grew by 44% in the 4 years preceding the lawsuit, not a single Black person held such a job.

Texaco flatly denied any systematic covert or overt bias. It steadfastly maintained that it was a color-blind company that valued diversity, treated everyone with dignity, and promoted employees without regard to race. The legal battle between Texaco and the Black plaintiffs might have continued indefinitely had not a disgruntled White executive who had lost his job in a corporate downsizing move leaked some incriminating audiotapes to the plaintiffs' lawyers. The plaintiffs' lawyers made the tapes available to the news media including national network news programs.

On the audiotapes, top company executives, one a former treasurer, can be heard sneering and laughing at Black employees, making negative references to Kwanzaa, a Black holiday festival, and referring to Blacks as jelly beans stuck at the bottom of the bag. The executives can also be heard threatening to destroy damaging evidence in the case. In early November 1996, excerpts of the tapes appeared in newspapers and were played on national network evening news programs.

A storm of public protest ensued with threats of economic retaliation, boycotts, and stockholders withdrawing their money. Texaco quickly moved for an out-of-court settlement. On November 15, 1996, Texaco agreed to pay out a total of $176 million to settle the lawsuit: $115 million to be paid in cash to the 1,500 current and former Black workers who sued; $26 million to be disbursed in pay raises over 5 years; and $35 million to be used for diversity and sensitivity programs for Texaco staff.

It would be naive to think that Texaco is one of only a very few organizations in the United States saturated with institutional race discrimination and bigotry. The kind of reprehensible behavior that went on at Texaco persists in far too many offices, law firms, universities, factories, and businesses. The tendency on the part of most organizations is to deny that racism exists until they are caught in a legally compromising situation (White & Cones, 1999).

Finally, spirituality was a source of strength for the men in the Hunter and Davis (1994) study. Being a man involved spiritual groundedness and a relationship between the I and the *We.* Infusing the I and the *We,* the men moved from the collective survival of the family to collective survival of the African American community with an approach to others that involved equality, faith, unselfishness, and respect. The configuration of the I and the We, collective survival, faith, and caring for others is congruent with Afrocentric philosophy. The Afrocentric view of masculinity emphasizes spiritual beliefs, the importance of human relationships, interdependent living, harmony with others, and survival of the collective We. In the Afrocentric context, spirituality is symbolized by a vibrant belief that a spiritual force acts as a connecting link to all life and human beings. Spirituality gives direction, purpose, and energy to all human endeavors. Spiritual power enables one to maintain psychological equilibrium during life's ups and downs. Soul is the essence of human beings; and soul force is fundamental to understanding the African and African American experience. From soul force comes the power, intensity, and will to survive oppression (White & Cones, 1999).

Historically, soul force has provided Black men with the courage to believe in themselves, face the world with a new day of hope, and help each generation discover fresh the meaning in the struggle against oppressive forces in American society (Wade-Gayles, 1997). In addition to spirituality, other psychological strengths which are part of the African American heritage involve improvisation, resilience, emotional vitality, humor that acknowledges the tragedies of life, and a healthy suspicion of the motives and dictates of Euro-American society. These strengths are essential in the Black man's struggle for a new day of hope to overcome the inordinate demands of growing up in America with its risks for unemployment, poverty, crime, and school failure (White & Cones, 1999).

African American men are expected to develop the ability to function effectively in two cultures (African American and Euro-American), in essence to be bicultural, which emphasize somewhat different role expectations. Negotiating the pathways between and within Euro-American and African American cultures requires an optimal integration of mainstream notions of aggressive, competitive, and domineering masculine values with the African American emphasis on spirituality, connectedness to others, collective survival, emotional vitality, resilience, and humor. Bicultural adaptive strategies are an essential of the legacy which Black men pass on to the next generation of young people to increase their chances of surviving and thriving as they renew the struggle for equality, respect, and fair play.

Until very recently, very little was known about how Black men defined themselves. Caldwell (2000) asserted that a lack of self-definition places African American men at greater risk for developing unhealthy coping skills in toxic environments. They were often defined by social scientists and White society in pathology-flavored terms: oversexed players, hustlers, drug dealers, violence-prone criminals, absent fathers, and emasculated victims. The African American masculine ideal presented in the Hunter and Davis (1994) project based on Afrocentric values is a goal Black men can strive for, but may not always reach. As a model of how African American men should think and act, it transcends Euro-American mainstream concepts of masculinity and offers a psychologically healthy alternative with its emphasis on spirituality, closeness to others, respect for human beings, and a vision of masculinity as a combination of the I and the We. When Black men are given the opportunity to define themselves, it is clear that viable concepts of manhood have developed in the Black community that provide Black men with a vision of what is important about personal identity, family responsibilities, and social values. Black men do not outright reject Euro-American notions of manhood. It is more the case that they combine Euro-American and African American masculine notions to create a set of flexible bicultural strategies to negotiate the challenges of adult life. Billingsley's (1992) study of the history of Black family life in America since slavery to the present indicates that even in the worst of times, Black men managed to develop a sense of dignity and self-worth and used flexible strategies in their quest to remain close to families and provide for their children.

GENERATIVE FATHERING SKILLS AND SKILL DEVELOPMENT

Involvement in the socialization process of children is a primary task for generative fathers. Father presence in the lives of children is multidimensional as companions, care providers, role models, moral guides, teachers, and is an important source of support for children's healthy development (Pruett, 2000). A growing body of evidence supports the belief that paternal warmth, nurturance, and closeness influences children's cognitive development, school achievement, and academic attainment. Some studies have demonstrated higher self-esteem, lower depression and anxiety, lower delinquency, and better peer relationships for African American children involved with biological or social fathers (Coley, 2001).

According to Palkovitz (1997), generative fathers need a battery of operational cognitive, affective, and emotional skills to promote children's ability to develop to their full potential. Major paternal skills include communication, teaching, caregiving, planning, providing, and sensitivity. An abbreviated description of paternal skills that are associated with positive outcomes in child development is presented in Table 3.1. Because Black children are expected to function effectively in two cultures, African American paternal skills should include bicultural guidance to enhance successful adaptation to Euro-American and African American social and economic environments. In recent years, child psychologists have added a category called human capital to the paternal skills pool. Human capital consists of skills, knowledge, and behaviors that can be passed on to foster achievement and success in U.S. society. Human capital involves financial status, educational attainment, employability, and social contacts which can be beneficial to children's educational and social development (Coley, 2001).

Generative fathering is a process of learning and discovery. Parenting is always on-the-job training where fathers learn skills by participating in activities that fathers and children can enjoy doing together. Continuous involvement by fathers with children enhances self-confidence, thereby in-

TABLE 3.1
Ways to Be Involved in Parenting

Communication	• Vacations
• Listening	• Holidays
• Talking to	• Saving for the future
• Expressing interest in child's activities	*Providing*
• Showing interest in child's friends	• Financial support
Teaching and Mentoring	• Housing
• Advising	• Clothing
• Role modeling	• Food
• Problem solving	• Medical care
• Giving choices	*Affection*
• Assisting in gaining new skills	• Hugging
• Teaching about cultural heritage	• Kissing
• Answering questions	• Cuddling
• Encouraging interest in hobbies	• Making eye contact
Care Giving	• Smiling
• Feeding	• Praising
• Bathing	• Showing patience
• Clothing	• Displaying emotional support
• Reaching things for children	*Sensitivity*
Planning	• Understanding children's signals and
• Birthdays	needs
• Trips	• Responding appropriately

Note. Adapted from Palkovitz (1997).

creasing the motivation for closer involvement and increased sensitivity to children's needs. Paternal skills can also be obtained in a growing number of formal skill development programs (Lamb, 1997).

The reading on African American fatherhood is sparse. Several authors have written books that give advice about fathering through the voices and experiences of other fathers (Harris, 2001; Hutchinson, 1995). These books give fathers and expectant fathers the opportunity to learn from others' experiences and pass on the wisdom based on lessons learned from trial and error. Madhubuti (1991) in his highly acclaimed book *Black Men: Obsolete, Single, Dangerous? The Afrikan American Family in Transition* asserts that Black men cannot depend on others to do our job of fathering our children. In his book, Madhubuti admits that many African American men learn about fathering from their mothers and the media. African American fathers need structured opportunities to learn about parenting through the experiences of other men.

According to Yale child psychologist Kyle Pruett (2000), generative fathering is a complex emergent process that evolves as children age. Generative fatherhood identity can only be achieved by a sustained involvement in parenting. Change is constant and complex as both child and father go through different developmental transitions as they evolve into what they will become. The role of the father changes as children age. A father doesn't parent the same child throughout life. Parenting skills that worked in early childhood may not work as effectively when a child becomes a rebellious teenager who is constantly testing the limits. Emergent generative fathering identity is constantly being shaped and reshaped as fathers encounter new experiences such as establishing rules for drugs, alcohol, sex, peer choices, and curfew. Fathers are likely to experience periods of disequilibrium and confusion as they struggle through growth cycles with children where they feel stuck and don't know how to solve problems with children who refuse to follow their dictates when it comes to completing their homework, cleaning up their room, and controlling anger.

Parental growth is reciprocal. Parents are changed by children as much as children are changed by parents. Ongoing interaction between parents and children fuels mutual development and drives them forward through successive growth stages, which result in skill development, wisdom, learning to care for others, and clarity of goals and direction. Successful skill building established by working closely with children builds a sense of competence. Conversely, if fathers are frustrated in their efforts to nurture children, they feel increasingly incompetent, which may decrease their motivation for active involvement. Fatherhood is frequently seen as a transition to adulthood. Babies have the power to change men, to make them more responsible, gentle, and settled into adult life. Young fathers who take responsibility for their children often report that it makes them more complete people. The opportunity to care for young children brings out a more nurturing and effective side of them (Pruett, 2000).

The driving force to become a successful generative father comes from motivation and commitment; what Erik Erikson (1950) called a faithfulness or fidelity to a self-chosen value system which one is willing to sacrifice to achieve. Some Black men are motivated by positive recollections of fathering experiences as children; others are motivated by understanding the sacrifices generations of Black men made in America so their children and grandchildren could have a wider range of economic, social, and educational opportunities. Genuine love for children, extended family pressures to be responsible, and understanding how much children need them can also be motivating factors for Black fathers to become emotionally involved, committed parents (Allen & Connor, 1997).

From a socialization, social learning theory, and sociocultural perspective, gender appropriate behavior such as fathering is developed through observation and emulation of models. The idea is that young men internalize images of fatherhood by observing others in real-life situations and through images symbolically projected in popular cultural carriers like movies and TV stories depicting people like Bill Cosby and other Black men in fathering roles. Internalized images regarding gender ideals shape behavior and cause people to perform in roles that are congruent with acceptable models. As they commit themselves to be a certain type of father, Black men are likely to seek out adult role models in a variety of social contexts. Biological fathers, social fathers, neighborhood elders, Black heroes, and even women, in some cases, can be models to observe and emulate. In his book, *Becoming a Dad: Black Men and Their Journey Into Fatherhood,* Leonard Pitts (1999) looked beyond his abusive, irresponsible, in-residence father role model. He found parental warmth, responsibility, accessibility, and commitment in his mother and admirable parental qualities in male acquaintances, older relatives, and colleagues which he desired to emulate. His biological father was a point of negative departure for what Pitts was motivated not to become. Black boys need exposure to role models and cultural images of fatherhood which move beyond stereotypes and shadowy figures who operate on the edge of criminal behavior, drugs, absent fatherhood, prison, and unemployment. They need to see strong African American bicultural role models in the extended family, neighborhood, and social circles to establish a clear picture of what fatherhood is like.

There is strong evidence to suggest that under the right circumstances most African American men are capable of becoming involved, nurturing generative fathers. Generative fathering is a choice. Social context can either enhance or impede men's goals and ability to develop nurturing attachments, be responsible decision makers, and construct mutually fulfilling bonds with their children. Encouragement or discouragement from extended family members and social networks can either weaken or strengthen a father's motivation to be involved with his children. For inner-city African American fathers, a strong alliance with the mother to mutually care for the child and community pressure, especially from the paternal grandmother, can be critically important in keeping fathers involved (Coley, 2001; Pruett, 2000). Recognizing and including these natural motivators is integral to keeping biological fathers involved even when the choice of disengagement presents as emotionally safer.

BARRIERS TO GENERATIVE FATHERING

Black men, especially young inner-city fathers, face a steep climb in their quest to become generative fathers. Numerous studies indicate that most men possess the desire and the capacity to nurture children, but motivation and commitment alone cannot assure responsible fathering behavior. For many Black men, the problem is not what they lack personally, but the barriers created by unemployment, inadequate schooling, household disruption (divorce, single parent, separation), and restrictive public policies involving child support payment and welfare rules, which have impeded their ability to take a more proactive role in child rearing. Resolving the conflict between fathering aspirations and opportunities in a society with a strong residual from racism is not easily accomplished (Allen & Connor, 1997).

The lack of family sustaining jobs in many communities denies African American men the possibility of sustaining an economically self-reliant family. This is particularly true for African American urban young men who are caught between society's expectations of fulfilling the provider role and scarce opportunities to do so. Young men who are unable to stay employed in jobs which can support their families are vulnerable to seeking recognition from street-oriented peer groups who are involved in marginal economic and social activities. Charles Ballard's many years of working with young American fathers in Cleveland, Washington, D.C., and other urban communities has convinced him that men who can provide for their families become more effective fathers (Levine & Pitt, 1995). Participation in the workforce in a job that pays a reasonable wage generates respect within the extended family and gives a man a sense of hope for a viable economic future.

The loss of work for large groups of Black men due to structural racism can have devastating economic and psychological effects. Work is an integral part of male identity in America. Work is more than just making a living; it also constitutes a framework for organizing daily behavior and developing discipline. If a man has a regular job, he knows where he is going to be and when he is going to be there. If he values his job, he organizes his time and plans ahead. In the absence of regular employment, life becomes less structured. Time is not well organized and often is spent hanging out, which can interfere with family life and building a long-term family plan for economic and social development. Many sociologists argue that today's problems in inner-city neighborhoods are fundamentally a consequence of the disappearance of work (White & Cones, 1999).

The quality of the mother–father relationship is an important predictor of paternal involvement whether or not the father resides in the home. Fathers who have close, amicable relationships with mom are more likely to be involved with their children. On the other hand, unstable relationships between parents makes it difficult for the parents to work together cooperatively to meet the needs of their children. When the parents are divorced, separated, never married, or not living together, mothers often have the power to control as gatekeepers, which they may not want to give up or share with the father (Lamb, 1997). When gatekeeping disrupts contact, fathers can drift away with the passage of time and develop new relationships that no longer involve their children (Pruett, 2000).

A powerful source of influence in the social circle of young African American inner-city males is the peer group. As the most important people in the lives of many young men, they set the standards for conduct. Peers can encourage or discourage responsible fathering behavior. If emotional commitment to a child's mother is perceived as a sign of weakness, a young father may be reluctant to bond with mother and child for fear of losing status in the eyes of his peers (Anderson, 1992).

Restrictive public policy rules for child support payments can prevent young African American fathers from having regular contacts with their children. A nonresident father who earns $700 a month take-home pay working in a fast-food restaurant can easily fall behind in his rent and child support payments during seasonal lay-offs. If he falls too far behind in child support payments and sees no possibility of catching up, he may disappear completely in order to prevent being apprehended by the authorities. This breaks the father–child bond completely and intensifies the mother's and her relatives' resentment of the father. Public policy officials need to be more receptive to the fact that many men can only partially fulfill the provider–breadwinner role (Furstenberg, 1995), but are willing to contribute to the well-being of children in nonmonetary ways such as babysitting, playing games, reading stories, cooking, and other household chores, and taking children to parks and visits to relatives.

Regardless of external circumstances, Black men with a strong commitment to parenting and who see fathering as a central part of their identity are likely to be more involved as fathers (Roopmarine & Ahmeduzzamen, 1993). Awareness of becoming a father can activate a sense of responsibility and pride. Many young Black fathers feel that becoming a parent was a life-changing experience that helped them reassess what was important. Engaged fathering improved their connectedness to family life and society as a whole. For some men, fatherhood is a concrete sign of transition to adulthood which opens up new avenues for personal growth and well-being (Allen & Connor, 1997; Pruett, 2000).

SUMMARY

Despite its complexity fathering is an important aspect of the definition of masculinity and identity to African American men. Complicated by history, socialization, economics, racism, and both social and personal challenges fathering is a natural part of the self-definition of African American masculinity and gender identity. Generative fathering allows men capable and willing to participate in the lives of children, in various ways, across their life span. The requirements for generative fathering are both psychological and social. There is a commitment of interpersonal resources like emotions and nurturance that are transmitted to children so that they may also demonstrate these feelings as healthy responses to a complex world for African Americans. Generative fathering requires a greater understanding of roles and identity as nonbiological fathers attend to an obligation to teach life skills to the next generation.

America was built by attempting to destroy the identity and masculinity of men of African descent. However, we write this chapter in defiant testimony to the resilience of African American men with the challenge to recreate those community systems of fathering when legal systems forbid us. Generative fathering systems are important if African American men are to participate in the transmission of African American culture and the nurturance of healthy children to sustain our communities.

REFERENCES

Akbar, N. (1998). *Know thyself.* Tallahassee, FL: Mind Production.

Allen, W., & Connor, M. (1997). An African American perspective on generative fathering. In A. J. Hawkins & D. C. Dollahite (Eds.), *Generative fathering: Beyond deficit perspectives* (pp. 52–70). Thousand Oaks, CA: Sage.

Anderson, E. (1992). *Street-wise: Race, class, and change in an urban community.* Chicago: University of Chicago Press.

Billingsley, A. (1992). *Climbing Jacob's ladder: The enduring legacy of African American families.* New York: Simon & Schuster.

Caldwell, L. D. (2000). The psychology of Black men. In L. Jones (Ed.), *Brothers of the academy, 30 up and coming Black males in higher education.* Sterling, VA: Stylus.

Cazenave, J. (1984). Race, socioeconomic status, and age: The social context of American masculinity. *Sex Roles, 11*(7–8), 639–656.

Coley, R. (2001). Invisible men: Emerging research on low-income, unmarried and minority fathers. *American Psychologist, 56*(9), 743–753.

Dollahite, D., Hawkins, A., & Brotherson, S. (1997). Father work: A conceptual ethic of fathering as generative work. In A. J. Hawkins & D. C. Dollahite (Eds.), *Generative fathering: Beyond deficit perspectives* (pp. 17–35). Thousand Oaks, CA: Sage.

Erikson, E. (1950). *Childhood and society*. New York: Norton.

Franklin, A. J. (2002). *From brotherhood to manhood: How Black men rescue their relationships and dreams from the invisibility syndrome*. New York: Wiley.

Furstenberg, F. (1995). Fathering in the inner city: Paternal participation and public policy. In W. Marsiglio (Ed.), *Fatherhood: Contemporary theory, research and social policy* (pp. 119–147). Thousand Oaks, CA: Sage.

Harris, P. Y. (2001). *From the soul: Stories of great Black parents and the lives they gave us*. New York: Putnam.

Hunter, A., & Davis, J. (1994). Hidden voices of Black men: The meaning, structure and complexity of manhood. *Journal of Black Studies, 25*(1), 20–40.

Hutchinson, E. O. (1995). *Black fatherhood: The guide to male parenting*. Los Angeles: Middle Passage Press.

Kambon, K. K. K. (1998). *African/Black psychology in the American context: An African-centered approach*. Tallahassee, FL: Nubian Nation.

Lamb, M. (1997). Fathers and child development: An introductory overview and guide. In M. E. Lamb (Ed.), *The role of the father in child development* (3rd ed., pp. 1–18). New York: Wiley.

Lee, C. C. (2003). *Empowering young Black males—III: A systematic modular training program for Black male children & adolescents*. Alexandria, VA: American Counseling Association.

Levine, J., & Pitt, E. (1995). *New expectations: Responsible strategies for fatherhood*. New York: Families and Work Institute.

Madhubuti, H. R. (1991). *Black men, obsolete, single, dangerous?: The Afrikan American family in transition*. Chicago, IL: Third World Press.

Madhubuti, H. R. (2002). *Tough notes: A healing call for creating exceptional Black men*. Chicago, IL: Third World Press.

Marsiglio, W. (1995). Fatherhood scholarship: An overview and agenda for the future. In W. Marsiglio (Ed.), *Fatherhood: Contemporary theory, research and social policy* (pp. 1–20). Thousand Oaks, CA: Sage.

Mott, F. (1990). When is a father really gone? Parent/child conduct in father absent homes. *Demograph, 27*(4), 499–517.

Palkovitz, R. (1997). Reconstructing involvement: Expanding men's caring in contemporary families. In A. J. Hawkins & D. C. Dollahite (Eds.), *Generative fathering: Beyond deficit perspectives* (pp. 200–216). Thousand Oaks, CA: Sage.

Parham, T. (2002). *Counseling persons of African descent: Raising the bar of practitioner competence*. Thousand Oaks, CA: Sage.

Pitts, L., Jr. (1999). *Becoming a dad: Black men and their journey into fatherhood*. Marietta, GA: Longstreet.

Pruett, K. (2000). *Fatherneed: Why father care is as essential as mother care for your child*. New York: Broadway Books.

Roberts, B. (1998). *Roberts v. Texaco: A true story of race and corporate America*. New York: Avon Books.

Roopmarine, J., & Ahmeduzzamen, M. (1993). Puerto Rican fathers involved with their school-age children. *Hispanic Journal of Behavioral Sciences, 15*, 96–107.

Thomas, I. (1998). *The search for meaning: Exploring Black male adolescents' relationship with adult males*. Doctoral dissertation, Harvard University, Cambridge, MA.

Wade-Gayles, G. (Ed.). (1997). *Father songs: Testimonies by African-American sons and daughters.* Boston: Beacon Press.

Winbush, R. A. (2001). *The Warrior method: A program for rearing healthy Black boys.* New York: HarperCollins.

White, J. L. (1984). *The psychology of Blacks: An Afro-American perspective.* Englewood Cliffs, NJ: Prentice-Hall.

White, J. L., & Cones, J. H., III. (1999). *Black man emerging: Facing the past and seizing a future in America.* New York: W. H. Freeman.

SUCCESSFUL BLACK PARENTING

Honeywine

i am quickly humbled
continually undergoing a rebirth
finding myself in the lavender depth
of one fond embrace
now the Goddess enters
for the deep is nothing to Her
but rushes thru me
i now understand the beauty of you
always healing   never smothering
the womb that i seek to nurture me

Interlude

the glow of pure love
is a rare emotion to find
it is the mind that has no doubt
and she tells him that he must return
because it is inevitable
she adores him by blocking external energy
for people frequently project their fears
as well as their inner beauty
and she protects him
a signal to return to warmth

shows him the way out
it brings spiritual potency
and i can no longer run
from inspiration
theirs or mine . . .

—Malia, May 21, 1995

Chapter 4

My Dad, My Main Man

Michael E. Connor
Emeritus, California State University, Long Beach

This chapter is dedicated to those African American men who are all too often ignored, overlooked, minimized and/or marginalized in both the popular and educational literature in discussions of fathers and fatherhood. Namely, those fathers of African descent who remain with their families through the hard times, those fathers who participate in the rearing of their children and work to maintain relationships with the mothers of their children, those who toil daily to help feed and clothe and provide shelter to their families are the focus of this chapter. As Staples (1986) wrote: "Rarely are we exposed to his more prosaic role as worker, husband, father and American citizen" (p. 1). These men face the racism, oppression, barriers, obstacles, and situations faced by men of African descent who reside in the United States, but for whatever reasons, they were able to or chose to stay with their families. Interestingly, as noted earlier, this population is routinely ignored in discussions of Black fathers, yet there is much to learn from them and about them. One can argue that if we are serious about understanding how to keep Black fathers connected with their families and their communities, it is likely this population of involved African American fathers has some (many?) answers. This chapter presents a review of relevant history pertaining to issues and barriers that negatively impact on Black fathers and interfere with meaningful interaction with children and families. Next, we address research that focuses on Black men who are involved with their children. Finally, men who were significant in my personal development (my father, my maternal grandfather, and some of my uncles) are offered as models in discussing Black men who are (were) present in the lives of their children and in the mothers of those children.

BRIEF HISTORY REGARDING AFRICAN AMERICAN FATHERS

In reviewing literature regarding Black males in the United States, one is hard pressed to find information that is not negatively oriented. Researchers usually emphasize father absenteeism and other perceived deficits including low aspiration/low self-esteem, unemployment/underemployment, educational deficits, alcohol and drug abuse, violence and aggression, and family disorganization (Lynn, 1974; Hetherington & Parke, 1975; Lamb, 1981), Interestingly, none of these deficits are discussed in the context of White supremacy and the resulting racism or White privilege. Seemingly, few "positives" happen in African American families and one is left to surmise that male–female dual-headed, intact families have never existed.

Dobson (1981) suggested the two primary social science approaches for studying Black families are the pathological and dysfunctional approach and the cultural relativistic approach. The former focuses on disorganized, unstable ("fragile" in the current social science literature) households and the latter focuses on family strengths, controlling for socioeconomic status. The pathological orientation remains the more pervasive model and continues to be well represented in the popular media (films such as *Finding Forrester* [2000] and *Drumline* [2002] are examples of popular recent films that include African-descended youth who were raised in father-absent homes).

During slavery evidence exists suggesting African (Blacks were not African American until *after* the Civil War) fathers were actively and directly involved in family life. For example, Genovese (1978) noted that slaves were willing to risk punishment in order to keep families together. He writes that slave owners were cognizant of this and often argued against separation of families because slaves worked better when their families were kept together. He notes, as relates to runaway slaves, that the importance of family life was second only to the resentment of punishment as reasons for running away. Gutman (1976) wrote that large numbers of slave couples lived in long marriages and most lived in dual-headed households. Thus, African fathers attempted, against great odds, to maintain their families.

After the Civil War, Harris (1976) found two-parent households to be dominant in the African American community, and the vast majority of the Black population resided in the Southern region of the country. During the late 1800s and early 1900s men and women of African descent moved North, in large numbers, *seeking a better way of life*. Because African Americans continued to experience the ravages of White racism and the vestiges of slavery throughout the South, they made the decision to attempt to "escape" and seek an environment that was more conducive to and accepting of recently freed Blacks. This Great Migration led to the urbanization and industrialization of masses of Black Americans in Northeastern and Midwestern cities. Data indicate that families, single men, single women and married men without their families participated in this move. Thus, some families were forever torn apart. Promises and dreams of an independent life off the farm and in the City were enticing. Unfortunately, the dreams quickly became nightmares: Although African American women were permitted domestic work, little was available for the masses of African American men (Genovese, 1978). Again, the pervasive White racism of the time and its resulting oppression of Black Americans are not seriously considered by social scientists as they study the Black Family. In fact, serious scholarship on White racism and White supremacy conducted by White social scientists is wholly lacking in the literature.

The years following World War I were harsh for Americans of African descent. Systematic exclusion from most aspects of American life was pervasive. "Jim Crow" was alive, well, and thriving throughout the country. Political, social, economical, and educational advances were slow in coming and painfully gained. The country, which fought a "Great War" to "make the world safe for democracy" made few and feeble attempts to include African descended citizens in the democratic process. At this time the primary composition of the Black family was dual-headed.

By the 1930s the country was in the midst of a Great Depression—unemployment of White Americans was at an all-time high of 24.9% in 1933. White families broke up, men were despondent, suicide and suicide attempts were not uncommon. White America came to understand the impact of poverty, the lack of work and despair—on White America. Unemployment and underemployment among "freed" African American males residing in the United States was twice that of White males and yet White America continued to show little understanding, compassion, or concern. It is as though Black folks created their own problems and must accept responsibility for resolving them irrespective of the wider educational-economical-social-political environment.

During the 1940s the United States was engaged in a second world war to make the world safe for democracy. African American males were willing to cross the seas and give their lives in defense of the country, when afforded the opportunity. Generally those who were drafted were placed in positions to be of service to Whites (cooks, valets, etc.) or were placed in extremely arduous and hazardous situations with great risk of bodily harm. Many of these fighting men displayed monumental courage in their segregated units, enduring harsh treatment from both their Nation's enemy and from White troops fighting for freedom abroad. Those Black men who stayed behind continued to experience problems finding and maintaining jobs in the war effort. Those who were able to locate work frequently had to migrate to other parts of the country, often having to leave wives and children behind (the jobs tended not to pay enough to support a family plus housing was difficult to find in segregated America). Thus, the displacement of families of African descent continued. Additionally, when White soldiers returned from the War, Black workers were often fired to make a place for White males to work. This led to riots in several cities across the nation.

Contrary to the common images depicted on popular television ("Happy Days," "Father Knows Best," "Ozzie and Harriet"), the 1950s were a time of heightened tension between White and Black Americans. White America continued to enforce Jim Crow laws across the land with Black Americans being afforded poor housing opportunities, minimal access to education, limited employment, and minimal protection under the law (see Allen, Als, Lewis, & Litwack, 2000, *Without Sanctuary* for a discussion of lynchings in the United States). As Bennett (1984) noted, the NAACP commenced an attack on segregated schools in 1951; Baton Rouge's segregated public buses were boycotted in 1953; Emmett Till, a Chicago teenager, was brutally murdered and disfigured in 1955; Rosa Parks refused to give up her seat on a Birmingham bus in 1955, and numerous churches, schools, and businesses utilized by African Americans were destroyed by White mobs. As Malcolm X noted, "the South is anywhere south of Canada" and, White supremacy was the rule of the land. In spite of the many obstacles before the Black community in 1950, 91% of African American families were two-parent headed. And, although numerous problems and limitations existed in segregated America, the Black community had functioning businesses, the extended family-kin network was strong, the Black church was vibrant, and Black students were attending historically Black colleges in large numbers. These African American students would become the force behind the Civil Rights Movement which, in turn, gave rise to the social movements of the 1960s and 1970s (e.g., the Free Speech Movement, the Anti-War Movement, the War on Poverty, the Black Power Movement, the Student Empowerment Movement, the Feminist Movement, the Fathers' Rights Movement, to name a few; four Black students at North Carolina A&T College began the sit-in movement in early 1960). The 1960s were a time of transition as the vestiges of Jim Crow were being challenged on several fronts. Slowly and as a result of numerous battles waged by Black Americans, the United States became more desegregated (integration remains elusive, at best). However, a significant toll was exacted during these turbulent times as relates to African American males. Namely, the leadership was destroyed. First, Medgar Evers was assassinated in 1963, Malcolm X was cut down in 1965, followed by the Reverend Martin Luther King, Jr. in 1968, and then Fred Hampton in 1969. Voices and actions from the masses of White America, particularly those who saw themselves as Christian and/or patriotic, were noticeably silent during the struggles against this rampant racism.

By the 1970s, the cumulative effects of White privilege, and the resulting poverty, racism, and segregation had taken a major toll on the African American family. Billingsley (1970) noted that while the majority of African descended families were headed by married men who were employed fulltime (underemployed), wages were so low that they were unable to pull themselves from pervasive poverty. By 1970, 33.3% of Black families were single-parent headed and by 1980, the percentage had swelled to 45.8 (Glick, 1981). Currently, the percentage of single-parent households in the African American community is 64% (U.S. Bureau of the Census, 1996). It can be argued that the direct attempts to control and to destroy Black families in general and Black males in particular that began during slavery continued into "freedom" through widespread and systematic discrimination in education, employment, and housing. With the growth of youth gangs and the introduction of drugs (particularly crack cocaine) during the 1980s and 1990s, the fabric of the African American community continued to deteriorate. Certainly, poor choices were made by some—"choices" in the context of an inner city sociocultural milieu characterized by poverty, substandard housing, lack of jobs, and inferior schools. In sum, given the numerous continuous significant barriers confronting the African American community in general and African American males in particular, what is surprising is not the large number of single-parent households, but that more African American homes have not been destroyed. That any males have remained in their families is a testament to the resilience of the spirit of the Black community. "The Black family is still around; it is not broken down. The miracle of the Black family is that it has survived and grown stronger over the years" (Willie, 1988, p. 5).

INVOLVED AFRICAN AMERICAN FATHERS

In reviewing research regarding African American fathers who are involved with their children, Cazenave (1981) indicated they believe that responsibility is the key to manhood. His sample notes that ambition, firm guiding principles, and being an economic provider are important. As relates to work, Glick (1981) indicated that as income increases, so does the proportion of men in intact first marriages. This stability is not related to being "well-to-do," but rather seems to depend on not being in poverty. Staples (1986), Connor (1986), Willie (1988), and Pinkney (1993) noted Black men describe their role in family life and marriage as egalitarian with respect to children, housework, and authority.

Connor (1986) surveyed working-class, African American men in stable relationships as relates to their attitudes toward their children and the mothers of their children. His sample shows active involvement with both mothers and children. They interacted and provided care for their children, financially supported their families, were interested in their children's education and futures, were involved with church, and took time to care for their children. Willie (1988) found that Black working-class parents feel so strongly about child-rearing responsibilities that they make "great personal sacrifices" for their families. They expect their kids to work to help out, to complete high school, to possess a sense of moral responsibility, and to stay out of trouble with the law. Home ownership is a major family goal; religion and cooperation for survival are basic.

Hunter and Davis (1994) found that family and family relationships are central to African American fathers' sense of and definition for manhood. McAdoo (1993) discussed four aspects of involvement that African American fathers accept as prerequisite for being a father. These include: being a provider, being a decision maker, participating in child socialization, and being a marital partner. White (1984) and White and Cones (1999) believe seven principles for living guide successful male involvement in family life. These principles, handed down by Black families over the years include:

1. Improvisation. The ability to be innovative, creative and resourceful.
2. Resilience. The ability to rebound from setbacks, gaining strength through adversity.
3. Connectedness to others. The sense of belonging to a wider network of family, kin, friends, and so forth. A support system that can include mentors, same gender peers, romantic relationships, and extended families.
4. Spirituality (not to be confused with religiosity). Deeply experienced feelings that give meaning and power to life. A "voice" of hope.
5. Emotional vitality. The "high" energy that exists in the Black Community, a zest for life seen in African American styles of dress, music, dance, language, athletics, and so on.
6. "Gallows" sense of humor. The ability to laugh and cry in order to survive (see Richard Pryor's work, for example).
7. A healthy suspicion of White folks. Many Blacks find it rather peculiar that so few Whites are willing to honestly confront the related issues of White privilege and White supremacy, especially those who see themselves as religious and/or patriotic.

Other studies have suggested African American fathers are warm, caring, nurturing, and supportive toward their children across SES and throughout the life span (Allen, 1981; Allen & Doherty, 1995; McAdoo, 1981, 1988). Allen and Connor (1997) discuss the concept of generative fathering as it relates to Black men. Generative fathering has its roots in Eriksonian theory suggesting that present-day fathers are responsible for future generations of dads. It posits that current fathers' activities have been influenced by previous generations of fathers, and future generations of fathers will, in turn, be influenced by these current fathers. Allen and Connor (1997) wrote that four major components are required to be successful in this endeavor. The *first* of these components is a set of prerequisites including motivation, skills and energy to parent; *second* is the development of patterns of responsible involvement for one's family; *third* is the sense of competence based on feeling confident of one's value to one's family; and, *four* is commitment—commitment to one's children to one's family and to one's community. This commitment includes an awareness that embraces self-sacrifice for family. As the authors noted: "Men who understand the sacrifices of their ancestors and who have thought seriously about what kind of ancestors they themselves want to be can make a commitment to generative fathering" (p. 62).

LESSONS LEARNED FROM MY DAD

I was, indeed, fortunate to have been born into a home and community where solid male (and female) figures were present. Thus, I was afforded an opportunity to observe how men act/react in relationship to children, to women, to other men, to their surroundings, to White privilege, to social institutions, to church, and to work issues. A variety of Black men (uncles, maternal grandfather, extended family networks, and, especially my father) were consistently around throughout my childhood, my adolescence, my young adulthood, and my adulthood. These men modeled the resilience, the spirituality, the connectedness to others, the improvisation, the emotional vitality, the gallows sense of humor, and the healthy suspicion of the White community as discussed before (White, 1984; White & Cones, 1999). Additionally, although the responsibility to future generations was not talked about directly, behaviors representing several of the components of generative fathering were evident, especially as relates to meaningful interactions with their own father and his siblings (my grandfather and granduncles), with the women in the environment, and with the many omnipresent children (my cousins, sibling, friends, and me). Each of these men was motivated and demonstrated the skill to parent; each developed a pattern of responsible involvement with their children; each was committed to family and to mate; and, each demonstrated competence in terms of being valued by family. In most cases, each of the men was married to or otherwise connected with a working woman. Thus, dual-worker households were the norm. My father's life, in particular, centered around family.

Russell Connor (1908–1988) lived his life in Northwestern Ohio. He was the second of four children. Dad spent his youth in Perrysburg and his adult life in Paulding County where my mother's family resided. Although my father left school after the eighth grade, he was an avid reader, thinker, and reflector of events of his time. He, like Black men of his era, grew up in a segregated, Jim Crow America. He was a willing and able worker, whenever he was able to find a job. He taught himself to do a variety of jobs including construction and automobile maintenance. He was a spiritual, ethical, kind man.

Throughout his adult life, my father held a variety of jobs, primarily in the janitorial-cleaning area. Usually, in order to make ends meet, he held two or more jobs at any one time. As my older brother and I were growing up, I remember my father getting up early every workday to make the 45-minute drive to Ft. Wayne, Indiana (driving time depended on the time of year, on the condition of his older car, and on road conditions as relates to mid-western winters). He typically came home, briefly interacted with us, ate, and went to another job. Weekends were spent working around the house (children were included in the work activities), interacting with my brother and me as relates to athletics, family, and extended family activities.

When I was eight, my father purchased the house where he resided until his death. Because White folks who owned the house would not sell it to him, he had to go through double escrow. That is, a White man, for whom my father worked, first bought the house (which had been condemned) and then sold it to my father. He then moved the house across the tracks where Black folks lived. Dad took the next several years repairing the structure, transforming it from a house to a home. He completed most of the work himself, working weekends and after hours as time, weather, and money permitted. For the tasks that demanded additional hands, my uncles were involved. We had no phone, no indoor bathroom, no television, and no heating (other than a pot-bellied stove in the middle of the house) until I was in high school. However, we had never had these "luxuries" so they were not missed. In fact, I assumed everyone lived much as we did! Nonetheless, we did have a connected family—meals together, and quiet evenings.

Also, there were other adult men continuously present, who were available to demonstrate and model appropriate male behavior. My mother's brothers, Uncle Bill, Uncle Robert, Uncle Charles ("Junior"), a sister's husband, Uncle Tommy, my maternal grandfather ("Pop"), and my father all provided clear and positive models of what Black men were about. All of them worked, and provided for their families. Each was married and generally had a meaningful relationship with his mate and with his own children;

each had a meaningful relationship with the children of the others; each worked to provide financially for their families; each had an interest in the outdoors—specifically, gardening, hunting, and fishing. Hunting and fishing were not considered "sport," rather, these activities were important means of helping to provide food for one's family—food to be shared with others. And, each had a sense of survival in an oppressive world. Along with my father, my uncles taught me to fish, to hunt, to grow food, and to take care of myself. Although we were poor, food was available—if one was willing to put forth the effort to get it, and if one knew how and where to seek it. The lesson conveyed: It is a man's place to put food on his family's table.

Much activity took place around and within the kitchen. For example, the men would come in from fishing or hunting, sit in a circle talking, smoking, drinking coffee and jiving, cleaning their game/catch. Usually one of them prepared a large cast iron skillet for cooking the meal (everything was deep fried), and almost mysteriously my mother or one of my many aunts would appear to take over the cooking. The men continued their discussions into the night, well after the food was consumed and the eating area cleaned for the next meal. These are among my best memories while growing up. I was afforded the opportunity to observe, learn, interact, and share. These interactions were often funny, educational, and intense. I came to understand and appreciate the "gallows" sense of humor, the sense of commitment to others, the improvisation, and the emotional vitality so evident during these activities.

There were numerous comments and lessons offered by my father which relate to surviving and perhaps thriving in life. Certainly, at the time some (most?) of the lessons were offered I did not possess the maturity, common sense, intelligence, or life experience to comprehend; however, somehow the words and lessons were tucked away in the recesses of my mind and as I grew they took on meaning and had value in how I came to conduct myself. Over the years I often find myself reflecting on the sage advice and common sense of some of the offerings—lessons and comments regarding work; White supremacy, racism, and segragation; male–female social relationships; and fathers and fatherhood.

WORK

My father believed that there is honor in work, no matter what you do. His philosophy was "No work can hurt you" and "You can learn about life and yourself from whatever work you do." One can glean important information about oneself (including skills required to complete tasks independently and cooperatively, skills needed to receive and to offer direction, responsibility, motivation and focus to remain on task, the value of productive activity) and about other people (differing value systems, differing approaches to tasks, differing problem-solving strategies, etc.) through work. He stated there is no job that is beneath me and I should not be embarrassed to do any type of work. He said on several occasions, "Work is what you do, it is not who you are." He also felt one can learn skills in completing labor, skills that would be of aid later in life, if you only took the time and attend to what you were doing. Thus, although I silently objected to some jobs I had (cleaning offices, washing dishes in a cafeteria; farm work; construction and painting; tending to lawns and gardens, including picking fruit and vegetables), each of these jobs offered valuable lessons, and transferable skills as a homeowner later in life. I learned that I could support myself.

My father admonished me to "Learn to take care of yourself and live within your means." Because both of my parents worked, my brother and I were provided with the opportunity to learn to care for our basic needs. My father participated in food preparation (and cleanup), washing and ironing clothes, keeping the house clean and keeping the yard clean. I was taught how to budget whatever money I accrued, and how to maintain household records. Additionally, I learned a valuable lesson regarding debt. Dad's position was, "if you do not have the money to pay with cash, you probably do not need what you think you want to buy." While we did not have much, what we did have was ours. He had no concept of "layaway," of credit card debt, of monthly car notes, or of going without electricity, heat, or food. He felt a man should anticipate his needs and work to provide for them. I learned that automobile and credit card debt represent wasted money and opportunity for "financial independence" as you are paying too much for what you are receiving. Additionally, I learned the importance of owning a home.

WHITE SUPREMACY, RACISM, AND SEGREGATION

As relates to the racism and segregation of the day, Dad indicated, "No one can beat you but you" and "White folks are not a problem unless you allow them to be." He noted that to be successful, I would have to be "twice as good" as White folks as they make up rules to keep us out and to minimize opportunity. "To get any chance in life, you'll have to be good, better than they are—and you are." He told me, "No one can control your mind, keep it clear and full of positive thoughts." He felt that while I possessed some athletic skills, that "education was your ticket to a better life." Thus, he pushed me (and my brother) to use our athletic abilities as a means to get an education. He seemed to recognize that athletic careers are fleeting and that as long as I was able to use my brain, I could survive. His position was if I tried my best and failed, I did not fail. Rather, if I worked to the best of my ability, that was fine and acceptable. By definition, the effort was "successful." Although I recognized the "system" was not fair, I did learn what it took to persevere. I came to understand life in America does not offer a level playing field and I should expect others to act as they do. This has been a valuable life lesson as it relates to my perceptions and experiences with the White privilege evidenced by the people with whom I work and interact.

Additionally, Dad believed that none of us (Black folks) has it "made" as long as any of us is suffering the consequences of American apartheid. He felt that Black folks have the responsibility to do their best in order to support future generations of the Black community. Always "try your best and feel good about your effort"—"you judge you before anyone else judges you." The effort you put forth will have an impact on others who are seeking opportunity. Finally, "race in America counts" and I am mindful of that fact.

MALE–FEMALE SOCIAL RELATIONSHIPS

"Do not disrespect women." Although my parents had disagreements in their marital relationship, I was never aware of my father saying or doing anything discourteous toward my mother. In fact, on several occasions, other adult males inquired as to why he "put up with" some of her actions. His response: "I cannot disrespect my wife without disrespecting myself and I have no intention of disrespecting me." My father was a quiet, dignified, polite man who genuinely loved his wife. He felt while he had the right to sometimes disagree with her, others did not have that same right. He admonished both my brother and me to "not disrespect women as long as you have my name." He felt it is important to try and develop a "partnership" with your mate. Recognize her strengths and skills and utilize them; appreciate her and what she offers you; model the behaviors you wish your children to emulate in their relationships with the opposite sex. Additionally, although Dad smoked cigarettes, he was a nondrinker. He felt that "alcohol dulls your mind and makes you do stupid things," and that "Black folks cannot afford to be dull-minded in (racist) America." "One must be ever mindful of who we are and where we live."

FATHERS AND FATHERHOOD

"The true mark of a real man is how he treats those around him, and the true mark of a father is how he raises his children." It is not about money and what you can buy for your children. Rather, it is about the time spent interacting, sharing, teaching, and learning from and with them. Certainly it takes money to provide and one needs to work to offer opportunity. Children are your "primary responsibility," and you must care for, nurture, provide for, and love them. He stated that I "should never be afraid to express my love" for my children (I came to understand that the most masculine thing a man can do is to love and care for his offspring). They are my "primary responsibility" and only I am "responsible to feed, clothe, and shelter" them. Others can help if they so desire, but I am responsible. Dad's position was that I would continue to father/parent my children until my death. I came to understand that having and rearing children is both expensive, rewarding, and can leave you quite venerable. I also understand the value, the pain, the joy, the excitement, the disappointment, the fear, the hope, and the love that comes from and with children.

DISCUSSION

The men I have discussed found the means to make their family relationships work. They were committed, they cared, they persevered, their families mattered, and they found strength in their many family associations and interactions. If social scientists are serious about understanding the ways and means to strengthen the African American family (and families in general as America could learn much from the African American community), it would be prudent to acknowledge and research the many men such as those mentioned here. It is likely they held/hold answers to many of today's pressing social problems. These men were able to remain with their families and maintain meaningful relationships with their children against considerable odds; they were able to make dual working households work (a significant issue in contemporary America); they lived within their means and had little debt; they overtly expressed care, love, and commitment to their children; they recognized and utilized the extended family and personal kinships; they were cognizant of the oppressive, racist environment in which they lived and they survived it; they were competent in terms of caring for themselves and their families; and, they cared for their children. There is much these men can teach us today, if only we were to listen, hear, and value their words.

Although this chapter focuses on involved African American fathers, it is important to note that each of the men discussed had a strong, supportive, African American woman who toiled alongside him. These fathers seemed to recognize they were not whole without their mate and they worked to keep their marriages and relationships together. In most cases, the women also worked outside the home in order to make ends meet. They seemed to recognize that a marital partnership was needed to confront and succeed against the significant odds confronting them. These men and their families have answers and solutions to some of the current issues confronting this society. Will they be asked? Will they be considered? Will they be heard?

REFERENCES

Allen, J., Als, H., Lewis, J., & Litwack, L. F. (2000). *Without sanctuary: Lynching photography in America*. Santa Fe, NM: Twin Palms Publishers.

Allen, W. (1981). Moms, dads, and boys: Race and sex differences in the socialization of male children. In L. E. Gary (Ed.), *Black men* (pp. 94–114). Beverly Hills, CA: Sage.

Allen, W., & Connor, M. (1997). An African American perspective on generative fathering. In A. J. Hawkins & D. C. Dollahite (Eds.), *Generative fathering: Beyond deficit perspectives* (pp. 52–70). Thousand Oaks, CA: Sage.

Allen, W., & Doherty, W. (1995). Being there: The perception of fatherhood among a group of African American adolescent fathers. In H. McCubbin, E. Thompson, A. Thompson, & J. Futrell (Eds.), *Resiliency in ethnic minority families* (Vol. 2, pp. 207–244). Madison: University of Wisconsin Press.

Bennett, L. (1984). *Before the Mayflower*. New York: Penguin Books.

Billingsley, A. (1970). Black families and white social science. *Journal of Social Issues, 26*(3), 127–142.

Cazenave, N. A. (1981). Black men in America: The quest for manhood. In H. P. McAdoo (Ed.), *Black families* (pp. 176–185). Beverly Hills, CA: Sage.

Connor, M. (1986). Some parenting attitudes of young Black fathers. In R. A. Lewis & R. E. Salt (Eds.), *Men in families* (pp. 159–168). Beverly Hills, CA: Sage.

Dobson, J. (1981). Conceptualizations of Black families. In H. T. McAdoo (Ed.), *Black families* (pp. 23–36). Beverly Hills, CA: Sage.

Genovese, E. D. (1978). The myth of the absent family. In R. Staples (Ed.), *The Black family: Essays and studies* (pp. 35–43). Belmont, CA: Wadsworth.

Glick, P. C. (1981). A demographic picture of Black families. In H. P. McAdoo (Ed.), *Black families* (pp. 106–126). Beverly Hills, CA: Sage.

Gutman, H. (1976). *The Black family in slavery and freedom, 1750–1925*. New York: Pantheon Books.

Harris, W. (1976). Work and family in Black America, 1880. *Journal of Social History, 9*(3), 319–330.

Hetherington, M., & Parke, R. (1975). *Child psychology*. New York: McGraw-Hill.

Hunter, A., & Davis, J. (1994). Hidden voices of Black men: The meaning, structure, and complexity of manhood. *Journal of Black Studies, 25*(1), 20–40.

Lamb, M. (1981). *The role of fathers in child development*. New York: Wiley Interscience.

Lynn, D. B. (1974). *The father: His role in child development*. Monterey, CA: Brooks/Cole.

McAdoo, J. L. (1981). Black father and child interactions. In L. E. Gary (Ed.), *Black men* (pp. 115–130). Beverly Hills, CA: Sage.

McAdoo, J. (1988). The role of Black fathers in the socialization of Black children. In H. McAdoo (Ed.), *Black families* (pp. 225–237). Newbury Park, CA: Sage.

McAdoo, J. (1993). The roles of African American fathers: An ecological perspective. *Families in Society, 74*, 28–35.

Staples, R. (1986). *Black masculinity: The Black male's role in American society.* San Francisco: The
    Black Scholar Press.
U.S. Bureau of the Census. (1996). *Statistical abstract of the United States.* Washington, DC: U.S.
    Government Printing Office.
White, J. L. (1984). *The psychology of Blacks: An Afro-American perspective.* Englewood Cliffs, NJ:
    Prentice-Hall.
White, J. L., & Cones, J. (1999). *Black man emerging.* New York: Routledge.
Willie, C. V. (1988). *A new look at Black families.* New York: General Hall, Inc.

Chapter 5

Intangible Assets

Claytie Davis III
University of California, Berkeley

Percy L. Abram III
Brentwood School, Los Angeles

> *In the chorus of negative reports and opinions, the voice of Black men themselves is rarely heard.*
>
> —White and Cones (1999, p. 3)

There is a crisis taking place in the Black community and few seem to care. We ask, "where have all of the positive Black 'real' models gone?" We chose the adjective *real* rather than *role* intentionally as role models do not seem to be working by our assessment. Recently, we each asked colleagues to name five Black men. We were not surprised by the predictable responses received. One individual gave the following names: "Martin Luther King Jr., Malcolm X, Kobe Bryant, Kevin Hill, and [the first author]." Another colleague had the following list: "father, grandfather, two friends, and MLK Jr." It is our contention that the latter list provides a closer approximation of what is necessary, though still not entirely sufficient for Black youth to thrive in a world that is not always affirming of Black people. The former list could be used to supplant lessons learned from people present in our lives, but is not as helpful as the latter as those individuals have the opportunity to provide feedback to the person. And it should be noted that the first list contains Kevin Hill—who is a fictional character on television. We need real Black men modeling behavior that is exemplary and facilitative of healthy development.

We believe our fathers and other male real models were instrumental in our development and that the tutelage we received is still applicable to young men today.

BOYS IN THE 'BURBS

We met in 1980 when the Abram family moved to "Shadowbriar," a pre-dominately White neighborhood in Houston, Texas. The Abram family was the third Black family to move into the neighborhood, which at the time was less than 10 years old. With few Black families in the neighborhood and our proximity in age (1 year difference) it was inevitable that we would be-friend one another. In the late 1970s through the early 1980s dressing preppy was the way to be in the suburbs. We were no different than any of the other kids around us—we wanted to be liked. Our personalities, on the extroverted side, and our sense of humor probably helped us get through middle school without the assaults of being called an "oreo" and "nigger" as often as other Blacks from comparable neighborhoods.

Although race relations in Houston were probably the same as they were in other places, class seemed to carry more weight in our neighborhood and school. We were unabashedly preppy in our dress and spoke what Bill Cosby would characterize as good English. Both which made us safe for our White peers to be around at school and in their homes. Although our mid-dle school had a significant proportion of African Americans it still felt seg-regated by the classes one took. Our only interactions at school with African Americans would take place at lunch, in Physical Education class, and on the way home on the bus. Navigating between the two groups was challeng-ing and yet empowering. The middle-school years were about establishing that academic identity and early bonds that you take to high school and be-yond. However, 5 years after moving to the neighborhood, and just as Percy was beginning high school, his father was transferred to the West Coast.

We didn't talk much during our high-school years. It wasn't until we were in college, with the advent of email, that we were able to reconnect and stay abreast of each other's lives. As we talked, we discovered that our past, present, and future lives had been running a parallel course. Al-though there were some differences in our histories it was hard to believe how much we had in common with regards to our social, educational expe-riences, and career goals. The most common theme we shared was the ac-tive presence of our fathers.

OUR FATHERS' HISTORIES

In 1903 William Edward Burghardt DuBois discussed the role and responsi-bility of the "Talented Tenth" in an essay of the same title. Although per-ceived at times as elitist and perhaps impractical, his ideas about what was necessary for the progress of the Black race, and specifically men, represent what our fathers had in mind for each of us. From our earliest remembrances we benefited from their foresight and belief that education was essential to our success. They made great sacrifices to ensure that we had whatever was necessary to be academically competitive. Thus, attending college and the pursuit of higher education was never an option, but rather an expectation. This was one of the many attributes handed down to us as being necessary in becoming successful young men, faithful husbands, loving fathers, and productive citizens.

Claytie Davis, Jr.

My father was born in Crowley, Louisiana, and raised in Port Arthur, Texas, in the southeastern part of the state near the Gulf of Mexico. Claytie Jr. was the oldest of seven children (5 boys and 2 girls). His mother was a full-time parent and his father, Claytie Sr., worked at the local refinery and moonlighted by repairing televisions out of his garage. My grandfather was a proud Black man and this trait was one of many that he instilled in my father who would in turn model the same for me. I learned the importance of saying "yes sir/ma'am" to elders, looking people in their eyes when I spoke to them, and being punctual (i.e., be early). Although not major, I believe these habits contributed to people developing trust for me, as well as confidence in me.

My father joined the military out of high school and would later attend and graduate from Rutgers University while working full-time. In addition to myself, my parents had another son, Corey, who is actually more like my father than I. My father and brother majored in business while I concentrated in the social sciences at the University of Texas. Corey received his BA in finance from Georgetown University and his MBA from Harvard University. I know my father is especially proud of both of us and probably takes pride in the paths that both of us have taken, although Corey had less questions to answer regarding his major. My father worked for Southwestern Bell for 29 years in numerous management roles until his retirement at the age of 53. His success in moving from a small segregated town in rural Texas to raising a family on his own in Houston was inspiring and at times daunting. And yet I believe Claytie Jr. provided my brother and me with the requisite tools to succeed.

Percy L. Abram, Jr.

My father was born in Canton, Mississippi, in the autumn of 1941. As was customary among the Black residents of Canton, my father was delivered at home by the town's only doctor, George Carmichael, his mother's brother. The scourge of the Jim Crow South took its psychological and economic toll on Canton's Black residents in those prewar years, but more personally and indelibly affected my father 2 years hence. Hemorrhaging from the labor of her second child, my paternal grandmother, Daisy Carmichael, drove with her brother past the local White hospital some 40 miles to the only hospital in the region that admitted Black patients, where she died along with her stillborn daughter in 1943.

After a small custody campaign, my father settled with his father, Percy L. Abram, Sr., his stepmother and sister in Los Angeles. My father graduated from Los Angeles High School, and California State University, Los Angeles. He married a high-school classmate, Sandra Orange, in 1964 and upon returning from service with the United States Army in Vietnam began a family that included two daughters and me. P.L. remained married to, and ultimately consoled my mother, until his death from lung cancer in April of 2000. My father created a passageway through which I was able to achieve a modicum of success. However, the economic circumstances that he developed pale in comparison to the strategic, ethical, and ecumenical lessons that have guided my personal and professional life. In many ways, his profound lessons about responsibility, dedication, and fatherhood resonate more in his absence.

ACADEMIC

We were fortunate to grow up in middle- and upper-middle-class neighborhoods and attend well-resourced public and private schools. However, this also meant that we were one of a scarce few Black students enrolled in advanced and honors-level courses. The effects were somewhat routine, our responses dramatic, and the outcome of this circumstance—when considered in toto—exceedingly positive. In the book *The Declining Significance of Race*, William Julius Wilson (1980) makes the case for the ascendancy of income and wealth as the primary determinant of one's economic and social opportunities while suggesting that race has become, in many ways, a superfluous consideration. Wilson's case for the former does, in fact, speak to the new economic realities of a burgeoning professional class; it quite pointedly neglects the interpersonal realities, academic disparities, and life choices that affect everyday life. As stated in the opening of this chapter, our dress and speech suggested that we were from the middle class. Our fathers worked to ensure that we might have opportunities not afforded them. Unfortunately, many of our brothers and sisters who we felt also belonged in the honors courses were not there in part because of their backgrounds. In fact, with the exception of maybe one White student, everyone on our street who attended our middle school was in the honors classes. And he probably chose to be in non-honors classes. Without the "right" address one has to have an advocate or a vocal parent. For example, when

Claytie Davis applied to Strake Jesuit College Preparatory—a private Catholic school—an entrance exam was required in addition to letters of recommendation. I received a 91% on my exam but was not admitted to Jesuit. My mother called 5 minutes after I received the rejection letter to ascertain why. She was told that because I had received a 70% on the entrance exam Jesuit was not a good fit. Obviously, after she pointed out the error, they apologized and sent out a letter of acceptance but what if she had not been there for me; or had made this call after all the slots for the freshman class were filled?

RACE AND IDENTITY

Claytie's Perspective

Learning how to succeed in spite of racial barriers were lessons taught to us at an early age. There were not many explicit discussions about race in our home but there was a consciousness about race, nonetheless. For example, every, and I stress, every Sunday I attended church at Wesley Chapel A.M.E. with my parents and brother. The congregation was all Black with the exception of perhaps one White family. The attributes that fostered my success in school were the same ones that caused distress at church. Following the eight o'clock morning service was Sunday school by age group. My dress, speech, and at times hair style were seen as peculiar. There were also the trips to Port Arthur, Texas, when my family visited the extended family. I often walked into the local grocery store, to hear the inevitable question, "where are you from?" It was obvious to the locals that although I was Black I was not from around there. I don't recall my father ever saying anything about why it was obvious to people that I was not from Port Arthur. It would have been easy for him to say, "you talk like White folks." His silence was more powerful and educational than any words that would have fallen on my adolescent ears.

At some point between the eighth and ninth grade I had, for lack of a better phrase, an identity crisis. I went so far as to relax my hair so I could "flick" it out of my eyes like my White friends. Reflecting on what it looked like, it is hard to believe that my father let me leave the house looking as I did. To be honest, I knew there was something not quite right. Every Sunday when I got dressed for church there was a nervous feeling related to how my hair would be perceived. Probably akin to a child today who comes home for the first time with their hair colored or a new tattoo. There was no reason for me to believe that my father was aware of Black racial identity development models; and yet his behavior belied a tacit understanding of the writings of people such as, William Cross (1971) and Thomas Parham

(1989). It was as if he knew I was stuck in a Pre-Encounter stage (see Cross, 1971, 1991, for a review of the racial identity stages and literature) and not willing to allow any of the Encounter experiences (e.g., racial epithets, being the only Black student in my class) move me along to the next stage. I'm not sure how my life would be different if he had attempted to prevent me from cycling through my identity but I believe the process of navigating my racial identity strengthened our relationship. I learned that my father loved me unconditionally and that regardless of who I associated with and how I dressed he supported me. In his mind I imagine he was saying, "If the boy wants to embarrass himself that is fine just don't embarrass the family . . . always remember you are a Davis." Over time I would begin to internalize this latter message more—pride in being a member of the family and appreciating the privileges afforded me.

Percy's Perspective

As Claytie describes above, and many African Americans continue to realize, growing up Black in a predominantly White area can have deleterious consequences to your sense of identity. I wince now when I consider the epithets I endured as an emerging adolescent. Among my "friends," the word nigger was exchanged with facility, never directed toward me, and always with the caveat that I was the exception. To be considered the exception was scarcely a consolation. I was loath to be regarded as anything other than Black in public. In private, I longed for a safer, more suitable racial identity. I felt tortured by this duality. Among my White friends, I was considered beyond Black, and among my Black friends, I was merely a "sellout." These discrete racial distinctions made growing up in Houston, Texas difficult. I found what appeared to be solace in our move to the suburbs of San Francisco at the end of my freshman year in high school.

The move was met with mixed success. Although still struggling to understand my place as one of perhaps 20 Black students in a high school of 1,400, I sought refuge in my studies. When I emerged after my sophomore year, I found that my peers in California did not have the attendant racial "baggage" that accumulates from growing up in the South (e.g., individuals espousing White supremacist views, looking fondly on the South's bygone era, and admitting anger for the "War of Northern Aggression"). However, in the early 1990s, California was at the forefront of action to curb any earlier gains made by people of color. The manifestation was a backlash among White families to affirmative action programs and diversity organizations, and a general tension among racial groups on campus. There was in my high school an acknowledgment that an acceptable response to these social and legal programs was to assert the legitimacy of Whiteness on campus. In my case, I noticed the proliferation of sympathetic views toward Neo-Nazi ideology. I was once confronted by a classmate and told in no uncertain terms that I was not welcome at the school.

PERSONAL INTEGRITY

Claytie's Perspective

There seems to be a lack of integrity among Black men. Not necessarily with regard to honesty but with individual integrity. The type of integrity that allows you to stand up in the face of enormous pressure and say "I want to study" or "I need to get into college." It is a sad indictment on our race that in the year 2005 there are still studies that confirm (and some that counter) that many Black youths, especially young boys, equate excelling in school with being counter to how they want to view themselves. We are reminded of a talk where Dr. Thomas Parham suggested that individuals ask themselves three fundamental questions: "Who am I? Am I who I say I am? and Am I who I ought to be?" These questions are difficult for even the most learned adults to answer; however, there are some means to helping young folks begin an exploration of them.

Personal integrity is a critical issue that allows us each to look ourselves in the mirror and feel good. On one occasion the first author and his brother were playing in the living room when my father called us into his office. He said he wanted to talk to us about something and that he had a question for us. The question would stay with me for the rest of my life. He asked, "What is the only intangible asset you have?" Partly because my brother and I were in fifth and fourth grade, respectively, and more that we weren't clear on what the word "intangible" meant, we thought we had done something wrong. After about 10 minutes of his asking us to "think," we gave up. He smiled and said, "The only intangible asset you have is your word . . . and once it is gone it is very difficult to get back." I think back on this lesson as I meet with young Black students at the university. Most students, ostensibly, come to college to get a good education which will lead to a good job. However, when you ask about their activities there is a disconnect between why they say they are in college and their behaviors. More than "keeping your word" with others, the need to be true to oneself is critical. Somehow in high school and college I saw myself as a student. My identity was clear and thus it was possible to recognize when I was off track. Part of being aware of oneself is recognizing when one is not "being oneself," but this is difficult to do if you have not begun addressing the first question, "Who am I?" and have no one to provide feedback—a real model.

Percy's Perspective

As a Black educator working in a predominantly affluent White environment, I must contend with small, insidious forms of prejudice directed at myself, or worse, other students of color. Recently, I spoke with a student who was discouraged by the lack of faculty training about issues of racism, prejudice, and injustice. In particular, during class discussions about texts that included, but do not necessarily revolve around, African American characters, she is asked to speak on behalf of the Black community. Often, when she presents information that challenges the collective wisdom of the group, her statements are subject to reprobative looks and contradictory retorts by students, frequently corroborated by teachers. These responses are corrosive and foster a milieu that discourages academic discourse and learning. Thus creating an environment where Black students in particular, and students of color more generally are reluctant to invest in the education process, declining academic performance, and lower expectations; an iterative process that can lead to decreased enrollment among students of color.

In addition to classroom scrutiny, students attending these institutions are subject to personal slights, misunderstandings, and ostracisms that affect not only academic performance, but self-identity and impressions of self-concept. These microaggressions often isolate students of color in predominantly White institutions and lead to their marginalization. In response, many academicians have found havens in departments that offer resources and support in their areas of intellectual interests. The ubiquity of Afro-American (Asian Studies, Hispanic/Latino) departments, as well as programs that foster multicultural education suggest that our institutions have evolved to find niches of academic and cultural freedom. These solutions can, however, restrict communication across disciplines and lead to less intellectual growth for individual scholars and the institution as a whole. We have also seen, more recently, a growing resentment among the population to these departments and the students who inhabit them.

Among public school students at the elementary and secondary level, the issues of microaggressions seem remote, even trivial. Currently, in my native city of Los Angeles, the racial composition of public schools paragons those of my father's hometown of Canton—of the 1940s. The White student population of the Los Angeles Unified School District is hovering around 10%, while the Black and Latino population in the district is approaching 75%. One might have suspected that, given the shifting racial and ethnic dynamic in America over the past 40 years, and the promises and aspirations of the civil rights movement, our public schools would trend toward greater understanding, collaboration, and integration rather than less. Although public schools in major metropolitan areas are often underresourced, mal-administered, and poorly staffed, parents often feel as if there are few alternatives.

Among middle-class Black parents, there may be more options for schooling, but the educational outcomes are often strikingly similar. In schools situated within middle-class neighborhoods, the Black–White and Latino–White gap continues to favor Whites, and in some areas the disparities are becoming more pronounced (see Ogbu, 2003). There have been numerous explanations for the gap (low teacher expectations, student apathy, absence of cultural capital, and contrary cultural norms), but none sufficiently or comprehensively elucidate how to address this critical issue.

RESPONSIBILITY

Although we grew up privileged in many ways our fathers didn't believe in "giving" us much. In order to play sports we had to maintain a minimum grade point average of B+ with *no* conduct problems. If we wanted an allowance like the rest of the kids in the neighborhood we had to mow the yard, vacuum the house, clean the bathrooms, and more. When the first author reached the age of 16 and had his heart set on getting a car like the rest of his friends it was a 50–50 deal. My father had informed me a few years earlier that if I wanted a car I would need to pay for at least half the purchase price and concomitant insurance. These were all important lessons. Learning the value of a dollar very early on and how hard it is to get significant amounts of money made us very aware that hard work would be necessary if we hoped to approach the level of financial success our fathers achieved.

FATHERING

Claytie's Perspective

In 2003 I was blessed with the birth of my daughter, Alexandra. There is no greater satisfaction for me than to walk into my house and hear her say, "Daddy" as she runs to give me a hug. Another passion of mine is golf. Yes, I was intrigued after seeing Tiger Woods dominate the sport and the ensuing Black celebrities out on the golf courses. I look forward to teaching Alexandra how to play and about the lessons she can learn there. Among my friends there is a running joke that I want her to be the next Michelle Wie, the 14-year-old phenom who plays in professional golf tournaments (men and women's) and can drive the ball as far as some of the men. In some ways I do want Alexandra (my daughter) to possess what Michelle Wie, Venus and Serena Williams undoubtedly embody—courage, determination, and a form of entitlement. It is this last attribute, entitlement, that I believe gets a bad rap. It is one thing to feel entitled to a new car at the age of 16, or to feel entitled to have your every wish accommodated. What I believe is missing from young African Americans more than from their White and Asian American peers is an entitlement to access (e.g., education). My goal is to raise my daughter so that she feels entitled to the best service, treatment, and resources; and anything less is unacceptable. And that is why I (we) "real" models must be there for her. It will not be enough for her to have the Williams sisters' picture on the wall. She needs a real person providing feedback, encouragement, and consequence. This notion of entitlement, however, begs the question of how do you prevent children from being spoiled. This problematic behavior is mitigated by being present and providing consistent and clear feedback.

Percy's Perspective

How then can Black men—emerging Black fathers—learn from the lessons of the past and formulate healthy, productive, satisfying relationships with their children given the structural limitations and the personal afflictions they leave? Among my family, the record has been mixed. My paternal and maternal grandfathers were apotheses of successful Black professionals and good fathers. They worked and lived with an ethic that encouraged financial prudence and social modesty; they demanded academic excellence and a stalwart belief in the virtues of progress through educational attainment; and lastly, assured that their children would have more opportunities than them. This promise, by and large, is borne out in their progeny. The anomalies include two uncles who succumbed to the emerging drug and gang culture of Los Angeles in the late 1970s and early 1980s.

One cannot discuss these limitations without acknowledging the immense progress Blacks have made collectively and individually since 1941. I have far more options as a result of my father's sacrifices, the changing racial climate, and by virtue of having received three advanced degrees. My father's wish, and the goal of most Black fathers, is to leave a more open, hospitable, and opportunity-rich world to their children than the one they entered. He succeeded in doing this for me as well as my siblings. My goal is similar, but I choose to add one small but complicated addendum. I am adamant that my daughter continues to view the possibility and opportunities that are available only in our democratic-minded society, while concurrently continue to hold its leaders, citizens, and participants accountable for its many failings. These ostensibly contradictory values wreaked havoc on the minds of two of my uncles and still weigh heavily on me. They remind us that promise comes not without pain and that my future aspirations are tethered to our recent past. So, as I ask my daughter to navigate the treacherous waters of racial classifications, interpersonal relationships and society's diffidence toward the issue, I am mindful that this is a heavy burden to bear. I am hopeful that I have prepared her as well as Percy L. Abram Jr. prepared me.

CONCLUSION

The lessons we have internalized from the examples of the Black men, specifically our fathers—real models—who have mentored, admonished, and guided us through adolescence and adulthood are that the failings, myopia, and cruelty of the individuals around you must not impede your willingness to set objectives and ultimately, attain them. However, this lesson is hollow unless we recognize the campaigns of those individuals, both historic and personal, and incorporate and inculcate their sense of justice into our lives and children.

As my colleague, coauthor and friend, Dr. Davis, recognized, one must establish a sense of community to remember the past, acknowledge while lamenting the impediments of the present, and build upon hope for the future. Dr. Davis' and my fortunes were a result of developing and maintaining that sense of community. The fortuity that placed us within one block of one another nearly 20 years ago and our resolve to continue and fortify our friendship has, undoubtedly, helped to make us more accomplished professionals, more devoted husbands, and better fathers. The Davises are the godparents to my daughter, Claudia, and are charged with continuing the legacy of Shadowbriar, wherever that may take her.

REFERENCES

Cross, W. E., Jr. (1971). The Negro to Black conversion experience: Toward a psychology of Black liberation. *Black World, 20*(9), 13–27.

Cross, W. E., Jr. (1991). *Shades of Black: Diversity in African-American identity.* Philadelphia: Temple University Press.

DuBois, W. E. B. (1903). The talented tenth. In B. T. Washington (Ed.), *The Negro problem: A series of articles by representative American Negroes of today.* New York: J. Pott & Co.

Ogbu, J. U. (2003). *Black American students in an affluent suburb: A study of academic disengagement.* Mahwah, NJ: Lawrence Erlbaum Associates.

Parham, T. A. (1989). Cycles of Nigrescence. *The Counseling Psychologist, 17*(2), 187–226.

Wilson, W. J. (1980). *The declining significance of race.* Chicago: University of Chicago Press.

White, J. L., & Cones, J. H., III. (1999). *Black man emerging: Facing the past and seizing a future in America.* New York: Freeman.

Chapter 6

Images of Black Fathers
From the Community

Kenneth W. Bentley
Nestlé USA

> *There is a man in my house*
> *He's so big and strong*
> *He goes to work each day and stays all day long*
> *Comes home at night, looking tired and beat . . .*
> *I think I'll color him father . . . I think I'll color him love.*
> —O. C. Smith, "Color Him Father." (1969)

In this chapter, comments and suggestions from a variety of African American fathers with varying histories are offered. These fathers are all professional men who believe in giving back and sharing.

In the south central Los Angeles neighborhood I grew up in, I never had problems finding positive images of Black fathers. I found them in my pastor Bishop William H. Graves and men in my church like Ralph Davis and Earl Dyer who told me that with God in my life I could do anything.

I found them in heroes like Arthur Ashe. I met Arthur when I was a 15-year-old sitting on a bench at the Los Angeles Tennis Club. I was the only African American in this important junior tournament and I was nervously waiting to play the biggest tennis match of my life. Arthur was the reigning U.S. Open Champion and when he walked up to me I was more than a little stunned. Dressed in his army uniform, Arthur introduced himself, wrote down his address and phone number then said, "if you ever need anything tennis or otherwise don't hesitate to get in touch with me." It was the start

99

of a friendship that lasted until he died. What I remember most from my conversations with this great man was the day he sat me down and told me that I should spend as much time working on my schoolwork as I did on my tennis. "Education not tennis," he said, "would be the key to your future." It was advice that served me well.

There were other less famous mentors like Booker Mooten at Crenshaw High and college professors Robert Norris and Dr. Joe White. These were men who believed in the words of Dr. Alvin Poussaint (1987) that "Black men must make a special effort to become spiritual and psychological fathers to needy Black children within their extended families and communities" (cited in Riley, 1991, p. 142). As much as I learned from these men, the greatest father figure I had was in the next bedroom.

James Bentley was the perfect example of a strong Black father. He went to work everyday—often working two jobs to support his eight kids. Despite working as many as 16 hours a day during the week, he still coached Little League baseball and Youth Flag Football on the weekends. I vividly remember being seven or eight and my father coming home with an old green truck. Every Saturday he would load that green truck with neighborhood boys and head for Harvard Park. A former baseball player in Negro Leagues around Arkansas as a youngster he would hit balls to us for as long as we wanted to stay on the field. But what stands out in my mind are not the sessions on the field, but what he told us during what he called "skull sessions."

During those skull or mental sessions he would gather us in one of the small classroom style rooms at the park. He would grab a piece of chalk and diagram on an old blackboard in the front of the room how to turn double plays or where to hit the cut off man—things that would make us better baseball players. But what I remember most about those sessions is when he would put the chalk down and talk to us about attitude. The importance of giving 100% every minute we were on the field. He talked about discipline and respect for authority. He urged us to have a healthy respect for the game and for ourselves. He told us we could do anything we put our minds to, but because of the society we lived in, we had to be better. We had to work a little harder. But it was ok he told us, because if we did, we would win and we usually did. At the end of each session, my Dad told us he was preparing us for next week's game, but, in fact, he was preparing us for life. He was my Dad, but he was also Dad to a neighborhood full of impressionable young men—many of whom have gone on to be successful in a variety of fields including fatherhood. My father passed away in 2003 a day after his 88th birthday, but the lessons I learned from those "skull sessions" will stay with me for the rest of my life.

The positive image of a Black father that was so evident in the Bentley household is one that I have held onto as I've entered into fatherhood. That image was challenged when my ex-wife and I divorced nearly 17 years ago. It was on my mind when I told my then 4-year-old daughter Christina that I would no longer be living with her everyday. As tears welled in her eyes I promised her I would still be there to pick her up when she fell. I went to nearly every PTA meeting, Open House, and parent conference. For 3 years I was on the sidelines for every swim meet. I made sure she had a voice in every critical decision I made including where I lived and worked and in my decision to remarry 3 years ago. A decision that added not only my wife Jelana to our family but her two kids, Al and Angelena as well. In the early years Christina spent summers with me and every other weekend. No matter how demanding our schedules have gotten over the years, we always reserved one day a week for dinner—even now while she's in college at UCLA. It's our "skull sessions." Our field or classroom is a local restaurant. Over a chicken burrito we review the week's schoolwork. But, just as important we talk about a variety of subjects. She talks about her friends and what she wants to do with her life. For me it's a very special time that most fathers don't have with their daughters.

Being a father you often don't know the effects of your work for years. You hope and pray that you're doing the right things, but you never know for sure. Two events let me know that I was on the right track. The first was receiving the "Father of the Year" award from the AKA's. The award from the African American female organization was not only for my work with my own daughter, but for all the work I had done on behalf of African American children.

The second thing was at my daughter's graduation party. She had just graduated from LaSalle High School in Pasadena, California and was soon to be a freshman at UCLA. When my daughter concluded her remarks to the 50 or so family and friends that gathered at our house she said, "I want to thank my Dad for always being there for me. I love him very much."

Being so involved in my daughter's life brought unexpected benefits. I became a mentor and father figure to two of her best friends, Marissa Millet and Melissa Kyle, both of whom had lost their fathers at young ages. I didn't realize the impact on them until I got a Father's Day card several years ago that said, "Some people feel sorry for me not having my own father in my life. But I know that I have been blessed to have Fathers like you in my life to love and motivate me as if I were their own. You've always supported me and encouraged me to become a successful Black woman. I appreciate everything you've done for me. I promise to make you proud. Love always, your other daughter Melissa."

There are many African American fathers who are not only raising their own children, but who believe in the African proverb "it takes a village to raise a child." The following is a sampling of those men and their stories of fatherhood.

Kenneth W. Bentley, the author of this chapter, is vice president, community affairs for Nestlé USA. As writer, Bentley has written 10 books including the highly acclaimed *Men of Courage I and II*, which profiled the inspirational stories of African American men. He has also written books profiling African American women and his series *Nestlé Very Best In Youth* tells the inspiring stories of young people of diverse backgrounds. For his work on behalf of young people Bentley has received numerous awards. He received his bachelor's degree from the University of California, Irvine and master's of arts in management from the University of Redlands. He lives in Los Angeles with his wife Jelana and their three children, Angelena, Alfred, and Christina.

Al B. Reid
Vice President, Corporate Development,
Abbott Laboratories
Northbrook, Illinois

I was born out of wedlock and my father chose to leave for whatever reason. Not having a father around shaped my experiences. I looked at his life and was determined not to make the same mistakes he did. Being a man means taking responsibility for your actions. He didn't. We have a good relationship now. When I turned 40 I wanted to spend time with all the people who had an influence in my life so I sent for my Dad. We spent a weekend together, just the two of us talking. My father really opened up. It was great for our relationship.

Until a few years ago my wife Cheri and I shared the parenting duties of our two kids, 9-year-old Christopher and 11-year-old Ariel. We both had demanding careers. But our son was struggling in school so my wife decided to take some time off from her career to get our kids squared away academically. It has paid off in a big way. Our son now is doing very well.

Though my father wasn't always around I did have some positive Black male influences in my life. My mother remarried when I was 11. My stepfather Alfred Green was an ex-military officer and had a positive influence on me. He made sure I did what I said I was going to do and when I said I was going to do it.

My uncle Lymon Bailey was my main role model. In my opinion he was the perfect example of a strong Black man. He had a long-term marriage and spent 30 plus years at General Motors, many of those years in management. He was also the first in his family to go to college. In my uncle I saw a man who was a good provider, a great protector of his family and friends, was self-disciplined and most importantly was persistent and worked hard for everything he got in life. My uncle and my stepfather were both strong role models. As I go about my life I often ask myself what would they do in certain situations.

People say that mothers give love at birth and kids have to earn a father's love. We need to dispel that. Fathers need to give kids unconditional love from day one. We have to be there for our kids. My father only saw me play one baseball game. I know how that made me feel so I try to attend all of my kids' activities. I remember one time I was in China on a business trip. I flew 18 to 20 hours to make it back in time for one of my daughter's school activities. I had to turn around the next day and go back to China. I was tired, but the smile on my daughter's face when she saw me made it worthwhile.

I believe in the "village approach to parenting." I am very involved with youth groups in my church. I've also been a Scoutmaster and serve on the board of director of Big Sisters and Big Brothers. I especially enjoy speaking at schools and to youth groups. When I do I tell young people my story—both the good and the bad. People that "make it" and don't give back . . . shame on them. The few of us who have slipped through the cracks need to be role models for young people. African American kids need to see strong Black men who are succeeding in fields other than athletics and entertainment.

I would like for my legacy to be as Dr. King said in his famous speech "I tried to help somebody." I want people to say that I was a loving person who tried to help his family and friends. I hope my kids will say, "My Dad was a good loving provider, who was a good role model and always stood for what was right."

Al Reid, prior to joining Abbott Laboratories held several positions of increasing responsibilities in finance, business development, and strategy in the health care industry. As an active member of the community Reid is a youth basketball/baseball coach, a Scoutmaster for Boy Scouts of America and participates in student mentoring programs. Al holds a bachelor's degree in communications from Clark Atlanta University and a master's degree in management from Carnegie Mellon University.

David McNeill
Executive Director, Baldwin Hills Conservancy
Los Angeles, California

My wife Rhonda and I share parenting responsibilities relying on each other's strengths, but not avoiding rising to new challenges that child rearing can bring. With her occupation as a flight attendant requiring considerable travel, I often have to take on the role of father and mother for our toddler son Cole Winston. I don't mind. It's great to be there for him and to have a close bond with my son that many fathers can't relate to and most mothers wish for their sons.

I am really excited about the Baldwin Hills Conservancy. We are in the process of building a state-of-the-art, two square miles of natural, park and recreation area. This is a great opportunity to have a lasting impact on an area I have lived in for 30 years. So much of Los Angeles African American history has happened in the Baldwin Hills area, that it will be great to have a place to make that history come alive.

I owe a lot of my success to lessons I learned from my father. He was a business professional and entrepreneur who took pride in providing for his family. He always enjoyed laughing and the simple things in life. I learned from him to take time out for fun with loved ones now because they will not always be there to reach out to you. Most of the lessons I learned from my father were later in life when I was ready to listen.

I played football from fifth grade through high school. From my coaches I learned the importance of discipline, teamwork, to believe in yourself, and to never give up.

Because so many people took time with me when I was growing up I try and be a role model for kids. I coach flag football at a local park and frequently speak at schools. I also try and take time to talk to young kids on my block. I think it's important to let kids know that they don't have to look far to find positive role models. They're in their home and down the block.

I get my strength and inspiration from my love of the human race and its capacity to do good things, coupled with a belief in God and the spirit working in everyone's life. When my career is over I want to be remembered as someone who cared about his community and worked to make a difference. Most importantly I want to be remembered as a father who loved his family unconditionally.

David McNeill has lived in the Los Angeles area all of his life. After receiving his Bachelor of Science degree in speech and communication from Oregon State University, he returned to Los Angeles to succeed in a wide range of professional positions including small business consultant, music industry executive, real estate agent, and a public affairs director for an environmental nonprofit organization. During the course of his diverse career, he has maintained a passion for projects and organizations that bring environmental education, recreation, and economic growth to the African American community.

DeWayne Wickham
Syndicated Newspaper Columnist
Owings Mills, Maryland

I was 6 years old when my parents died. Because they died under tragic circumstances I've blotted most memories of them out of my mind.

Despite growing up without my father there were many fatherly figures in my life. There were men who made a strong effort to make me be manly. That means to accept responsibility, to be there for your family, to take financial responsibility for your family, and to be a strong disciplinary figure.

My mother's brother, Conroy Chase was someone I looked up to. He was a Merchant Marine and traveled all over the world. When he was in town he'd come around and sit on the porch and talk to my brothers and I about our family history. He also told us about his life, both the good and the bad.

Parren Mitchell, the first Black Congressman from Maryland was another important figure in my life. I met him when he was a college professor at Morgan State University. We'd sit for hours and talk about life and responsibility. He was the first person I heard use the term *race man*, which referred to a strong and prideful way a man looked at his race.

My wife Wanda plays the dominant role in raising our 11-year-old daughter. She is the consummate mother. Wanda is our daughter's primary instructor and is the reason she is excelling in school. My role is to be the strength of the family. To be the primary breadwinner. To help set the standard of behavior and to provide a sense of security. Because I work out of my house I'm home nearly every day and I can impact my daughter's thought process. It's a new experience for me. I had far less interaction with my first two daughters.

In 1997 I founded the Woodholme Foundation, which provides mentoring and college scholarship for young people with low high-school grades and tons of potential. I've been where these kids are. Unless someone helps them they are destined to be part of the underclass. At Woodholme we try and bring them back into the fold. These kids initially see me as a middle-class guy who can't relate to their problems. But when they hear my story they understand I've been where they are and even worse.

My inspiration comes from these kids. When I read their scholarship applications I see my story in them. My eyes often well up with tears. I want to help them grow and prosper in the worst way.

I hope people will look at me as a person that whatever I did I did it from the heart not the mind. And I did it with no pretense of glory. As a journalist I want to be remembered as a disturber of the peace. That I shined a light in dark places. That through my writing I advocated for a more open and transparent society.

As a father I want my kids to know that what I did for them was from the
heart and out of love. I didn't do it because of a court order or societal pressure. I want them to know that I did what I was supposed to do to the best of
my ability.

DeWayne Wickham is a columnist for *USA Today* and the Gannett News Ser-
vice. Wickham is the editor of *Thinking Black: Some of the Nation's Best Black
Columnists Speak Their Mind*. He is also the author of *Woodholme: A Black
Man's Story of Growing Up Alone, Fire at Will*, and *Bill Clinton and Black America*.
Wickham is one of the founding members of the National Association of
Black Journalists and is currently a journalism professor at North Carolina
A&T.

Donald Henderson, M.D.
Los Angeles, California

To be a good father you need patience, compassion, a lot of love and a central faith or spiritual belief in the goodness of people.

I was blessed to have loving parents. My father really taught me about
leadership. He was quiet, but strong. He showed that you don't have to be
demonstrative to be an effective leader. He also taught me about self-
sacrifice, about working hard for the benefit of others. My father worked
three jobs. He was a high-school administrator, ran a newspaper distribution company, and renovated old houses. I worked alongside him renovat-
ing the old houses. He taught me how to do electrical and plumbing re-
pairs. As we worked he didn't say much. He led by example. He let his
deeds do his talking.

My parents have passed on, but not a day goes by that I don't think of
them and the lessons they taught me.

When my ex-wife and I divorced 6 years ago we never brought the children into the negative issues. I only said positive things about their mom.
Most of the time during my marriage I spent a lot of time building my medical practice. My wife did most of the rearing of our kids, Shasta now 19 years
old and Donald II, 23 years old. But, the first year after the divorce I became
the primary caregiver as my ex-wife began to build her career. I took the
kids to school. I came home from work early to help with their homework.
It affected my relationship with the partners in my practice. But, my priorities changed. Work and money were secondary, my family came first. In the
process I became a better father and a happier person.

In addition to my father, Dr. Tim Scott had the biggest effect on me. Dr.
Scott got divorced when he was a student at Meharry Medical School. Despite
his demanding schedule he took custody of his two sons and daughter. I

watched how he dealt with his kids. I saw how he handled the ups and the downs. He was very involved in their lives. He took them skiing and on houseboat trips. His daughter has joined him in his Ophthalmology practice.

As a doctor my patients become my extended family. I feel my role is to not only be a mentor to my own family but others as well. It is really gratifying to have parents bring kids to me to talk with them and mentor them. A number have gone on and become doctors and nurses. My good friend Dr. Ewart Brown moved to Bermuda. When he left he told his son, who had just graduated from medical school, that if he had any questions or needed any guidance to call me. We talk frequently.

There is no road map for success in being a father. Though life experiences do play a heavy role. I was so fortunate to have great parents. They told me they loved me every time I talked with them.

I want my kids to say that I was the best parent I could be. My son is in college and at times I do get upset by him. Recently I gave him one of those talks about not spending so much money. When I finished he said, "Dad I love you." No matter what our differences are we end every conversation with I love you.

Dr. Donald R. Henderson is a gastroenterologist in Los Angeles, California. He is a leader in the local medical community. He has dedicated himself to providing excellent health care, preventive health care, and health promotion to underserved populations.

Erikk Aldridge
Director, Community Affairs, The Walt Disney Company
Los Angeles, California

There are three characteristics of a good father. The first is dedication. It's important to be dedicated to being the best Dad you can be. When it's time to be a Dad all of your thoughts and energies should be focused on being a Dad. The second is patience. Children are like balls of clay. It takes time to mold them into the best person they can be. Finally, a good father needs to have enthusiasm. Children will feed off you. If you are proud and enthusiastic, they will be too.

My wife Tiffany and I have demanding careers. So we share the parenting responsibilities of my 8-year-old son Chase and 4-year-old daughter Drew. I get my daughter dressed in the morning and then I take her to preschool. Despite my work schedule I take time to be involved in both of my kids' daily schedule. I want to be aware of their habits and moods so if something is wrong I will know immediately.

Growing up, my parents were very involved in the lives of my two brothers and me. My father was a disciplinarian. He had to be with all the things going on in the Los Angeles area. The biggest thing I learned from him was a strong work ethic. He's an engineer. He got up every day and went to work. No matter what was going on at work he still took time to coach our baseball team. He made sure whatever we did we were dedicated to succeeding. I remember when I was seven or eight he took us to the park and hit ground balls to us for what seemed like hours. He wanted to show us that to be successful you had to do something over and over again.

My source of inspiration comes from my family. My mother has 11 brothers and sisters. Growing up, no matter what I did I always felt like I had this large family unit backing me up. My wife and kids push me now to do better and better. It's important that each generation gets better.

Part of making sure each generation gets better is being a role model to kids outside of your family. I learned so much from my Little League coach James Henry. He was the most fearless person I have ever met. He was confident—some people say cocky. He made all of us feel invincible. He took a team of 11 and 12 year olds from Inglewood, California to within two games of the Little League World Series. He told us if we believe in ourselves anything is possible.

As often as I can, I go back to where I played Little League. I not only bring balls and bats and tickets to Los Angeles Dodger games but I try and pass on some of the lessons I learned to those kids. It's my way of paying back people like Coach Henry. It's important to give back. I believe that whatever you give it comes back to you twofold.

As African Americans I think it's important that we prepare our kids for society. That means setting the bar a little higher. As they go through life other people will do that so it should start in the family.

I hope people in the community will say I was a good neighbor who volunteered when he saw a need. I want my kids to say, "My Dad was always there. He didn't let anything interfere with him being at my events."

Erikk Aldridge before joining the Walt Disney Company was director of community affairs for the Los Angeles Dodgers and the Los Angeles Lakers. A graduate of the University of California, San Diego he majored in psychology and was a starter on the baseball team. Aldridge serves on many charitable and civic boards and is a volunteer Little League baseball coach.

John B. Woodruff
Sr. Contracts Negotiator
Raytheon Corporation
Los Angeles, California

My source of inspiration and strength comes from the generations of Black men that persevered despite tremendous odds. I often look back at the Black men in the south central Los Angeles neighborhood that I grew up in. Many were overqualified for the jobs they had. I remember reading about Mack Robinson, Jackie's brother. He was an Olympic silver medalist and had a degree from Oregon, but he had to take a job as a janitor. He later did great things, but he humbled himself and held on long enough until he could do better.

Consistency is the most important aspect of parenting. You have to consistently be there for your kids. To keep kids from getting confused you have to give them the same message all the time. For example with our son we always stressed good values like taking responsibility for your actions and treating others as you want to be treated.

My job in raising our son John, now 27 years old, was to be the disciplinarian. My wife Renee respected my judgment in this area and didn't interfere.

My father taught me the meaning of responsibility. He always said, "Do what you are supposed to do on a daily basis." Sometimes you may not want to, but you have to. I remember when I was young we moved into a new house. My Dad spent all weekend fixing up the house. I knew he was tired, but on Monday mornings he was up and dressed by 4:00 a.m. and on his way to work. Being a father means you have to make sacrifices.

My Dad worked so much trying to take care of us; he didn't have time to spend with me outside the home. It didn't bother me. I understood. He provided food and shelter for a wife and five kids. That was more than most of my friends could say about their fathers.

My football and track coaches became my surrogate fathers. They were men of great character who were great role models. The one that comes to mind is my football coach Mr. DeWitty. The Los Angeles Rams had a program that allowed one paid adult to bring five kids to the games at no cost. Every Los Angeles Rams home game he would pick up me and four other kids and take us to the Los Angeles Coliseum to see a professional football game. On the way to and from the games, Mr. DeWitty would use that time as an opportunity to talk to us about the importance of staying in school and staying out of trouble. He had a tremendous impact on my life.

Role models are extremely important—especially in the Black community. I try to do my part by coaching Little League teams and heading up a church group that mentors young men. I try and create an environment that breeds self-confidence and responsibility.

I work hard, but I was fortunate enough to be able to spend time with my son John outside of the home. I got a lot of personal satisfaction out of coaching his sports teams, going to his church youth programs and school events. I know it meant a lot to him, but it meant a lot to me as well. I had the opportunity to watch him develop and I also participated in that development.

One of the things I am proudest of on my job is that people know they can depend on me to do what I say I'm going to do. If I have a proposal or project due I'll stay up all night to make sure it is done right and on time. I hope that by my actions I have taught my son to be responsible and consistent. I also think he knows that even though I was hard on him at times I always wanted the best for him.

John B. Woodruff has been employed in various capacities in the pursuit of delivering cutting-edge technology such as Global Positional Systems (GPS), along with Military Electronics and weapon systems to the U.S. Government and their NATO allies worldwide. Woodruff received a Bachelor of Science degree from Pepperdine University and a master's degree in management from California State University at Dominguez Hills. Active in the community, he serves in a leadership capacity at his church and has coached Little League baseball, youth basketball and been a Cub Scout Leader.

Louis S. Smith
School Social Worker
Burlington, New Jersey

I was watching television many years ago when I heard Rev. Jesse Jackson say the first sign of a dying civilization is when the elders don't care about the youth. That statement had a profound effect on me. I've dedicated my life to young people.

My parents divorced when I was young. My father spent many years working for CORE, first as the director of the Philadelphia office then as the Mississippi State director. Medgar Evers was working for him when he was killed. Because my father was moving around with the civil rights movement he wasn't there when I was growing up. He never went to a Boy Scout event or saw me play football. I remember being in a barbershop and people were talking about how great my father was and I just went off. I told them a great man wouldn't abandon his family. I wanted a father who was there for me not fighting battles a thousand miles away.

My Dad moved to California when I was in high school. After starting Operation Bootstrap in Los Angeles he began teaching at the University of California, Irvine. I'll never forget the day he called me shortly after I graduated from high school and asked me to join him at UCI. I said "no way." All of a sudden he wanted to be part of my life and I was having none of it. But, knowing my love for football, the next time my father called he told me UCI had a football team and if I went to school there I could be on the team. It wasn't until I got to California that I discovered that UCI did not have a team and had no plans to develop one. My father was such a great communicator that once I was there I saw a different side of him. We spent hours talking about all sorts of things. For the first time I saw the qualities that made him such a special person to so many people. My father died in a tragic car accident several years after I graduated from UCI but I'm glad we had a chance to build a special bond.

I learned from my father the art of good communication—especially in dealing with young people. I communicate well with kids because I listen. I learn a lot from kids. I also learned from my father that it's important to be there. I never want my kids, 13 year-old Kyle and 26 year-old Louis IV, to experience the hurt I had so I'm there for every one of their events—even Girl Scout functions.

The words "I can't" aren't spoken in my house. I tell my kids to try anything their heart desires. They won't always succeed. But, my job is to be a safety net to catch them when they fall.

My son's mother and I divorced when he was one. His mother moved to Mississippi shortly after that. No matter what I was doing I called him every Thursday evening at 7:00 p.m. I called other times, but I wanted to make sure he knew that every Thursday at 7:00 p.m. he would get a call from his Dad. Often his mother wouldn't let me speak with him, but I called anyway. When he turned six I got custody of him and he lived with me until he went to college. I was very involved in every aspect of his life. I went to all of his sports events. I became a track referee so I could be more involved in his track meets. My son really made me feel good several months ago. He's a father now with a 4-year-old. Not long ago we were sitting around talking and he said, "Dad now I know why you were hard on me growing up. You were just preparing me for the world."

Even though my father wasn't around, growing up in the projects of Philadelphia there were plenty of strong African American role models who prepared me for the world. Charles Lee was one of them. He had his own family, but he still took time to coach and sponsor a youth football team. He took a special interest in me and he became a lifelong mentor. He wrote to me while I was in college and helped get me my first job. I owe him a lot.

I want to be remembered as someone who gave more than they took. I want to be remembered as a good father and a good husband to my wife Trudy. I believe in karma. If you treat people right—especially young people—good things will happen.

Louis Smith was born and raised in Philadelphia, Pennsylvania to parents who instilled in him the importance of "giving back." He received his Bachelor of Science degree from the University of California, Irvine and a master's degree in social work from Rutgers University. He serves on the Board of Directors for the Boys and Girls Club of Burlington County and is the coordinator for Special Olympics.

REFERENCES

Riley, D. W. (1991). My soul looks back, 'less I forget . . . A collection of quotations by people of color. In A. Poussaint (Ed.), *The challenge of the Black family* (p. 142). New York: HarperCollins.

Smith, O. C. (1969). Color him father. On *O. C. Smith at home.* New York: Columbia Records.

Wickham, D. (2002). *Bill Clinton and Black America.* New York: Ballantine Books.

Chapter 7

David Leroy Hopkins:
The Face of Conscious Manhood

Thomas A. Parham
University of California, Irvine

Existence has a face on every side, and every face teaches a lesson. Those who truly understand existence do not separate the faces from the lessons, say the knowledge holders.

—Peters (1983)

His face is chocolate brown. His hair is salt and pepper gray. His eyes sparkle with a gratefulness for the life he has been blessed to live. His smile is as eager to connect with a family member or good friend, as it is to greet a perfect stranger. His mouth utters words that marvel at new information, that chuckle at life's inconsistencies, and that hold steadfast to opinions forged out of the stubborn ways elder men come to know what they know.

He is handsome, yet unassuming; intelligent, yet street-wise; medically challenged, yet robust in his thirst to embrace each new day. This is my father-in-law, David L. Hopkins, who has taught many lessons in responsibility, perseverance, manhood, family, unconditional love, respect, and giving. In this chapter, I share with you some perspective on his life and our relationship, and why he characterizes a strong level of intergenerational support that most of America believes is nonexistent in the African American community.

CONTEXT

My own father's life ended much too early. William D. Parham lost his battle with lung cancer in late 1971 at the age of 53. While my siblings and I did have an opportunity to travel from Los Angeles to Washington D.C. to visit

113

with him in the hospital shortly before he died, that week, and another 2-week summer visit in 1968, were too short. More importantly, they were insufficient to make up for the years we had spent apart during my childhood, due to his marital separation from my mother. My mother and father's relationship, when seen through the eyes of a child viewing family photographs, was magical. Each of them dawned movie star looks and were glamorous enough to grace the cover of any style magazine, and I will be eternally grateful for their union. But try as they might, my mother could never subdue her anxiety of worrying about my father's unpredictability when alcohol consumption would taint his otherwise pleasant disposition. Although her own safety never seemed too much an issue, mom was not willing to risk the safety of her children, and that, more than anything, led to her separation from him in September of 1958, when I was just 1 month shy of my fourth birthday.

Sadie Parham, my mother, was an extraordinary woman who did a superb job of raising four children by herself, with no other financial support beyond the paycheck she earned by working for the government for 32 years. She was mother and father, and I owe her so much. But try as she might, there were things she simply could not teach me. Those lessons are reserved for interactions between fathers and sons, and the unavailability of my own dad delayed much of that instruction until I was well into my adult years and professional career. Once the lessons began, however, there was meaning in the instruction that provided wisdom and insight equivalent to any I had gained in my formal studies.

The landscape of American life is littered with broken dreams and unused potential of African American males. They begin life with enormous possibility of potential endowed in them by the CREATOR. However, the harsh realities of their existence, where juggling assault on the manhood, intellect, sexuality, and emotional comfort zones are all too common, claims a disproportionate number of casualties. Marable (1984) underscores this dilemma quite clearly as he writes that the essential tragedy of being Black and male (in this society) is our inability, as men and as people of African descent, to define ourselves without the stereotype that the larger society imposes on us. Like many of you, I too have been a victim of these intellectual and emotional assaults, yet somehow, I found a way to not allow these microaggressions to derail my progress. I am clear that my relationship with my father-in-law was one factor that helped to sustain me during some of the trying times.

Despite life's circumstances that claim so many victims, there are those African American men who manage to successfully navigate the pathways to productivity and success. This story is about one of those individuals, David Leroy Hopkins, a Chester, Pennsylvania native and Camden, New Jersey "homeboy," who is an inspiration and role model to me. You won't find his story in the glamour or style magazines of *Ebony* or *Essence,* although you should be able to. But by society's standards, he was not "celebrity" enough to warrant such consideration. But the lessons he taught through his adulthood years will have a much more profound impact on me than 100 issues of those popular magazines.

BACKGROUND

Growing up in South Jersey, David Hopkins was raised in a loving household with his mother, and two sisters, Mildred and Vivian, in a neighborhood with numerous other extended families. His mother Gertrude and he were extremely close, and despite her single-parent status, he believed her to be a tower of strength. David had almost no interaction with his father, who was not around during his childhood. Perhaps, it was these early experiences that reinforced the value and importance of family for him, and helped him develop a sense of manhood that was forged out of childhood experiences he cared not to replicate in his own life as a husband, father, and grandfather.

While there was a very responsible side to David, he had a well-rounded adolescence and early adulthood life. In his generation, males of African descent did not have access to many white-collar jobs, private schools, country clubs, or expensive vacations to exotic places. Their activity was confined to the inner cities and urban cores of America. David made the best of those spaces and developed several hobbies or leisure pursuits around games like cards, pool (billiards), watching sports, and gambling. Occasionally, he would visit a nightclub to take in the entertainment of the evening, and maybe indulge in an alcoholic beverage or two. Although he enjoyed what he called "the good life," he never fell victim to the ravages of the streets nor did he allow himself to get caught in the self-destructive cycles of violence, alcohol and drug abuse, that ruin so many lives of Black men.

FORGING A RELATIONSHIP

My relationship with David Hopkins began from afar a year or so after I had relocated to Philadelphia, Pennsylvania to take a faculty position at the University of Pennsylvania in 1982. I learned that he was informed about my relationship with his oldest daughter Davida through a conversation with Davida's mom Loretta. His response was simply to say, "I've seen him on TV," in reference to the news interviews and public affairs shows I was occasionally asked to do for local television. On another occasion, we all attended a Philadelphia 76ers basketball game, where we shared an evening of sports, cheering, laughter, and fun.

But perhaps, our relationship was cemented when I came to dinner at their home in early 1985 and announced my desire to marry his daughter, and through some very disclosive conversation, shared much of my values and background as I asked for his and my future mother-in-law's blessings. The sincerity with which I spoke that night brought me a high level of respect from Hopkins and his wife, which was surprising in the short time we had known each other. But my candor was what he respected. He was less impressed with professional titles or positions, and more enamored with genuineness, authentic self-expression, and a humble posture that showed deference to their positions as family elders, despite my position as an Ivy League academic, psychologist, scholar, and as a grown man.

THE CHARACTER OF A MAN

David Hopkins' identity was not defined by his educational attainments, although he did graduate from high school in New Jersey around 1940. Rather, his identity was defined by being a devoted husband, father, grandfather, and friend. He and Loretta Primas were married in 1944 during World War II. Three months later he was shipped overseas where he completed his military service in the Army. After returning home to the United States, David held several jobs, mostly in the realm of manual labor. He worked as a construction worker, and a shipyard bricklayer. Although the work was taxing and physically demanding, it provided a source of income through which he could meet life's basic necessities. Subsequently, he secured an opportunity as a Camden Police Officer, and was eventually promoted to Detective. This was a particularly interesting role for David, as it was the first, steady, nonmanual labor position he held in his life.

If the truth be told about his intentions, I believe that he was a reluctant entrant into the world of law enforcement. However, whatever reservations he harbored, he dismissed because the position provided a good living and wage, full benefits for he and his family, and a legitimate, if unexpected opportunity for a Black man with only a high-school diploma as an educational foundation.

The police officer role was an interesting one for David Hopkins, and he genuinely enjoyed contributing to the safety of his community. Unlike many of his past and contemporary members of the law enforcement family, he took pride in never having to discharge his weapon in the line of duty. He ultimately left the force some 14 years later, however, as the injustices perpetrated by his own fellow officers against citizens he was sworn to protect were too much of a burden for him to tolerate.

He also spent some time in the insurance business, and became the first Black insurance consultant for Metropolitan Life Insurance Company in the South Jersey area. The position with Metropolitan Life was an opportunity of a different sort. Beyond the status of a white-collar lifestyle, it allowed him to relocate his family out of Camden about the time when the riots were escalating in the inner cities of America.

He tutored under a good friend and eventual political powerhouse from New Jersey, John L. Watson, who had achieved some measure of success in that business. David was soon doing very well himself. Ultimately however, his interests drew him back into a career in the law enforcement field, this time on the defense side as an investigator for the state of New Jersey's public defender's office, and he retired from that role in 1989.

Dependability was his mark, as he provided faithful service in a career that afforded him predictable wages, hours, and benefits. Those hours were important for a family man whose wife was much happier with him at home in the evenings rather than out selling insurance policies after the dinner hour, when she wanted him to be home. Although some men might consider such a request a challenge to their authoritative manhood, Daddy made no such attribution. He simply lived his life in ways that both fulfilled his obligations as a man, and adjusted to compromise with sensitivity to the feminine energy that shared his life space. David Hopkins always knew that relationships were about compromise. But unlike a number of men, he never approached compromise decisions with a begrudging compliance. He viewed his marital relationship as a partnership, and if he believed a decision to be in the best interest of that partnership (regardless of what he personally wanted or thought was necessary), then whatever outcome followed was fine with him. That was a key ingredient to a successful marriage that lasted 51 years. In an age of "disposable marriages" that might last a year or two; or the "7-year itch" that couples never get to scratch because their relationships rarely reach that plateau, David Hopkins taught a constant lesson in endurance.

RELATIONSHIP DYNAMICS

There are a number of texts that seek to provide the keys to a successful relationship. Hooks (2004) talks about the need for Black men to abandon the patriarchal and sexist ways they relate to their partners. Similarly, Hopson and Powell-Hopson (1994) talk about intimacy, communication, and trust as ingredients necessary to sustain a relationship over time. Although these resources are important tools in the intellectual arsenal of relationship dynamics, David Hopkins had no such resources on which to rely. He simply used his own common sense, a standard of moral decency and integrity, and motherly advice as the template for guiding his behavior.

David Hopkins always insisted that good relationships were a partnership that two people participated in. He and my mother-in-law were partners in love, work, child rearing, and extended family support. They exercised a collaborative model of decision making, and communicated with each other about both major and minor decisions. Convergence of opinion was most common in their household, but on those occasions when divergent disagreement would insert itself into the conversation, they found a way to work through it, even if that meant acquiescing to one or the other's insistent demand.

INNER SELF-ASSURANCE

Unlike many people in society, David Hopkins' identity was not defined by material possessions. He was neat and clean in his appearance and dress, but not at all consumed by the latest fashion or fad. He dressed in conservative attire with just a hint of style to accent his engaging character. The absence of a materialistic mentality seemed to help David Hopkins develop and maintain an independence of thought that served him well. He never appeared too concerned about the opinions of others, beyond those closest to him. The validation he sought came from a close circle that included his own mother, his siblings, his spiritual connection to the CREATOR, and his own moral compass.

When it came to automobiles, David Hopkins was all American. Foreign sports or luxury vehicle trends never seemed to suit his taste. Instead, he preferred domestic transportation, and during his adult life never strayed too far from the Buick, Chevrolet, Pontiac, or General Motors family. I suspect he held some measure of patriotism in his purchases. Buying cars from countries he had fought against in World War II just never seemed to sit right with him. Instead, he was content and determined to support the American factory worker who brought their manufactured products to the marketplace. Interestingly, he was also cognizant of the Black male's position within the American workforce, and how so much of what was available in terms of career opportunities was determined by race and class. Yet, he found no incongruence in supporting an American workplace that was blatantly racist and sexist in its employment practices.

CRYSTALLIZING ONE'S IDENTITY

The analysis provided by Marable (1984) highlights a larger dilemma than simply confronting society's image of African descent men. They must also be careful not to accept those derogatory stereotypes as road maps they follow in navigating their way through life. The challenge here centers around who and what men of African descent use as a source of validation for their manhood. Growing up in the 1930s, 1940s, and 1950s afforded men an interesting array of lifestyle choices, particular for a Black male in the inner city. There was poverty, crime, street hustles, and the fast life of excesses. Conversely, there was a more subdued lifestyle, where honest work, regular family life with a mix of appropriate leisure activities, and child rearing were more the norm. David Hopkins was skilled enough to carve out an existence in both worlds, and like most men, he had a choice to make. Would it be the rich legacy of his community or the distorted reflections of society's view of the Black male and his cycle of self-destruction? David Hopkins chose the former. The violation of what I later came to know as his "inner spirit," and the threat of losing the affection and company of a woman he loved, helped him to make the more responsible choice. Unquestionably, Mom Loretta putting her foot down and insisting that he curtail his "street life" was a powerful influence on his decision making.

Even if the life of Black males has been spent confronting negative images, one might reason that the energy doing so is a healthy posture to assume under the circumstance. In that regard, it could be reasoned that a man's life direction is influenced in part by self-determined pursuit of one's humanity that defines the character of a man in positive rather than negative ways. David Hopkins was such a man.

LIFE ADJUSTMENTS

Among the rich blessings I have received in recent years, was "Daddy" coming to live with us in the last 7 years of his life. That decision was engineered by my wife and I 3 years before, when we decided to purchase a home large enough to absorb an elder parent at some point in the future. My father-in-law was the beneficiary of that decision when my mother-in-law, Loretta Hopkins, passed away after a long battle with breast cancer. Their marriage lasted 51 years. While the pain of her departure from this world lingered until his own passing, 7 years later, my wife Davida and I reasoned that Daddy would be much better off with us, than living by himself in New Jersey, some 2,500 miles away. Close proximity also allowed us to monitor his medical conditions and connect him to physicians who could treat his diabetes and high blood pressure.

Clearly, we took some measure of pride and delight in transitioning into caretaker role with Daddy. What was equally clear, however, is how the reciprocal benefits of his presence in our household began to pay dividends almost immediately upon his arrival. David Hopkins was a source of elder wisdom available in the moment. He was another vehicle by which we could fulfill our intuitive obligation to repay our parents for all the ways they had contributed to our growth and development as youth and young adults.

Interestingly, the presence of my father-in-law also mirrors what Nobles (1981) has described as "an instrument of culture." In discussing the strength of the African American family unit, Nobles talks about the "legitimation of beingness," where elder parents serve as a source of connection, attachment, validation, worth, recognition, respect, and legitimacy for adult children. This was clearly the case in our lives, as Daddy (and my own mother who lived close by) was a reference point for how life's challenges should be managed, and how well we measured up to a parental standard set in the previous generation. Interestingly, the template for success had less to do with reaching positions of prominence and influence, and more to do with reflecting those values and characteristics most highly valued in traditional African American and African families. In fact, Hill's (1971) book on the *Strengths of The Black Family* closely parallel the standard of aspiration we were measured against. First, Daddy believed that "family came first" and there was nothing more important than family, except God. Whether he was extending a helping hand going grocery shopping, providing transportation for an errand, or just visiting periodically to touch base with that network of biological and extended family members, this was a priority. Hill referred to this as "strong kinship bonds." Second, David Hopkins always knew it was his duty and obligation as a man to provide for his family. Whether he needed to work one job or three in order to make ends meet, he did it proudly. He believed in being on time, giving an honest effort, and being reliable in the discharge of one's duties. Hill wrote about the "strong work orientation." Hopkins insisted that his children excel in school, and each of his three daughters were college educated. He imparted those same lessons to his grandchildren, which I could clearly see in his interactions with our daughters Tonya and Kenya. The remarkable way he preached the value of education is important, given that he was not college educated himself. The correlational research that talks about the relationship between level of parent's educational attainment and that of their children doesn't seem to capture African American families, and it did not reflect ours at all. Daddy also stayed very current by reading two and sometimes three newspapers per day. He loved politics and conversing about current issues of our day. He also took seriously the necessity to vote and never failed to exercise that right, or to instill that value in his children. This is what Hill (1971) was talking about as evidence of a "strong achievement orientation" in Black families. Furthermore, David Hopkins never relegated himself to any rigid gender role distinction about what was appropriate for him to do. He was as comfortable lifting heavy objects or taking out the trash as he was washing dishes or cleaning house. While he and my mother-in-law did settle into roles prescribed for men and women, they also crossed those boundaries in frequent instances, in order to ensure that a task was done. He was comfortable preparing baby formula, changing diapers, or cooking a roast. In fact, both he and my mother-in-law worked during their marriage and he bore no resentment about the shared "breadwinner" status, nor did he appear to feel threatened by her wage earning potential. Hill referred to this strength as the "adaptability of family roles." David Hopkins believed in God, and found his faith operationalized in the daily interactions he had with others. He was kind, generous, giving, and always willing to extend a helping hand. While in New Jersey, he was a regular church goer, but the inability to find a church that mirrored his place of worship back home in New Jersey, made his church attendance in California more sporadic. However, during those times when he returned home to the family church, St. Johns Baptist Church, in Camden, New Jersey, he was in service every Sunday. He and my mother always taught us the importance of going to church, keeping the faith, and acknowledging God's blessings—what Hill referred to as a "strong religious orientation."

He was a companion and source of support for our youngest daughter Kenya, who now had daily access to a second generation of adult role models and family tradition through her maternal grandfather. Their bond was solidified early in her life, as he would take a playful, and sometimes "teasing" approach to daily activities. From the time she was an infant and toddler, until she was a preteen, he would constantly joke with, playfully insult, and even tease her on occasion. Kenya, in turn, would provide a reciprocal amount of joking and teasing, after, of course, she "fussed" at him in the special way a child engages her grandparent.

Interestingly, Kenya's grandmother Loretta, and her mother Davida, would occasionally caution Daddy against excessively engaging his grandchild in that way. While mom Loretta was concerned about him teasing her too much, Davida's worry centered more on the potential effect their reciprocal teasing would have on Kenya being able to view her "Pop-Pop" with the level of respect, reverence, and deference accorded family elders. But David Hopkins would hear none of it. His worldly eyes could only see love for his grandchild, and his experience knew children grew up too fast in this world, and he wanted to keep her young at heart and spirit for as long as possible. This was a similar dynamic to what I observed in the interactions with our oldest daughter, and his oldest granddaughter, Tonya.

The dynamics of our family life after Daddy's relocation paralleled the generational support concept described in the literature (Chatters & Taylor, 1993). In the text entitled *Aging in Black America*, Chatters and Taylor discussed the adult child–elderly parent kinship bonds that provide a network of intergenerational support for members of the family unit. They also remind us that intergenerational support is influenced by proximity and degree of closeness. Proximity was assured through David Hopkins' relocation to our home; the degree of closeness was nurtured through both years of parent–child interactions with my wife Davida, and a relationship he and I developed once we became members of each other's family.

While living in our home carried with it no financial obligation or assistance, Daddy insisted on paying for his individual expenses, even as we managed his affairs. He also contributed to the management of the household in ways that attended to the smallest of details. Whether taking out the trash, grocery shopping, picking his grandchild up at school or taking her to an after-school appointment, T-Ball practice, or the dentist, he was always ready to lend a helping hand. Clearly, his support of his family was unwavering, even until the day he was called home to be with the Lord and his late wife.

CLOSING

Within the course of adult African American male development, the need for external validation has many men seeking to ground their identity in distorted images of maleness. It takes a strong character and inner strength to resist the lure of those social roles in deference to a more constructive persona. David Leroy Hopkins, in a life lived with truth, integrity, and righteous character, was able to achieve genuine manhood.

He offered a definition of manhood where dominant masculinity characterized by aggression toward other males and violence toward women was not the template used to measure worth. Rather, his was a manhood shaped by: a partnership with his wife; a nurturing and loving relationship with his children and grandchildren; a willingness to work as hard as necessary to provide for his family; and a heart that knew no boundary when it came to supporting extended family and friends. Indeed, his face is connected to the lessons he taught, and those of us whom he touched are better for having shared his space.

REFERENCES

Chatters, L. M., & Taylor, R. J. (1993). Intergenerational support: The provision to parents of adult children. In J. S. Jackson, L. M. Chatters, & R. J. Taylor (Eds.), *Aging in Black America.* Newbury Park, CA: Sage.

Hill, R. (1971). *Strengths of the Black family.* New York: National Urban League.

Hooks, B. (2004). *We real cool: Black men and masculinity.* New York: Rutledge Press.

Hopson, D. S., & Powell-Hopson, D. (1994). *Friends, lovers, and soulmates.* New York: Simon & Schuster.

Marable, M. (1984). The Black male: Searching beyond stereotypes. In R. Staples (Ed.), *The Black family: Essays and studies.* Belmont, CA: Wadsworth.

Nobles, W. W. (1981). African American family life: An instrument of culture. In H. P. McAdoo (Ed.), *Black families.* Newbury Park, CA: Sage.

Peters, E. (1983). *African openings to the tree of life: Life giving principles.* Oakland, CA: The Warren Press.

Chapter 8

Bill Cosby: America's Father

Anne Chan
Stanford University

If there were an award for "Father Laureate" of the United States, the award would indisputably be given to Bill Cosby. His portrayal of a loving father on *The Cosby Show* captivated the nation's imagination to such an extent that he has become an enduring icon of the ideal American father. Cosby and fatherhood are virtually synonymous, with his book *Fatherhood* breaking records as the fastest selling hardcover book (Fuller, 1992) and *USA Today* hailing him as "Father of our nation, every Thursday night . . . the USA's ideal dad" (Britt-Gibson, 1986, p. 1). *The Cosby Show* has become part of mainstream American cultural symbolism and vernacular, with the word "Cosby" often used to denote a happy, healthy family or a good father. This image of the perfect "Cosby" family has even been celebrated in literature in John Updike's (1990) novel, *Rabbit at Rest*: "On *The Cosby Show* rerun, the Huxtables are having one of those child-rearing crises bound to dissolve like a lump of sugar in their warm good humor, their mutual lovingness" (p. 336).

The popularity of Cosby and his show was truly phenomenal: The show ranked first, not only in the United States, but also in countries as diverse as South Africa and the Middle East. During its heyday, it was widespread in its popularity across an entire spectrum of demographic groups. The show not only had a loyal following of 60 million people who stayed home on Thursday evenings to watch it, it was also lauded for "saving" the family sitcom (hitherto declared to be a dead television genre) and was credited for enabling NBC to become the #1-ranked network for the first time in NBC's history (Fuller, 1992, pp. 20–22). *The Cosby Show* also ranked first in the Nielsen ratings for all of its eight seasons—an unprecedented accomplishment (Fuller, 1992).

The show garnered extensive praise for its positive portrayal of Black parents and family. Hence, it is logical to ask how the show has impacted public perception of Black fatherhood and masculinity.

BACKGROUND OF THE SHOW

Starring Bill Cosby as the amiable father of the Huxtable clan, *The Cosby Show* was a half-hour situation comedy featuring an upper-middle-class Black nuclear family headed by an obstetrician (Cliff Huxtable) and his lawyer wife (Clair Huxtable), the loving parents of five children, Sondra, Denise, Theo, Vanessa, and Rudy. As the series progressed, additional family and friends were included in the cast of characters, including grandparents, in-laws, and grandchildren. Much of the action in the show revolved around comedic situations in the family; the primary setting for the show was the Huxtables' comfortable and well-furnished New York brownstone.

The show premiered in 1984 and ran for eight seasons, breaking records and creating new benchmarks along the way. Not only was it a trailblazer in its weekly portrayal of a loving, healthy, intact nuclear Black family, it was also the first time in television history that American viewers were exposed to consistent images of successful, upper-middle-class, professional Black parents who cared deeply about their children and who were competent and committed to parenting.

THE ROLE OF TELEVISION IN STEREOTYPING
AND COUNTERSTEREOTYPING

Before analyzing the television portrayal of Black fatherhood on *The Cosby Show*, it is first necessary to understand the nature of stereotyping as well as the role of television in fostering or challenging stereotypes.

Theories about stereotyping provide a useful backdrop for analyzing the presentation of Black images and stereotypes on television. The psychological utility of stereotypes in demarcating self from other was first recognized by journalist Walter Lippmann (1922), who coined the term *stereotype*. Drawing upon prevailing psychoanalytic theories of the time, Lippmann understands the utility of stereotypes as "the projection upon the world of our sense of our own value, our own position and our own rights. The stereotypes are the fortress of our tradition, and behind its defenses we can continue to feel ourselves safe in the position we occupy" (p. 96). Allport

(1954) elaborated on the self-serving functionality of stereotypes "as a justif-
icatory device for categorical acceptance or rejection of a group, and as a
screening or selective device to maintain simplicity in perception and in
thinking" (p. 192). Likewise Hewstone and Giles (1986) have argued that
stereotyping presents a means for people to create and confirm their expectancies about others.

Each of the foregoing theorists have outlined the utility of stereotypes,
both in confirming expectancies about outgroups as well as in maintaining
distance between self and other. It is certainly plausible that television functions as a means for supporting and furthering these psychological goals,
thus creating ripe conditions for intolerance and prejudice. In fact, as the
most popular medium for information and entertainment in the United
States, television has been a formidable force in presenting, maintaining,
and confirming stereotypes about Blacks.[1] A silent dispenser of powerful
images and quick soundbites, television can easily serve to fortify our positions, induce simplistic thinking and judgment, as well as reinforce negative expectancies of others. One study of reference group identification, for
example, found that identification with the TV character Archie Bunker
led to an increase in authoritarian thinking and beliefs (Evuleocha &
Ugbah, 1989).

A few scholars have argued, however, that television can, on occasion,
serve as a counterstereotyping force. Evuleocha and Ugbah (1989) defined
counterstereotyping as "any attempts to deviate from traditionally existing
exaggerated beliefs associated with a category of people" (p. 202). *The Cosby
Show* is often acclaimed for being one of the few examples of counterstereotyping on television. Its weekly half-hour portrayal of an intact, upper-middle-class Black family headed by warm, loving, successful parents is
often cited as a major benchmark in television representations of Black fathers and families.

The very nature of television as a simulacrum of *our* reality serves to encourage an intimacy with the characters who enter our lives each week;
such familiarity may then result in subtle changes in attitude, beliefs, and
cognitions about self and other. This sense of familiarity and intimacy is notable in research on audience reactions to *The Cosby Show.* One participant
reported, "He's [Cosby] so likable, and I get the feeling if he were your
neighbor or your relative, you'd love to see him come in. I do, anyway. I
think he's just a real nice guy" (Jhally & Lewis, 1992, p. 19). This blurring of
television and reality is further encouraged by the very title of the show,
which leads viewers to identify Dr. Heathcliff Huxtable as the real-life Bill

---

[1]It has been estimated that more than 90 million people in America own television sets
and the average American watches an equivalent of 52 days of TV per year (*Just The Facts,*
2000).

Cosby and the Huxtables as the real-life Cosby family (Jhally & Lewis, 1992). This point is nicely illustrated in one viewer's reaction to the Bill Cosby/Huxtable character: "I think that's the way he is really, in real life, with his own kids. I'll bet that's how he is. . . . That's how he is as a father, he's not acting" (Jhally & Lewis, 1992).

What remains to be seen, however, is the impact of this counterstereotyping effect on public perception of Black men/fathers: did *The Cosby Show* succeed in debunking stereotypes of Black fathers or was the show merely televised artifice that failed to penetrate beyond the level of entertainment? Given the subversive nature of stereotyping, did the show, in any way, indirectly or unconsciously serve to foster stereotypes of Black men?

The aim of this chapter is threefold: first, to examine images of Black fatherhood and masculinity on *The Cosby Show*, second, to examine evidence that points to the positive/counterstereotyping impact of these images, and third, to deconstruct and critique these images for possible deleterious effects on perceptions of Blacks.

STEREOTYPES OF BLACKS ON TV
BEFORE *THE COSBY SHOW*

In order to truly appreciate the contributions of *The Cosby Show* to television history, it is first imperative to review the portrayals of Blacks during the first two decades of television prior to the show. For the most part, the roles relegated to Blacks were demeaning and stereotypical—Blacks were primarily portrayed either as minstrels, maids, or fools. Judging by the level of protest engendered by the casting of a Black actor as a judge in a 1963 episode of *Perry Mason*, it was evident that White audiences were far more approving of seeing Blacks in stereotypical working-class roles of Uncle Tom and the mammy than in middle-class, white-collar roles (Evuleocha & Ugbah, 1989, p. 201).

Between the late 1960s and early 1970s, sitcoms featuring all Black casts or Blacks in central roles were produced. Although Black actors were given more prominence in these productions, their characters were still stock stereotypes (Evuleocha & Ugbah, 1989, p. 201). Moreover, the majority of the Black characters in these sitcoms were of lower socioeconomic status (e.g., *The Jeffersons*, *Good Times*, and *What's Happening*) or were in subordinate positions to Whites (e.g., the Black adopted sons in *Different Strokes*).

The 1980s continued this dismal trend of depicting Blacks in subservient positions. Even though they were now portrayed as intelligent and quick-witted, they were nonetheless featured in occupations that served Whites (*Benson* was the aide to a White governor and Nell Carter played the smart housekeeper of a White family). Perhaps one of the most unfortunate characterizations from this period was that of Mr. T, the "super masculine menial, brainless eunuch" (Evuleocha & Ugbah, 1989, p. 201) who was depicted as having a phobia of flying but was constantly being tricked and sedated by the other (White) members of the A-team into taking a flight.

TELEVISION FATHERS AND FAMILIES BEFORE
THE COSBY SHOW

The father figure was a stock character in early sitcoms like *Life of Riley*, *Make Room for Daddy*, *The Honeymooners*, *Father Knows Best*, and *Ozzie and Harriet*. These sitcoms featured the father figure as the center of dramatic and comedic action; characters and stories were specifically written to revolve around this central figure. This convention was later utilized in *The Cosby Show*, where the father, Dr. Huxtable, is the true axis of the show. Like the depiction of Blacks on network television, portrayals of television fathers were, for the most part, stereotyped along predictable racial and class lines.

According to Glennon and Butsch's (1982) comprehensive analysis of 218 television families from 1946 to 1978, working-class fathers (such as Archie Bunker in *All in the Family* and Lars in *I Remember Mama*) tended to be portrayed and ridiculed as bumbling, inept, and loutish, while mothers in these families were portrayed as capable and strong. Cantor (1990) noted that this stereotype has been most recently seen in the show *Roseanne*, where the mother is clearly the dominant figure and decision maker in the house. Despite being portrayed as loutish and foolish, the television working-class fathers still endeared themselves to viewers. Particularly noteworthy in this regard is the character of Archie Bunker, the loud, oafish father in *All in the Family*. Archie Bunker was openly bigoted and racist, yet still maintained a loyal fan base.

In contrast to the working-class families, sitcoms with White middle-class families (such as *The Donna Reed Show*, *The Adventures of Ozzie and Harriet*, *Leave It to Beaver*, *Father Knows Best*) presented fathers as dedicated superdads who could confidently handle any crisis (Glennon & Butsch, 1982). Unlike the more acrimonious marital interactions portrayed in the working-class families, middle-class sitcom fathers were shown to be in harmonious and cooperative relationships with their wives.

Interestingly, sitcoms first presented single-parent households with fathers (*Bachelor Father*, *My Two Dads*) rather than mothers (*Julia*, *One Day at a Time*, *Kate & Allie*). Cantor (1990) noted that this single-father portrayal is perplexing given that the number of actual households with single dads was miniscule compared to the number of households headed by single moms.[2]

Depictions of family interactions of Blacks and other minorities were characterized by discord between males and females, aggressiveness in parents and children, female-dominated households (regardless of whether a male was present), and little supervision and love for children (Berry, 1992). The most prominent pre-Cosby Black fathers were featured in *Good Times* (1974–1979) and *The Jeffersons* (1975–1985). Much like their White working-class counterparts, the Black fathers in these two sitcoms were unfavorably portrayed. The father in *Good Times* is incompetent, does not contribute financially to the family, and is clearly subordinate to the mother. As Cantor (1990) noted, the father is unemployed in the first episodes, and is then quickly killed off after he finally finds a job. In an even sadder and more demeaning portrayal, George Jefferson of *The Jeffersons* is depicted as an upwardly mobile man who has succeeded in moving beyond his working-class status; yet he is also depicted as hating Whites and is regarded by his loved ones as an idiot. The underlying message of this show appears to be that a Black man can make it in a White world but he is *still* considered as less than capable and intelligent, even by his own family.

More often than not, the figure of the Black television father was denoted more by his absence than his presence (Merritt & Stroman, 1993). When present, Black fathers prior to *The Cosby Show* were, for the most part, shown to be irresponsible, shiftless, incompetent, and lacking power and respect within their own families. The functionality of television in confirming negative expectancies was clearly in operation here. These television representations of Black fatherhood served to foster continued rejection of the outgroup: They are consistent with the pervasive stereotype of Black fathers as the urban, inner-city hoodlum who has fathered several children and has abandoned them all (White & Cones, 1999).

BILL COSBY: QUEST FOR THE BLACK MASCULINE CHARACTER

Although Bill Cosby is best known for his work on his namesake show, he had a distinguished acting and comedic career long before he became memorialized as "America's Dad." In 1965, he made television history when he was cast as the first Black performer in a starring role on the drama series *I*

---

[2]*Julia* is particularly notable in two respects: she was the first single mother portrayed in a sitcom and she was also the first Black woman to star in her own series (Cantor, 1990). Some have argued that this portrayal of a single Black mother raising a son bowed to the "antimale, emasculating pattern of traditional prejudice" (MacDonald, 1983).

Spy. Cosby's character as a United States secret agent (paired with another White agent) was also revolutionary in its being free of the usual racial stereotyping of minstrel and fool, and of a depiction of a Black man as a protector, rather than as the perpetrator of crime. Cosby portrayed a capable spy who could hobnob comfortably with heads of state and foreign agents (MacDonald, 1983). After *I Spy*, Bill Cosby played a middle-class, educated, high school track coach and bachelor in his namesake show, *Bill Cosby Show*. This character again broke free of traditional representations of Blacks by depicting a Black man who was responsible, educated, gainfully employed, and a capable problem solver. In 1972, Bill Cosby premiered his Saturday morning children's show, *Fat Albert and the Cosby Kids*. Based on Cosby's childhood memories, the show aimed to teach ethics, responsibility, and values. The show was progressive for its positive portrayals of Black children, but it was nevertheless very well-received by audiences.

Subsequent to *The Cosby Show*, Bill Cosby has attempted several television ventures, including the comedic host of *Kids Say the Darndest Things* and *You Bet Your Life*. However, none of these ventures have captured the hearts of the public as did *The Cosby Show*.

In many of his productions, Bill Cosby should be credited for going against the grain of traditional television stereotypes and creating dignified representations of Black men. His entire career trajectory is distinguished by his efforts in depicting Black masculinity in positive terms. In terms of audience response, his efforts can be regarded as largely successful; the fact that he is now synonymous with American fatherhood is testimony to what he has achieved.

At the same time, Cosby's version of Black masculinity has always been somewhat "gently neutered"—his characters express no patriarchal wrath nor testosterone rage and have thus remained attractive and acceptable to White audiences. Most of his characters have been funny, somewhat goofy, in control, and always safe—thus providing a wide comfort zone for the majority culture (R. Chrisman, personal communication, November 9, 2002). Bottom-line, although he ever so gently challenged audiences in subtle ways, the key to his success has been his conformity to an acceptable White vision of manhood and family. This adherence to audience comfort and safety is well demonstrated in the magic formula of the widely successful *Cosby Show*.

POSITIVE IMAGES OF BLACK MASCULINITY AND FATHERHOOD ON *THE COSBY SHOW*

One of the most notable achievements of *The Cosby Show* was that it showed positive, healthy images of Blacks during its weekly visit to American households. Rejecting the stereotype of Black families as rancorous and aggressive, *The Cosby Show* instead provided a consistent picture of an intact Black family thriving on loving interactions between parent and child, husband and wife. Challenging the view of the absentee, unemployed Black father who has no concern for his family, the show presented its audience with a strong father character who was loving, always available to his children, in control, and successfully employed as a doctor. Overturning the stereotype of the hypersexualized, wanton Black man, the show depicted a loving Black man who was a supremely faithful, loving, trustworthy, and dependable husband.

Most notably, the character of Dr. Huxtable gave audiences a new image of Black masculinity and fatherhood: one of sensitivity, good humor, openness, caring, confidence, and gentleness. At the same time, Cosby gave the Huxtable father an endearing humanness by depicting a Dad who sometimes made mistakes and who was at other times less than enthralled with his children. Despite these minor (and very forgivable) fatherly lapses, Dr. Huxtable was clearly depicted as being the parent in charge and in control. In fact, one study found that directing communication was provided far more by Cliff ($n = 76$) than by Clair ($n = 3$) and supporting communication was again offered far more by Cliff ($n = 56$) rather than Clair ($n = 15$) (Larson, 1993). Another study of the interactions in the show found that father–child interactions far outnumbered mother–child interactions (Merritt & Stroman, 1993).

The character of Dr. Huxtable was also counterstereotyping in his close relationships with his children (he was often depicted interacting positively and communicating with his children and their friends) and in his household activities (he was depicted as a great cook and was often seen in the kitchen donning an apron).

The other Black male/father figures in *The Cosby Show* were similarly depicted in positive terms. In fact, the males in the family were often portrayed expressing an extraordinary depth of feeling and sensitivity. One memorable scene featured the three Huxtable males being embarrassed by their attempts to impress women. Bogle (1988) wrote, "The episode ended with the three Huxtable males sitting together on the sofa, eyeing one another furtively, then affectionately wrapping their arms around each other. What appeared perhaps to be a tame episode really was something quite new to TV: a rare glimpse of Black fathers and sons relating warmth and regard for one another" (pp. 263–264).

Likewise, although Bill Cosby commands attention as the loving father of the Huxtable clan, the show presents another significant positive father/grandfather figure in the character of Cliff's father, who is equally loving and committed to his grandchildren and wife, and who is dignified, wise, and sensitive. Later in the series, other loving Black fathers are introduced through the characters of Sondra's and Denise's husbands. These characters provided a powerful backdrop of fatherly love that is consistent, stable, respected, and generational.

All in all, these positive portrayals of Black fathers resulted in the creation of television characters that Whites liked and identified with. For some viewers, these likeable characters may have encouraged a conscious or unconscious re-examination of their assumptions and stereotypes about Black fathers. This appears to be the case with one White viewer who stated his opinion about the show in a research study, "I think it's good for people to see Black families can own nice homes and have careers and have nice clothes and have goals for their children, where for so long, it was never even thought of, considered" (Jhally & Lewis, 1992, p. 32).

Cosby's intent in creating his show was for the Huxtable parents to serve as role models for the millions of viewers who tuned in. Cosby, who earned his doctorate in education from the University of Massachusetts and who wrote his dissertation on using visual media as a teaching tool for children, has stated that the show is about "parents who love the children, who give them understanding. It is about people who respect each other" (Johnson, 1992, p. 60). It appears that he succeeded spectacularly in achieving this goal: The parenting skills of the Huxtables have been so admired that episodes of *The Cosby Show* have been used as guidelines for teaching parenting (Fuller, 1992). The Huxtables have even been lauded as model parents by popular psychologist Dr. Joyce Brothers for being firm but loving disciplinarians (Brothers, 1989).

These external indicators point to the show's success in creating television parents who were parenting role models. However, in terms of countering established racial stereotypes, did the show provoke a deeper change in public perception of Blacks?

THE COSBY SHOW AS A POSSIBLE COUNTERSTEREOTYPING FORCE: IMPACT ON WHITE VIEWERS

According to social learning theory, television models can shape learning and behavior (Bandura, 1977). For Bandura, television is a major influence in the development of children via its modeling effects. Bandura calls this form of learning "abstract modeling." Using this model, one could postulate that seeing positive imagery and interactions on shows like *The Cosby Show* could teach children to act in positive ways and to see Blacks in a positive light. Alvin F. Poussaint, a Harvard professor and a psychological consultant for the show, suggested that the show's gentle approach to race is paradoxically more impactful than a direct, hard-edged approach: "This show is changing the White community's perspective of Black Americans. It's doing far more to instill positive racial attitudes than if Bill came at the viewer with a sledgehammer or a sermon" (cited in Waters, 1985, p. 54). Reep and Damprot (1989) further suggested that though Cosby's creation was an exception within the mainstream of television, the high impact of his nonstereotypical fatherly portrayal may reduce or impact stereotypical perception more than other (more numerous) stereotyped Black characters.

There is some limited support for these ideas through experimental as well as qualitative research. One prosocial study examined the effects of sitcoms on children's prosocial behavior and found that an overwhelming majority (94%) of the children in the study were able to understand moral lessons contained in an episode of *The Cosby Show* (Rosenkoetter, 1999). Rosenkoetter followed up with a second study to see if there was an association between television viewing and children's prosocial behavior. Interestingly, prosocial sitcom viewing was found to be one of three predictors of prosocial behavior (the other predictors were grade and gender). Other modeling behavior studies have similarly shown some change in children's sex-role stereotyping through the use of counterstereotypical images (Eisenstock, 1984; Johnston & Ettema, 1982).

Studies of amygdala[3] response to Black and White faces have also provided limited support for the possibility of counterstereotyping. One study of amygdala activation (Phelps et al., in press) found differential amygdala activation to ordinary Black and White faces based on unconscious social evaluation (as measured by the Implicit Association Test) as well as a potentiated startle eyeblink to Black, as opposed to White faces. Repeating this experiment with pictures of famous, highly regarded Blacks (such as Bill Cosby), the researchers found a reduction in the mean response time in the IAT, and no evidence of eyeblink startle response to the faces of the Black celebrities. The authors of this study believe that these results point to the effect of culturally acquired information on the connection between social learning and brain function. However, the learning involved appears to be confined to a tiny fraction of Blacks who are celebrities and does not appear to generalize to all Blacks.

It is impossible to gauge the full impact of *The Cosby Show* on White perceptions of Blacks, particularly given the difficulty of isolating the effects of the show in research experiments. Although there is tentative support for the notion that *The Cosby Show* is a counterstereotyping force, the available research on this topic is very limited.

---

[3]The amygdala is often described as the fear center of the brain; unconscious stimuli (such as fear triggers) can measurably arouse the amygdala.

CRITIQUES OF *THE COSBY SHOW*

Detractors of the show have contended that the show fails at counterstereotyping; some have even gone so far as to assert that the show fosters modern racism.

A major critique of *The Cosby Show* is that it has failed to address important Black social issues. As Taylor (1989) put it, "they inhabit a visibly Black world, whose Blackness is hardly ever alluded to" (p. 26). Other critics have accused the show of being "colorblind": that it is *Leave It to Beaver* in Blackface or that it is not "Black enough" (Fuller, 1992). This sense of colorblindness may perhaps be the reason why Fuller's study found that more than 69% of their predominantly White American schoolchildren sample considered the Huxtables to be "typically" American; yet more than half of their American respondents denied that they are a "typical Black family" (Fuller, 1992). One comment by a White South African is particularly telling in this regard:

> I must say that when we first watched the show it did seem rather strange to see how "normal" everyone was. It didn't take long before we stopped thinking of the Huxtables as a Black family and began to relate to them as one would to any show about a middle-class family. It really helped us to better understand the fact that they were in fact no different from us, despite the color of their skins. (Fuller, 1992, p. 113)

Another South African, a Johannesburg television executive, opined that *The Cosby Show* was No. 1 in the South African ratings because it "was not about race but about family values" (Taylor, 1989, p. 177). This colorblindness appears to have pervaded the show from the outset: One of the earliest reviews of the show described it thus: "In unadorned outline, this is just another family sitcom with lovable Mom and Pop struggling to raise their frisky but lovable children. . . . This particular family happens to be Black but its lifestyle and problems are universal middle-class" (O'Connor, 1984, p.). The show's colorblindness has led some to argue that Bill Cosby "transcends" race and is therefore not perceived as a Black father (Jhally & Lewis, 1992). The comments from one research respondent appear to support this argument: "He's what I think a father should be; and a mother. . . . They both are there for their kids. That's what it portrays to me. . . . I don't think of them as Black. . . . They're just people and they are nice and they treat their children good and they seem to get through all the situations pretty well" (Jhally & Lewis, 1992, p. 45).

Indeed, the show was so unstereotypically "Black" that Cosby may have even been perceived as being atypical of Black fathers. One comment from a research participant provides some support for this point:

I don't think Cosby is stereotypical Black. . . . I mean they really don't make much point to the fact that they're Black. And certainly don't do Black stereotypical things like *Good Times* used to do. But I think *Amen, 227,* are more that way. They talk the slick Black accent, and they work on the mannerisms, and I think they make a conscious effort to act that way like they are catering to the Black race in that show. Whereas Cosby, you know, definitely doesn't do that. He's upper middle class and he's not Black stereotypical. There's a difference in the tone of those shows, completely. (Jhally & Lewis, 1992, p. 102)

Perhaps the televised medium through which *The Cosby Show* exists may have served to heighten the sense of unreality about the Cosbys rather than to break down stereotypes of Black fatherhood. In this light, *The Cosby Show* may have unfortunately served to *reinforce* stereotypes of Black fatherhood rather than to debunk them. The comments from one focus group participant are particularly compelling in this regard: "That show shows a really unrealistic view. I mean, can you think of anyone whose wife is a lawyer, and the husband's a doctor? I'm talking anyone. I mean, that's blowing off the spectrum. And then if you talk about Black or White children, or anybody, that are raised in this area, there's no way that they can really get the proper upbringing" (Jhally & Lewis, 1992, pp. 28–29). Another White respondent, when queried about the reality of *The Cosby Show*, provided this telling comment: "My God, you're going to bring a crack house into Cosby? Come on, where do you think all the crack houses are? Who in hell do you think's running the crack houses? You think these are all White people selling dope? No! It's all his people selling dope, running the crack houses, and having all the problems. But we're not going to talk about that in this show. This is the show that ignores 100 percent of all the problems that exist in this country" (Jhally & Lewis, 1992, p. 29).

Other critics have charged that the show did not change stereotypes of Blacks, but instead provided a "Black comfort zone" for White viewers (Carter, 1988) that "lulled" them into "the assumption that the races were at peace with one another, that inner city blight and decay as well as social tension and racial inequities had ceased to exist, that indeed America's past history of racism had vanished" (Bogle, 1988, p. 268). In this regard, these arguments suggest that the show has not succeeded in counterstereotyping but has in effect served to further "fortress" (Lippmann's term) and shield Whites from facing and understanding Black social issues. Worse still, the show may have actually *reinforced* modern racism by trumpeting the myth of social mobility through the affluence of the Huxtables. According to Jhally and Lewis (1992): "The Huxtables' achievements ultimately lend credibility to the idea that 'anyone can make it,' the comforting assumption of the American dream, which is a myth that sustains a conservative political ideology blind to the inequalities hindering persons born on mean streets and privileging persons born on easy street" (p. 8).

Indeed, there is some anecdotal evidence that the show's counterstereo-typing imagery has had adverse consequences for some viewers. Lamented one father who needed to explain to his children why they do not live like the Huxtables: "I do know that this is just entertainment. But my kids think it's the way we should live. That is unfair. It is unfair for me to explain to my son that, no, Mom is not a lawyer, dad is not a doctor, and these things don't work that way. I think it's really sad" (Inniss & Feagin, 1995, p. 700). One Barbadian survey participant echoed similar concerns: "The image of the father as 'happy go lucky' is not necessarily the same for us and Barbadian children may judge their parents on this basis. So, too, the free-dom and material possessions of the children could encourage our kids to aspire for these, leading to breakdown in family life and morality" (Payne, 1994, p. 243).

These comments also provide support for Jhally and Lewis's (1992) cri-tique of the show for equating success with prosperity: "This dubious equa-tion means that African Americans are trapped in a position where any re-flection of a more typical Black experience—which is certainly *not* upper middle class—is stereotypical" (p. 138). Jhally and Lewis point out that Bill Cosby/Dr. Huxtable's image as a positive role model and a successful father is largely dependent on his class status as an upper-middle-class profes-sional. They argue that this equating of upper-middle-class status with nor-malcy traps Black viewers into buying into a value system where they will in-evitably lose—they describe it as "cultural and political suicide" (p. 122). They urge a rethinking of television representation of Blacks such that there is less distortion and forced choice in class structure, and where im-ages of a successful Black working-class family can be seen.

Another problem with the representation of Bill Cosby as superdad is that the parental focus shifts subtly and subversively away from the mother of the family. The character of Mrs. Huxtable "is a combination earth mother and genius, and in the economy of sexual and family relations, these talents serve only to subsidize Bill's gentle patriarchy. This suggests that the price paid for benign patriarchy is the subordination of the wife's talent and temperament. This is a rather conservative ideological position for Blacks—or for anyone, for that matter" (R. Chrisman, personal com-munication, November 9, 2002). The subordination of Mrs. Huxtable to Mr. Huxtable, of mother to father, means that her role either as mother or as a contributing breadwinner, does not, in the end, matter in the hier-archy of things at the Cosby household. Feminist scholars such as Phyllis Japp have critiqued the Cosby super-Dad portrayal for diminishing and undermining Mrs. Huxtable's value, power, and significance as a bread-winner and mother.

In response to the critiques to the show, Alvin Poussaint (a Harvard psy-chiatrist and consultant for the show) replied:

It should be apparent by now that *The Cosby Show* presents a high level of positive images that are far ahead of other Black sitcoms, and it is racist to suggest that the series is merely "Father Knows Best" in Blackface. The Black style of the characters is evident in their speech, intonations, and nuances; Black art, music and dance are frequently displayed. Black authors and books are often mentioned; Black colleges and other institutions have been introduced on the show, perhaps for the first time, on network television.

There is ample evidence to suggest that the show has raised Black self-esteem, it has simultaneously lessened stereotypical views of Blacks among Whites. It is even possible that *The Cosby Show* will produce changes in American attitudes that are not yet apparent. (Poussaint, 1988, p. 74)

Bill Cosby himself has responded to the criticism of his show's color-blindness by asserting the abilities and means for Blacks to be like the Cosbys: "To say that we're acting White means that only White people can do this. It denies us being Americans" (quoted in Fuller, 1992, p. 123). Another defense of *The Cosby Show* has pointed out that "there is value in letting White America understand that blackness isn't necessarily a pathological condition" (Raspberry, 1984, p. A27).

IMPACT OF *THE COSBY SHOW* ON BLACK VIEWERS

The earlier arguments for and against *The Cosby Show* have, for the most part, centered on the show's impact on White viewers. Research on the reactions of Black viewers is much less well known. Some important differences between Black and White audiences, have, however, been noted by the researchers.

The colorblind reactions to the show (as outlined in the previous sections) do not appear to be salient for Black viewers. The Black viewers in Jhally and Lewis's (1992) study overwhelmingly saw the Huxtables as "really black" (p. 53), as opposed to seeing them as a universalist family that transcended race. In fact, some Black participants in their study were perplexed and even offended when asked about their awareness of the Huxtables' race. One upper-middle-class Black female reacted to the question thus:

How aware? How aware? . . . Just look at them and you can see that they are Black. You're not talking to White folks now. What kind of question is that for Black folk? (Jhally & Lewis, 1992, p. 53)

Other respondents attributed the "blackness" of the show, less to the skin color of the actors, and more to subtle characterization of their mannerisms and speech. Notes one respondent, "If you take the two shows [*Cosby* and *Family Ties*] and, you know, put 'em side by side and give them the same scripts, I don't think they could come across as what happens in the Black script and then the same thing would be the same in the White script. . . . There's just something about the way Blacks do things, say things, react to things that Whites would do in a different way. . . . Or sometimes it's the relationship between the father and the son" (Jhally & Lewis, 1992, p. 54).

Reaction to Bill Cosby and to the show among Black viewers may depend on socioeconomic status as well as other factors. A few studies have indicated that *The Cosby Show* has not been effective in reaching Blacks from lower socioeconomic levels. One study comparing two TV fathers, Cliff Huxtable and James Evans (a lower socioeconomic, unemployed, and more stereotypic Black father in *Good Times*) found that a majority (87%) of Black youths in the study identified with James because they found him to be stronger and more manly, whereas Cliff Huxtable was thought to be effeminate and weak. The author of this study concludes that "While it may be true that *The Cosby Show* is presenting new definitions of Black manhood and Black family, the failure of the show to address class status differences may be affecting the show's ability to actually deliver those images to the lower class audience as anymore than entertainment" (Berry, 1992, p. 119).

Similar reactions were found in the survey of Barbadian adults. Some were impressed with Cliff's relationship with Clair, while others were repulsed by his lack of authority in heading his household (Payne, 1994). The response of one male participant in the survey is particularly telling: "I feel that while the father is portrayed as 'nice,' he doesn't seem to exert the leadership that men are traditionally expected to. In that sense I think he represents a negative example for young boys" (p. 241).

In contrast, other studies have shown positive receptions to Bill Cosby and his show. Qualitative research on audience response to *The Cosby Show* has provided some anecdotal evidence that the show challenged some Black viewers to rethink their perceptions of themselves. For instance, one study of study of Caribbean perceptions of *The Cosby Show* elicited the following responses (Payne, 1993, pp. 235, 237):

- Watching this show can remind us that Blacks do more than steal hubcaps and snort cocaine. (Male, nonmanual, 26+)
- Being Black does not mean you have to be a sportsman or a policeman as most programs tend to project Black people as being. (Female, nonmanual, 26+)
- Generally provides a positive example of Black family life which are so different from other Black comedies where there are absent fathers who are generally irresponsible ones. (Female, manual, 26+)

These responses indicate that the show challenged some viewers' previously held assumptions about Blacks and provided alternatives to stereo-

typed ideas of Blacks. In another study, many Black viewers talked about
identifying closely with the characters of Cliff and Clair: "I can see some of
my father in him because he's got this restraint. It says, 'I'm not going to get
angry.' . . . Those types of things, those are real situations I can hear my parents, I can hear my father, I can hear people that I've grown up with, doing
the same thing. Or thinking the same things, maybe not saying it. . . .
There's something when it's extremely real, you know, some of the stuff is
actually in real life versus imitating it. . . . I don't like to think when I watch
that show, and I really don't have to think. It's really all right there" (Jhally
& Lewis, 1992, p. 52). In fact, Jhally and Lewis observed that Black audiences blurred the distinction between Bill Cosby and Cliff Huxtable much
more than did White audiences. As one respondent in their study commented, "He portrays a good father, yeah, and he portrays a good father
not only on this program but it follows him off the set and on the set. . . . He
always has time for the children. If they got a problem, he's always there"
(p. 49). Although Jhally and Lewis (1992) assert that Black audiences have a
higher level of identification with the Huxtables than do White audiences,
this assertion may need a more fine-tuned analysis in terms of socioeconomic and class differences in Black viewers' identification with the
Huxtables.

CONCLUSION

As befits a television show of its prominence and significance, *The Cosby
Show* has had its share of critical praise and blame, with one camp lauding it
because it "recodes Black ethnicity around the father figure and the strong
nuclear family" (Real, 1989, p. 120) and the opposite camp excoriating it
for fostering modern racism:

> As long as *all* Blacks were represented in demeaning or peripheral roles, it
> was possible to believe that American racism was, as it were, indiscriminate.
> The social vision of "Cosby," however, reflecting the minuscule integration of
> Blacks into the upper middle-class, reassuringly throws the blame for Black
> poverty back onto the impoverished. (Gates, 1989, p. H40)

One of the most salient critiques of the show is that the beloved Huxtable Dad does little to represent the experiences of Black fathers who are
invisible in mainstream media and in the public consciousness, but are very
much present in the lives of their children and families. These fathers may
not be "Cosby Dads" in terms of class or socioeconomic status, but they are
every bit as dedicated, motivated, capable, responsible, and concerned as
the Cosby father figure. These invisible fathers are excised from the public

consciousness in many different ways; worse still, they are brushed aside and forgotten when any type of statement or representation about Black fathers is made. Case in point, Cosby's recent controversial remarks about Black parents at an NAACP dinner painted working-class Black fathers as an irresponsible and thoughtless lot: "The lower economic people are not holding up their end in this deal. These people are not parenting. They are buying things for their kids—$500 sneakers for what? And won't spend $200 for 'Hooked on Phonics' " ("Bill Cosby Live," 2004). A week later, in a speech at Stanford University, Cosby reiterated this theme, noting that some Black children "have been raised like pimps" ("Bill Cosby Live," 2004). Such remarks from the most famous American Father in television history, serve not only to stereotype *all* Black fathers as uncaring parents, they also work to further reinforce the invisibility surrounding the dedicated and caring Black fathers who do not fit this stereotype. Hence, although it could be argued that the Bill Cosby show counterstereotypes Black fathers in its representation of a loving, responsible father figure, it is also ironic that Bill Cosby himself serves to negatively stereotype all Black fathers in his public statements.

In all fairness, although the Cosby show has rightly been criticized for its limitations in addressing complex issues of race, class, and gender, it would be remiss to dismiss the triumphs of this show, most notably the groundbreaking presentation of positive images of Blacks and Black fatherhood on network television. In particular, the achievements of this show cannot be assessed without a consideration of the sociopolitical environment of the mid-1980s in which the show came into prominence. It is important to recognize that the counterstereotyping efforts of *The Cosby Show* took place within a cultural milieu that was both conservative, that had a widening gap between rich and poor, and that was reeling from the savings and loans scandals. This was *not* a fertile ground to launch a new sitcom with groundbreaking images of an upper-middle-class Black family. As John Downing (1988) pointed out, "to be as good as it is *and* to have gotten past these barriers is a major achievement in itself" (p. 68).

In examining this issue of counterstereotyping and *The Cosby Show*, it bears us well to remember that television is a unique distinctive genre that both shapes and is shaped by social values, mores, and expectations. Television programming is the by-product of two interacting poles of demand— that of the producer and that of the consumer. As both an economic and social commodity, it represents current social values as well as shapes them. Seen in this light, I would argue that the issue of counterstereotyping in *The Cosby Show* cannot be determined strictly in dualistic, either/or terms. Rather, its legacy will be necessarily complex and mixed, with some viewers learning to be more tolerant and others less tolerant, with some Blacks aspiring to be like Bill Cosby and others rejecting his role modeling (Berry,

1992). Perhaps Bill Cosby, the often appointed "Dad" of America, will be the salient image that will "override the less significant stereotypical portrayals of all other Blacks on television" (Reep & Dambrot, 1989, p. 556). It is just as plausible that his show will not have any lasting impact on the American consciousness. The ultimate outcome, in all likelihood, lies somewhere in between.

ACKNOWLEDGMENTS

Many thanks to Professors Robert Chrisman, Jennifer Eberhardt, Michael Connor, and Joseph White for their valuable feedback and insights regarding this chapter.

REFERENCES

Allport, G. (1954). *The nature of prejudice.* Cambridge, MA: Addison-Wesley.

Bandura, A. (1977). *Social learning theory.* Englewood Cliffs, NJ: Prentice-Hall.

Berry, V. T. (1992). From good times to the Cosby show: Perceptions of changing televised images among Black fathers and sons. In S. Craig (Ed.), *Men, masculinity, and the media* (pp. 111–123). Newbury Park, CA: Sage.

Bill Cosby live. (2004, May 25). *Wall Street Journal,* p. A16.

Bogle, D. (1988). *Blacks in American films and television: An encyclopedia.* New York: Garland.

Britt-Gibson, D. (1986, December 23). Cover story: The Cos, family man for the '80s. *USA Today,* p. 1.

Brothers, J. (1989, March 4). "If you want to be a better parent . . ." *TV Guide, 10,* 22–25.

Cantor, M. (1990). Prime-time fathers: A study in continuity and change. *Critical Studies in Mass Communication, 7,* 275–285.

Carter, R. G. (1988). TV's black comfort zone for whites. *Television Quarterly, 33,* 29–34.

Downing, J. D. H. (1988). "The Cosby Show" and American racial discourse. In G. Smitherman-Donaldson & T. A. van Dijk (Eds.), *Discourse and discrimination* (pp. 46–73). Detroit: Wayne State University Press.

Eisenstock, B. (1984). Sex-role differences in children's identification with counter-stereotypical televised portrayals. *Sex Roles, 10*(5/6), 417–430.

Evuleocha, S. U., & Ugbah, S. D. (1989). Stereotypes, counter-stereotypes, and Black television images in the 1990s. *The Western Journal of Black Studies, 13*(4), 197–205.

Fuller, L. K. (1992). *The Cosby show: Audiences, impact, and implications.* Westport, CT: Greenwood Press.

Gates, H. L. (1989, November 12). TV's Black world turns—But stays unreal. *New York Times,* p. H40.

Glennon, L. M., & Butsch, R. (1982). The family as portrayed on television 1946–1978. In D. Pearl, L. Bouthilet, & J. Lazar (Eds.), *Television and behavior: Ten years of scientific progress and implications for the eighties.* Washington: U.S. Department of Health and Human Services.

Hewstone, M., & Giles, H. (1986). Stereotypes and intergroup communications. In W. Gudykunst (Ed.), *Intergroup communication.* London: Edward Arnold.

Inniss, L. B., & Feagin, J. R. (1995). "The Cosby Show": The view from the Black middle class. *Journal of Black Studies, 25*(6), 692–711.

Japp, P. M. (1991). Gender and work in the 1980s: Television's working women as displaced persons. *Women's Studies in Communication, 14*(1), 49–74.

Jhally, S., & Lewis, J. (1992). *Enlightened racism: The Cosby show, audiences, and the myth of the American dream.* Boulder, CO: Westview Press.

Johnson, R. E. (1992, May 4). "The Cosby Show" ends after 8 years with a vital message to all young Blacks. *Jet, 82,* 56–61.

Johnston, J., & Ettema, J. (1982). *Positive images: Breaking stereotypes with children's television.* Beverly Hills: Sage.

Just The Facts. (2000). Action For Media Education. Retrieved June 6, 2002, from http://www.action4mediaed.org/justthefacts/justthefacts.html

Larson, M. S. (1993). Family communication on prime-time television. *Journal of Broadcasting and Electronic Media, 37*(3), 349–357.

Lippmann, W. (1922). *Public opinion.* New York: Macmillan.

MacDonald, J. F. (1983). *Blacks and White TV: Afro-Americans in television since 1948.* Chicago: Nelson-Hall Publishers.

Merritt, B., & Stroman, C. A. (1993). Black family imagery and interaction on television. *Journal of Black Studies, 23*(4), 492–499.

O'Connor, J. J. (1984, September 20). Cosby in NBC series on a New York family. *New York Times,* p. C30.

Payne, M. A. (1993). Barbadian adults' perceptions of eighteen popular U.S. television programs. *Perceptual and Motor Skills, 77*(3), 771–775.

Phelps, E. A., O'Connor, K. J., Cunningham, W. A., Funayama, E. S., Gatenby, J. C., Gore, J. C., & Banaji, M. R. (in press). Performance on indirect measures of race evaluation predicts amygdala activation.

Poussaint, A. F. (1988, October). The Huxtables: Fact or fantasy? *Ebony, 74,* 72–74.

Raspberry, W. (1984, November 5). Cosby show: Black or White. *Washington Post,* p. A27.

Real, M. (1989). *Super media: A cultural studies approach.* Newbury Park, CA: Sage.

Reep, D. C., & Dambrot, F. H. (1989). Effects of frequent television viewing on stereotypes: "Drip, drip," or "drench"? *Journalism Quarterly, 66*(3), 542.

Rosenkoetter, L. I. (1999). The television situation comedy and children's prosocial behavior. *Journal of Applied Social Psychology, 29*(5), 979–993.

Taylor, E. (1989). From the Nelsons to the Huxtables: Genre and family imagery in American network television. *Qualitative Sociology, 12*(1), 13–28.

Updike, J. (1990). *Rabbit at rest* (1st ed.). New York: Knopf.

Waters, H. F. (1985, September 2). Cosby's fast track. *Newsweek,* 54.

White, J. L., & Cones, J. H. I. (1999). *Black man emerging: Facing the past and seizing a future in America.* New York: Routledge.

Part III

PROBLEMATIC RELATIONSHIPS

Mingus

smells of sweetness lead me to my past
as powerful music enters my soul
it helps almost pushes kindly forces me to create
movement and gesture combined with perfect faith
full moon pushed along passion
as a Brown Woman in red soaks in china rain at midnight
she presses play on a random tape
3 or 4 shades of Mingus roll off her breath
and i too am looking for the flowers that bloom
empowerment wrapped in that sheet of music
while the Black butterflies emerge
taking flight on the Underground Railroad we all
need time we all need truth
funk soul jazz love it's all relative.
            it turned out not to be a session of free form improvisation
                    but set pieces perfectly performed
                a lyrical interlude transformed by passion
                    leads me to my knowledge of self
            you can see forever when you reap what you sow
            there's a profound eroticism in such a freedom
                it brings divine suppleness and strength
                    i am when all is fierce
                rebirth of incense and gardenias

i gather the stories of the sacred circle
and they tell me to turn around and go home to the waking of my soul
once there i find that the land is still giving birth in the silences
images float by on a dragonfly
forcing me to embrace the power of language and it is deep
like the moving sea between shores remind me
that nothing is worth more than today.

—Malia, December 21, 1996

Chapter 9

A Father's Call: Father–Son Relationship Survival of Critical Life Transitions

Ivory Achebe Toldson*
Ivory Lee Toldson
Southern University and A&M College, Baton Rouge, LA

THE CALL

Far too many young African American males grow up to be men in homes without their fathers. I did not, but for most of my son Achebe's life, he did. Day-to-day separation from my children, especially my son, created regrettable and painful gaps in our relationship continuity.

Achebe's mother, a remarkable woman and mother, responsibly reared him in the tradition of African parenthood and values. With my diminished role as a nonresident dad, I cannot amply thank her for the dedication and devotion she displayed to ensure that my marginal presence would not marginalized my son's manhood.

Desperate to fulfill my responsibilities as a father to my son, and determined not to fit the absentee model that unfairly stains the image of Black fatherhood, I was nevertheless bound by the understanding that a nonresident dad cannot fully provide paternal sufficiency. It is an unfortunate consequence of marital dissolution that I will live with for the rest of my life.

Long after making the decision to breakup with my son's mother, I was tormented with the deep agonizing feeling of being incompletely connected to Achebe. He was so young, not much beyond toddler age.

It was different with my daughters. I believed my relationship with them had irrevocably formed and that comforted me. As heartbreaking a decision it was to make, I did not believe that the marital disruption could di-

---

*Ivory A. Toldson is now a professor at Howard University in Washington, D.C.

minish the bond between us. Albeit crushing, my girls knew the meaning of separation and divorce. Achebe did not.

When my son informed me that he and I had been invited to contribute to a compendium of writings on father–son relationships, I consented with intrigue but not with full enthusiasm. Even in the moment, before tendering an affirmative response, I knew the project would wake up ghosts from the past and reactivate painful and not fully healed wounds. As a psychologist, I also knew that this was procedural to healing, and I responded, "Yes, let's do it."

It is time to relive and celebrate the pleasure and pain intricate to our relationship. I believe this to be a therapeutic undertaking that will enable us to more fully appreciate and experience what is apparent to us, and to others who know us. Withstanding the cruel and painful vicissitudes of family separation and divorce, we have grown to love, respect, and admire each other, unconditionally. Framed in the African linguistic tradition of *Call and Response*, we have written this chapter by calling and responding to each other, to tell the story of our father–son relationship survival.

A RITE OF PASSAGE

For his 13th birthday, I wrote Achebe a letter, formatted in verses like a poem. Unformatted, it reads thusly:

> But for the need to fulfill the provision aspects of my role as a man, I would be with you this day, the occasion of your birth thirteen years later.
>
> How well I remember you, the little muscle bound infant man, who on your first day of life began asserting your will by nearly turning yourself over.
>
> You grew quickly and unlike your sisters, you exerted far more energy on the household. Running through the house, sliding down the stairs on your belly, tearing up your share of household articles; you were all boy, people would say. You loved to spring back and forth from a standing position on my knees, pushing and pulling against the strong grip of my hands.
>
> Your mother didn't understand all that energy. She didn't think you were as bright as your sisters early on. I assured her you were equally smart, if not smarter. I could tell then that you would be good at numbers, that you would express beauty in music, in poetry, drawing and in manners.
>
> And now, ceasing to be a child, I gleam with pride as you rebirth as a man. Our African forefathers left many proverbs or sayings to advise us in order that we might dignify our manhood.
>
> One falsehood spoils a thousand truths, be honest they would say. There is no medicine to cure hatred, our forefathers advised. A little subtleness is better than a lot of force. On the same note, they said, it is the slow, steady, misty rain that floods the river. Be easy in the expression of your will to conquer life's treasures, reminding us that a roaring lion kills no game.
>
> About suffering they said, no matter how long the night, the day is sure to come. Our forefathers knew the intoxicating power of love and how it

can make you do foolish things. They said, when one is in love, a cliff becomes a meadow, and don't be so much in love that you can't tell when the rain comes.

Be yourself. Don't wish to be like others who you cannot be like. Our forefathers said a frog wanted to be big like an elephant and burst.

Strive for unity with other blacks against others of power who oppress us. Our forefathers said, when spider webs unite, they can tie up a lion.

Be relaxed and flexible in your opinion and permit differences to prevail. Our forefathers said, some birds avoid water, but ducks seek it. They also noted, too much discussion means a quarrel.

Cross the river in a crowd and the crocodile won't eat you, is another way of telling us that there is strength in unity which overcomes danger and fear. Spare your heart, your tongue and your lips from the sharpness of ill-spoken words. If your mouth turns into a knife, they said, it will cut off your lips.

Withhold contempt for people and don't try to change people other than by example with your own life. Our forefathers said, if you try to cleanse others, like soap, you will waste away in the process.

When Kunta Kinte, from Alex Haley's famous *Roots*, completed his manhood training, his father, Omoro, gave him two female goats as his present. Soon, both were pregnant and kunta hoped for twins so he would have six goats. While it seemed that Omoro had only given his son two goats, Omoro knew that over Kunta's lifetime, the two goats would multiply into a whole herd.

I give you my son, I wrote to Achebe, one hundred dollars worth of mutual fund shares. If you receive 18% return on your money, that means your one hundred dollars will double every four years or double 13 times by the time you retire. At that time your $100 dollars could be worth $409,000. So if at first it seems that my gift to you is the equal of two goats, remember the compounding power of Omoro's gift to Kunta. I give you Achebe, as Omoro gave Kunta, a whole herd.

I love you and Happy Manhood Day. Daddy.

WHAT'S IN A NAME?

Our African forefathers believed that there was a material and physical affinity between a man and his name. They considered pronouncing a name as an act on the soul. The name gives birth to a new generation through which the life of the ancestors is transmitted. The name does not perish and permits one a certain immortality as long as the name is called among the living.

I was my father's first son. His first name was Henry, but my first name was Ivory. My brother next to me was given the name Henry. As it turned out, he was almost the clone of my father, and I was temperamentally more like my mother, even though all six of my father's sons carried his muscular stature. I envied my brother for having my father's first name when I was the first son. I had long declared that my first son would be named after me. With the development of an African consciousness, at points in my life I pondered abandoning my birth name for a more obviously African name.

Achebe was born in Philadelphia, Pennsylvania when I was a Professor of Counseling Psychology at Temple University. By that time, I had decided not to take on an African name, reconciling that the name Ivory commanded intrigue and images of power, strength, and beauty intrinsic to the African heritage. My coming into the knowledge of our ancestral Egyptians' love of ivory necklaces and bracelets put me at ease with my first name. Our ancestors used ivory as amulets to adorn themselves in life and placed them in graves to signal their belief in life after death.

Continually embodied with a blossoming African consciousness, when my son was born, I gladly forfeited my middle name "Lee," and gave him the name, Ivory "Achebe" Toldson. It was around the time that I had read the eye-opening and mind-opening book, *Things Fall Apart*, by the African writer, Chinua Achebe (1958).

His mother agreed that Achebe was the perfect middle name for our son and so we called him, not Ivory, but Achebe! Until he recently emerged as a professional, it was almost as if his first name was Achebe. With the satisfaction I had found in my first name, assigning my son the middle name of an African literary icon seemed to compliment the advanced stage of Black identity that defined my consciousness.

The naming consummated the rebirth I felt when Achebe was born. It was a powerful spiritual connection between us that would struggle to maintain itself through years of postmarital discord and other life transitions.

LIKE FATHER LIKE SON

We moved back to Baton Rouge, Louisiana in 1974 when I accepted a professorship in the Department of Psychology at Southern University. Achebe's mother and I met at and graduated from Southern. Achebe was still arm-carrying age and loved to ride my shoulders whether in my arms or straddle my neck above my head.

"He who touches a father touches a son" according to an Ethiopian Proverb. More than anything I wanted my son to be like me, no doubt my own unconscious desire to be idealized. The muscular form of his body at birth reassured me that he would mirror my athletic build in adolescence. However, as he grew, I witnessed his transformation to a slender grandeur consistent with his maternal line.

Despite his nonathletic body type, I was determined to impose my athletic fascination for baseball, basketball, football, and tennis on him. After a few years of practicing with him it became clear that among all the notable things he was, he was not athletic. In this way Achebe was not like me, but I was not disappointed. I recalled Kahlil Gibran's (1973) verses in his book *The Prophet*, who spoke thusly on children:

Your children are not your children.
They are the sons and daughters of Life's longing for itself . . .
You may strive to be like them, but seek not to make them like you . . .

It was not until I abandoned my self-idealistic wish for Achebe to silhouette me that I could begin to appreciate all the things he was that I was not. Yet, ironically, at the same time, I could see even more clearly how very much he was just like me.

Much to his advantage, Achebe did not have to throw off the shackles of an inferiority complex as I did. His boldness, courageousness, and intellectual confrontational style use to stun me. I was raised in a manner that required me to subdue my assertive spirit fearing the wrath of White people toward the "uppidy" of my hue.

Developing a state of African consciousness was a long and perplexing intellectual and spiritual process for me. Achebe was born into a family environment characterized by a high state of African consciousness and his paternal grandfather was a well-known civil rights activist in the State of Louisiana. Achebe, since discerning his personality, exuded a confidence that I admired—a level of confidence that will probably always be beyond my reach, possibly not even in my nature.

Like me however, he is passionate about the note, fascinated by words that evoke awe and surprise in speech and writings, drawn to artistic beauty, and is near helplessly attracted to beautiful women. I married two beautiful women. He married one. It took me a long time to learn I only needed but one.

I believed my adulterous sins were at one time unforgivable. I know it was confusing and annoying to Achebe to meet many of the female companions who entered my life for brief periods following my divorce from his mother. He had to unfairly compete with them for my attention. I recall our one and only father–son Boy Scout wilderness weekend camp out. It was the first time I experienced him being overtly angry at me. We had a "back to nature" good time, sleeping in a tent with no lights, telephone, or television. Catching a critter to compete in a critter race was a highlight, as well as the campfire serenade. Because I was missing the company of the female in my life at that time, I ended the weekend outing a half-day early.

On the drive back to the city Achebe was seething with anger. He persistently pressed, "Why are we leaving early?" Nothing I said satisfied him. Of course I did not tell him the real reason, and he did not dishonor me by telling me what I am certain he already knew. Boiling silence heated with Achebe's anger made the less than one hour drive back seem like days in hell.

I never forgave myself for cheating him of time with me that day and all the times after that. I have forgiven myself for being the womanizing scoundrel I was. Having total confidence in the grace and forgiveness of God who has removed all the shame and guilt of sin in my life, I take this means to sincerely ask my son's forgiveness: *Forgive me Achebe for not always choosing you over other interests in my life including the poor excuse I often gave of my busy work schedule.*

THE SUICIDE CRY

Postmarital volatility strained communication between Achebe's mother and me, however she willingly, unselfishly, and consistently apprised me on what was happening with my children. While it was especially gratifying to hear about their developmental and academic successes, I always felt a sense of loss; a sense of being on the outside looking in, witnessing my children developing from afar.

When Achebe was 5 years old, his mother told me that he unabashedly and innocently asked one of his aunts, "When are you and my uncle getting divorced?" His aunt, astonished by his question, assured him that she and his uncle did not intend to divorce. Achebe responded, "But my mama and dad divorced!"

It was apparent that to him that divorce was a normal progression of the marriage cycle. It was not whether or if, but *when* will you divorce. Jolted into a new found understanding he started to unravel the meaning of marriage. Increasingly I could see he was deeply troubled and hurt that his mother and I did not live happily together in the same home.

It seemed as if my heart dropped out of my body when one day I received a call informing me of a suicidal gesture Achebe had made. He secured a knife from the kitchen of his home and threatened to slit his stomach to terminate his agony and pain. Against his resistance, his oldest sister took the knife from him.

I rushed a couple of miles to his side and found him subdued and sobbing with his sisters by his side. I hugged him, probably for the first time in a long time. Not like a baby, I hugged him like a son who needed his father. I tried to convey my deep and abiding love for him and how unbearably painful my life would be without him. I wanted Achebe to know that I was there for him and that I would always be there, that I loved him and that I would always love him despite the fact I did not live with him anymore.

That he internalized the meaning of what the father–son duo Eddie and Gerald LeVert (1995) sang about in the song, "I Got Your Back," long before the song was conceived and recorded, was important to me:

I know you have those days when it seems like the whole world's against you, nobody's with you. You know the days when it seems that you wake up on the wrong side of the bed—wished you were dead. But I'm the one to pick you up when you're down, help you get your feet firmly on the ground. I got your back and I'll go to the wall for you.

I got your back and I'll take the fall for you. I got your back . . . I care for you and I'll be there for you.

ON THE ROAD AGAIN

Even to me, it seemed that I was always gone; somewhere. After the divorce I traveled even more. Professionally, it was timely. Therapeutically, it was necessary to my emotional stability. But it was not enough. I rather quickly made a mess of my life. Too many women, too many nights out, too many intoxicants, too many get-away weekends to anywhere, and not nearly enough time with Achebe and my daughters.

Seeking to put my life back together, in 1981 I went on-leave from my position at Southern University. I accepted a postdoctoral research fellowship at The Ohio State University in Columbus, Ohio.

I went to Columbus with no personal connections or established social network. In addition to the academic opportunity, I went to be alone to heal from the postdivorce affliction that had virtually brought my personal and professional life to a standstill. I needed to become a better father to my son and daughters. Achebe and I frequently exchanged letters and spoke on the telephone during the year. His letters and phone conversations warmed my heart and made the cold Ohio winter bearable.

I returned to Southern in 1982 on a high professional plateau. Doubleday recently released *Roots of Soul: The Psychology of Black Expressiveness*, a book I coauthored with Al Pasteur. Achebe, who was 9 years old, attended a book signing ceremony at Southern University in recognition of my work. I introduced him and my daughters to the crowd of enthusiasts. He beamed with pride and I felt redeemed, although promoting the book kept me on the road again and again.

That same year, I purchased my second home, the first I surrendered in a property settlement to Achebe's mother. Achebe was excited to visit me at what I had described for him as his second home. Upon the initial visit, he found present a female companion of mine and her preschool age daughter. He immediately became indrawn and soon disappeared. I found him crying outside the front entrance to the house. Although I knew what was wrong, I had to ask, "What's wrong?" He tearfully replied, "I want you and my mama to get back together."

We walked around the neighborhood and talked. I told him that I loved him and regarded him as a very important part of my life, even though his mother and I were no longer married. I had to prepare him for the possibility that he might be sharing a stepmother and stepsiblings with me, but they would never take me away from him.

I do not believe he was convinced. Whenever he called the house for me and I did not answer the call, he would demandingly ask the receiver, "May I speak to MY daddy." Early on, he never greeted the receiver, signaling that he wanted an exclusive relationship with me, and that he was not interested in sharing me with other occupants of my new household.

THE SECOND TIME AROUND

It is better, because I was a better man, a better father. I married my second wife, not just because she was a beautiful woman whom I loved beyond measure, but because I sensed her capacity to love my children as if they were her own. I knew that overtime Achebe would come to realize he was not losing his father, he was gaining a second mom—not a mom to replace or rival his mother, but a different mom, a stepmother who loved him enough to allow him to have me exclusively, as long as he needed.

When I remarried, the day was perfect, except that my children did not attend my wedding. I was hurt, but I understood that Achebe's mother and I once loved each other and that emotionally letting go does not necessarily coincide with a legal divorce decree. At first I was angry with Achebe's mother but I have now forgiven her for the hurtful things she did. I hope she has forgiven me or can forgive me for the far worse and more numerous hurtful sins I committed against our marriage.

I knew that for Achebe to respect and love me, he had to be sure that I respected his mother and regarded her with esteem. Much of his childhood, he had seen us verbally combative and engaged in cold wars with each other. I knew it was important for his mother and I to demonstrate to him and our daughters that we could be still be kind to each other, despite our divorce. I wanted them to see that we highly regarded each other, and could cooperatively share the affection and love our children had for each of us. That way, I surmised, they might one day share us with new found loves in our lives.

We called a truce and ended the postmarital discord. I knew Achebe's mother and I had done the mature and sensible thing when Achebe commented to a peer embroiled in parental divorce, "At least my parents don't hate each other!" It was important that we as his parents do this so he and his siblings might avoid repeating the sins of our past.

A student was killed at the high school Achebe was attending. This was a difficult time for him. He made the choice to accept an option I afforded him and used my address as his domicile to transfer to a high school in my neighborhood. I issued him a key to the house and assured him he was not a guest, but that he was at his second home.

Most nights he slept at his mother's, but he started to blend in the new family I imposed on him as a function of remarriage. He decided to return to the school from which he had transferred the next fall. While I feared for his safety, I delighted in his courage to face the fire of community and school life marked by economic depravity and the attendant crime, violence, and unhealthy indulgences often associated with being poor. He emerged undaunted and unscathed.

Achebe has successfully blended into two new families, mine and his mother's who remarried a scholarly academician with high levels of African consciousness and revolutionary scars to go along with it. Achebe is comfortable at home with all of us.

ANGELA'S DEATH

Our African fore parents noted that the death of a young person is like an uprooted plant that will never bear fruit. They regarded such a death as particularly sad. So it was with Angela's death. She was my oldest daughter, Achebe's oldest sister, the sister who intervened in that critical moment to preserve his life. Her death wreaked unimaginable devastation on all of us. There was a peculiar irony in the theme of the eulogy her pastor beautifully delivered at her home going ceremony: "A Noon Day Sunset," he called her death.

I have never known pain sharper than that I experienced when my Angela died in 1991. My mother, Achebe's paternal grandmother, died in 1990; my paternal grandmother (Achebe's great grandmother) died in 1992. My oldest brother, Achebe's uncle, died in 1993, and my brother second next to me died along with his wife and grandchild in a vehicular accident in 1994. Collectively their deaths didn't hollow me as Angela's death did.

A day or so following Angela's death, Achebe's stepfather called me. He urged me to consult with Achebe because Achebe had been observed in social interactions that suggested he was disconnected from the reality of Angela's death. Because I knew he was on the front-end of the grief cycle characterized by denial I had no fear that he was plunging into a state of cognitive decompensation. It was his way of dealing with the pain early on. When most of us had come to terms with Angela's death, as much as that is possible, Achebe showed us how to memorialize Angela with angelic beauty. In this moving tribute to Angela in her cosmically transformed state, Achebe wrote four years after her death:

> When I was a child, I would gaze into the heavens for hours. The clouds, sun, moon and stars were my companions. For some inexplicable and mysterious

reason, looking up into a cloudy canopy or a starry deck heaven would transform my state of loneliness, melancholy and detachment to that of serenity, peace, and tranquility. The Heavens were my divine family, a place of repose from turmoil and vexation. Looking at the expanse of the heavens was like deja vu. I had a vague memory of my existence in a remote dimension of space-time, before 1973 when I had eternal peace, before my spirit became circumscribed by flesh.

I often felt as though my mortal family was being absolved of harmony. The demons of my flesh began to ossify my soul. I longed to attain my premortal existence; to have the eternal peace that I was certain I once knew. I saw my fate on my epileptic sister's dresser. I began a journey that I thought would be my last when my efforts were thwarted by my sister, walking in on her baby brother crying, gagging, and trembling. Her tears at the sight of my morbid condition were my reviviscence. The support she gave me in consciousness was my effervescence. Now, almost twenty years later, it is my tears that submerge the soil that covers her, 1991 to date, hoping to generate the same consequence, to no avail.

Twenty years later, I still look into the Heavens now to find her brilliant dispersions. Twice each day I see her cross the horizon—once as she ascends into the Heavens and again as she descends out of view. In her mortal life, she adorned a cold, damp and dark world with resonance and life, mystically creeping above the horizon climbing ever so steadily to her zenith above the Earth. She immersed the world with her vital energy; enchanting, vibrating, and illuminating her subjects as they exalted at her Heavenly presence. Then she alighted, remitting her throne at the zenith to celestial darkness, slowly creeping beneath the horizon to join our divine family. I dream, creating in my mind's eye her return, waking to face the horizon, awaiting, deliberating, and anticipating her reconnaissance, the restoration of her effervescence, the prevalence of quanta. Inexorably, my fate lies in celestial motives.

What a daughter, what a son! His embrace of a cosmic consciousness is emotionally evoking, and spiritually converting. His words has helped me to smile when I remember Angela, and helped me to cover the hole in my heart that can never be filled. Achebe has already returned to me comfort that I have given to him.

PROUD MOMENTS

On the Sunday morning Achebe was baptized, I was traveling from Tallulah, Louisiana visiting my parents, and almost missed his holy submersion, but I was there.

I was there when he graduated from high school, an urban school with all the entrapment zones that cut short the lives of many young African American men. I was immensely proud to see his name, my name, on the graduation program, and knew he was well on his way to a successful manhood.

I was there for him to share with me his coming of age sexually as an adolescent. The fact that safety and mutual consent were important sexual values he practiced was especially gratifying. Although medical paternity has never been determined, I am possibly the father of another son who was born when I was of early teenage years. I did not want Achebe to make mistakes I made and was proud to see in him the emergence of responsible manhood.

I was there when he received his baccalaureate degree from Louisiana State University, and celebrated with him the attainment of his master's and Ph.D. degrees from Penn State University and Temple University, respectively. It was during his graduate study at Penn State that I helped him to drive from Baton Rouge to State College, two times. It was a special time of bonding and reflection. No topic was off the table. Sex and intimate relationships, politics, history, racial loyalty and heritage, academic erudition, we talked about everything.

Achebe's wedding was a gala to remember. It signaled for me a final letting go. The Bible prepares us for this. Matthew 19:5 states, "For this cause shall a man leave his father and mother, and cleave unto his wife, and they twain shall be one flesh." The fact that he was marrying a beautiful Jamaican born, New York City reared, Tulane University trained attorney was indeed reassuring. His wedding brought together our realigned family trees where we demonstrated the ability to share his joy with mutual respect, cordiality, and cooperativeness. It was several wonderful hours to behold and I was never more proud that he was my son.

We trained in the same intellectual discipline at the master's and doctoral levels, on target for both of us to be licensed psychologists; we both have professorial status at the same university, and receive an equal share of each other's telephone calls and emails; we both deliver psychological services in a psychology practice I own and one day plan to pass on to him.

We have already coauthored two published works (Toldson & Toldson, 1999; and Toldson & Toldson, 2001), this being the third. Some say he speaks like me, some say he writes like me, some say he meditates to music like me; some even say he looks like me. But I say he exceeds me in all these things. He has authored a haunting and poignant novel that illustrates the plight of young black men in the United States entitled, *Black Sheep*. Achebe has successfully written grants, and is on the edge of an avalanche of scholarly publications related to his grant activity.

Truly the "apple doesn't fall far from the tree." As the song goes, "I'm just like him and he's just like me . . . together we can conquer the world. I'm so proud of all you've done, cause you're my heart, you're my son. In my book you're number 1" (LeVert & LeVert, 1995).

SON'S RESPONSE

Perfection From Chaos

For all the wrong reasons, the story of Ivory Lee and Ivory Achebe Toldson seems perfect for a compendium on Black fatherhood. On the surface, many of our friends, colleagues, and even family members, see us as simply the case of an ambitious son following in his noble father's footsteps. We have the same name and profession. We often remind others of one another. Usually, when people find out who my father is, they feel like they have a better understanding of how I became me—'like father, like son.'

To a certain extent, the forgoing is true, but nothing heretofore stated alone makes our story compelling. In fact, the stanch similarities that exist between my father and I often conceals the true story and gives people the illusion that our father–son journey is, and always has been, perfect. To the contrary, my father and I have a relationship that has endured many uncertain, disorderly, and painful periods.

However, as quantum scientists suggest, *chaos* is the natural order of life, from which all things perfect spring forth. In Einstein's radical science, he warned us against imposing order to achieve perfection, and advised us to appreciate the beauty of chaos. In that view, my mission is not to impose order on my life and experiences with my father, but to redefine your perception of perfection. Through these stories I want to reveal that the odyssey of Ivory Lee and Ivory Achebe is perfect for this compendium, simply because we are not.

A CHILD OF THE BLACK REVOLUTION

But for God's grace, a lame shot, and the dogged will of my maternal grandfather, I might not exist as I do today. The White fascist, who shot my grandfather after he became the first Black man to vote in North Louisiana, tried to kill him, his legacy, and his lineage. But the racists failed, he triumphed, and went on to raise my mother, who grew up to be a champion for Black reparations. My mother passed the legacy on to me, so in a sense, Black power is my birthright. Other 'would be' decedents of countless slain heroes are not fortunate enough to exist, and today, the Black community bewails their absence.

My maternal and paternal grandfathers were both activist ministers in North Louisiana. As children, my mother and father picked cotton on faltering plantations, at a time when southern Whites were still riding the waves of *The Birth of a Nation* and exploiting the "but equal" clause in *Plessy v. Ferguson*. In the 1950s, my parents lived in terror. My mother's home was torched because my grandfather led a Black voting rights campaign. My father's brother was kidnapped and arrested by police when he cursed a White teen who cursed him first. Since North Louisiana police officers were notorious for lynching, my paternal grandfather and his brother-in-law armed themselves to defend my uncle's life. They were prepared to kill or die before idly allowing murderous police to lynch my uncle.

In the 1960s, my parents met at Southern University at the height of the civil rights movement, and married at the brink of the Black power era. It was a time when Black Americans were trying to find meaning in a nation reeling from Hoover's COINTELPRO, hero assassinations, and the Vietnam War. As conscious and curious African Americans, my parents sympathized with the Nation of Islam while holding steadfast to Christian roots; flirted with name change while honoring their family legacies; and entertained the White-devil notion, while accommodating hippies. Eventually, they had two daughters in 1968 and 1969, and their only mutual son in 1973. My mother and father gave us all ethnic middle names that started with A—Adjoa, Azenna, and Achebe.

As a toddler, my father cut a line in the center of my afro, draped me in a little dashiki, and called me by my Nigerian tag, Achebe. My first book was Mari Evans' (1975), *I Look at Me*. To this day, I have my original copy from when I was only 4 years old. On the last page, I colored the flag with red, black, and green crayons, and wrote 'Achebe' on the page that stated, "It's nation time!" The same year, my mother documented me telling a preschool-mate that I was from Africa. When the kid challenged me, I told him, "My great, great, great, great, great-grandfather was from Africa, and my great, great, great, great, great-grandmother lived with him." Apparently, my mother and father's teachings countered the social vestiges of White supremacy. I keenly remember being proud to be Black.

By the time I started first grade, society and my family changed. Divorce was at an all-time high for Black Americans and my parents fit well within the statistic. Also, at the brink of the Reagan 80s, African tags became passé and the notion of Black Power got lost somewhere between a Jheri-curl and a cardigan sweater. The U.S. political prisoners and the exiles in Cuba got the message, "The revolution is dead," Black scholars took a little slice of Reaganomics, and the poor Black community took crumbs, guns, and crack.

In elementary school, I began to wonder if my family's Afrocentric leanings were misinformed and eccentric. I wanted to fit in with my peers and adapt to the changing society. My middle name embarrassed me, and the idea of wearing a dashiki to school was laughable. I no longer had the audacity to challenge my peers on our African origin. Instead, I blindly accepted school lessons that taught me to revere racist savages like Columbus and White supremacists like Woodrow Wilson. Also, subconsciously we

learned to admire Black people with light skin and 'good hair.' Although I
was too young to articulate my doubts, I often questioned the relevance of
having a 'Black identity.' Ironically, at the time, my father was poised to be
an authority on Black identity when he wrote, *Roots of Soul: The Psychology of
Black Expressiveness.*

I was in the fourth grade when my father released *Roots of Soul.* I was
proud to see my name in the acknowledgments. He gave me an autographed copy that read, "Son, someday I want you to take the ideas and
principles in this book to a new level of scholarship." At only 9 years old, I
could not fully grasp the 'ideas and principles,' in the book or conceive of a
"new level of scholarship." However, with chapter titles like, *Rock Steady
Baby,* and the assortment of "Ya Mamma" jokes, the book was a hit at my elementary school. I was proud to have a *famous father,* although I did not know
exactly what he stood for. I loved and adored him as any son would his father, counting and cherishing every minute we spent together. As a child, I
wanted to be like my father, although he was a bit of a mystery. Secretly, I
feared that one day I would lose him to his ambition.

By the time I entered high school, crack was epidemic in the hood and
Black-on-Black crime was soaring. I went to a predominately Black high
school with mostly White teachers and an aging principal who was losing
control of the school. Many students openly smoked weed and sold drugs
on school grounds. After a drug dealer was stabbed to death in front of me,
my mother suggested that I use my father's address to change schools.

My father lived only 15 minutes away from my mother, yet I felt they lived
worlds apart. My mother raised me in a working-class community, with a
moderate level of street crime that rose steadily each year. My father lived in
the suburbs among what I considered rich folks. I was comfortable in my father's home, but I did not feel like a core family member. My father, stepmother, half-sister and half-brother seemed to enjoy a level of extravagance, to which I was not accustomed. They openly accepted me into their
world of fine dining, name-brand clothing and family vacations; aspects of
life that my mother considered superfluous. Although I enjoyed visiting
their world, I usually felt like a misfit.

At the beginning of the 11th grade, I returned to the school that I tem-
porarily abandoned. Trying to make sense of the violence and complacency
in my community, I revisited my Black power roots. The task was easy, because the modest library in my mother's home included *The Autobiography of
Malcolm X, A Message to the Black Man, The Isis Papers,* and scores of other
books to awaken the sleeping Black warrior within me. In addition, my
mother married Dr. Imari Obadele, the president of a provisional government for "New Africans," called the *Republic of New Africa.* Brother Imari was
a former political prisoner, who received a Ph.D. from Temple University.

He introduced me to grassroots movements and Black Nationalism. His stories of directly confronting the government invigorated me. As a teen with a diminished fear factor and exposure to community violence, I did not want to boycott buses like King; I wanted to take an axe to the oppressor like Nat Turner.

The same year, I became a staff writer, and eventually the editor, of my high-school newspaper. I wrote articles on Black empowerment that drew controversy and acclaim. My editorial entitled *Heed the Word* hailed Garveyism, and my article entitled *Let's Get This Party Started* advised the 'thugs' to stop killing each other and direct their aggression toward the "real enemy."

At the time, the first Bush was president, conscious rappers started wearing African medallions, and I began listening to *Public Enemy* and *X-clan*. I protested our school-sponsored rally for the first gulf-war by wearing a pocket-size American flag upside down on the crotch area of my jeans. Later, my White American history teacher told my class that slavery would be wrong now, but was *acceptable* for that time. I argued, she scathingly condemned me, and I literally kicked her butt as she passed my desk. She then sent me to the White assistant principal who gave me a slap on the wrist, told me I was a critical thinker, and advised me to save the debating for college.

Next year, as a senior, my White English teacher rejected my research topic on FBI covert activities against Black organizations. I warned her that I had Black political connections and would fight her decision. She reluctantly approved my topic and gave me an A for my research with no comment. At my high-school graduation she ardently gripped my shoulders and told me, "You could be something great, if you'd just get rid of your anger." I wondered if she ever shared those words with any of my Black male classmates who brought weapons to school and fought one another. Why was my anger more menacing than theirs?

To me, my anger was constructive and my mother and stepfather understood. But I never mentioned my anger toward my father—not even to myself. Near the end of my senior year, I only used my last name when I absolutely had to. A part of me wanted to abandon the proverbial 'slave-name,' but another part of me wanted to abandon my father. I began to deny my father's contributions to my development and criticize him for being a "buppie." I accused him of having a vague, "jellyfish" approach to Black empowerment, and believed him to be disengaged from the Black community. Notably, I had not yet read *Roots of Soul*, and discounted his very humble beginnings.

In college, I continued fighting at Louisiana State University. By my sophomore year, I became the Black Culture Committee chair and sparked controversy when I invited a Nation of Islam minister to a meeting. One

White student blasted me in an editorial and I blasted back with a 'mightier' pen. Later, I received threatening phone calls that were more humorous than scary. My mother became the national co-chair of N'COBRA (National Coalition of Blacks for Reparations in America). When I visited home with a college frat brother, my mother played an anonymous voicemail message that said, "So you niggers want reparations? How 'bout I give you some chicken and a piece of cornbread." My frazzled frat brother clamored, "It feels like we've time warped to the 70s."

My fraternity brother was implying that the revolution died in the 1970s, however the revolution pressed on in my home. Still, I believed that the revolution had died in my father's heart, and never really existed in his home. I harbored stereotypes of him from high school, even after he became a more active part of my life in college.

At the time, I was getting to know my father better, but I did not necessarily want to be like him; or whatever I thought he was. But unlike high school, I was not a tough kid roughing a fierce milieu without my father's guidance. Like it or not, in college, I was riding my father's coattail, driving his sports car, working in his office and wearing his name. The prevailing image across campus of me being a "daddy's boy" was unsettling—especially when I posed as a neorevolutionary. I did not like people believing that I grew up with a silver spoon in my mouth, yet I often entertained 'campus cuties,' bidding for a ride in my *daddy's car*.

In a sense, I had a split conscious and two dads influencing two different sides of my personality. My revolutionary stepfather guided the part of me that sparked controversy, while my 'bourgeois' biological father guided the part of me that cruised campus in a "fly whip, picking up chicks." In that view, I was trivializing the personas of two very remarkable men who were more similar than different. In time, I realized that I did not know either one of my fathers as well as I thought.

I was a junior in college when I matured into the advanced stages of Black identity. I read *Roots of Soul*, and for the first time I understood it beyond the humorous hooks. It helped me to see the struggle beyond race wars, and delve into my African conscious. Also, I began to see past the fruit of my father's labor and understand his mission. At the time he was providing psychological services to the poor and underserved. Eventually, he became a father who spurred my African intellect. Undoubtedly, his greatest gift to me was not the sports car.

To date, my father and I have published two articles built on the African-centered psychology premise (Toldson & Toldson, 1999; Toldson & Toldson, 2001). We continue to develop African-centered paradigms for poor and underserved clients. My father's legacy in our community is unparalleled and I am proud to bear his name. I am also proud of my history, which qualifies me to be a child of the Black revolution.

NO FEARS, NO TEARS

I was an emotional toddler who expressed my love for my parents with hugs and kisses. My feelings were intense and fragile. I cried often and I had many phobias. I feared ghosts, the dark, and most of all, I feared being alone. Every night I slept in a sleeping bag on the floor in my sisters' room. I was too afraid to sleep alone. When forced into solitude, I created imaginary friends, but when the images became too vivid, I began to fear them too. When I was only four, my fear of abandonment and my worries about my parents fighting, drove me to the brink of insanity. In a reluctant suicide attempt, I swallowed one of my sister's pills and threatened to slash my stomach with a kitchen knife.

As a child, I had many female qualities, although I did not have homosexual feelings. In fact, my intense emotions spurred my attraction to girls at a very young age. I had my first 'girlfriend' at only 4 years old. Every time I kissed her, other rough and tumble boys at the daycare called me *gross*, but I loved her and did not mind expressing it.

As I grew into childhood, my father pushed me to be more assertive, and at times, more aggressive. When I was 8 years old, my elementary school suspended me for fighting. My father cheered, I reciprocated, and we bonded. For his approval, I often tried to be more aggressive. Soon, I realized I had a high threshold for pain. Between the ages of 8 and 11, I made frequent trips to my family physician for doing such things as jumping ramps with my dirt bike, jumping off roofs, and climbing barbwire fences. To this day, I have two small bald spots in the back of my head from childhood head injuries.

As a nonresident dad, my father did not recognize my quiet penchant for danger. And although I do not consider my childhood high-risk behaviors to be "cries for attention," at the time, I craved my father's approval. Perhaps, on a subconscious level, many boys become aggressive to gain approval from men who teach them, "Crying is for girls." I learned my lessons well, and by the time I reached middle school, I learned to endure both physical and emotional pain without tears.

In high school, I had many reasons to cry, but I never shed a tear. When I was in the ninth grade, my grandmother died in my home after battling with Alzheimer's disease. That morning, my mother advised me to go to school in spite of the tragedy. On my way to the bus stop, I fought tears, but by the time I reached school, I *looked* normal.

Two years later, Angela, my sister who had epilepsy, became physically disabled and mentally challenged from repeated seizures, medication side-effects, and ineffective surgeries. My mother spent her days at my sister's bedside, and her nights praying for my sister's recovery. I spent my days being autonomous, and my nights being strong. At the time, I believed that autonomy and strength was what my mother needed from me, so that she could focus on my sister's health. But in my simplistic view, autonomy meant *no fear*, and strength meant *no tears*.

Between the ages of 16 and 18, I became stronger, yet more estranged from my father and my emotions. Nothing significant happened to create a rift between us—except for the fact that *nothing significant* was happening between us. He had a new wife and two new children. I had the new identity of a young man with emotional aloofness and fearlessness. In fact, the new me regarded my emotional distance from my father as a badge of honor. Not unlike many rap artist who boastfully speak scorn upon their fathers. Tupac (1994), for example, claimed:

> Had to play catch by myself, what a sorry sight, a pitiful plight,
> So I pray for a starry night
> Please send me a pops before puberty
> The things I wouldn't do to see a piece of family unity
> Moms always work, I barely see her
> I'm startin' to get worried without a pops I'll grow to be her
> A different father every weekend
> Before we get to meet him they break up before the week ends
> How can I be a man if there's no role model?
> Strivin' to save my soul, I stay cold drinkin' a forty bottle.

Like Tupac, I *stayed cold*. As a child, I counted the minutes my father and I spent together, but as a teenager I counted the weeks we spent apart. In the same way, as a child I strove to be like my father, but as a teenager, I admired our differences. I saw my father as a suburban socialite with a family who adulated extravagance. I, on the other hand, was a young man who understood the hardships of growing up with death and disease in a working-class community. In addition, I attended a violence-ridden school with open drug use and drug dealing. I took pride in everything that was working against me. Once again, my pain became my pride.

I also prided myself on self-sufficiency. When I was 16 years old, I bought a used car with my own cash. At 17 years old, I had two jobs and too many ambitions. I was a penny-pincher who vigilantly saved money. In fact, just before I graduated from high school, I completely cut off contact with my best friend over a simple money issue. My soul never settled long enough the think about my callousness. I had become good at letting go.

I graduated with honors and started college. During my first semester at Louisiana State University, two important things happened: My father started acting more like a father and my sister's fight with epilepsy ended tragically with her death. I did not know how to emotionally deal with either one of these events.

My mother called me at about 4 a.m. to tell me of Angela's death. I spent the morning thinking about the last conversation I had with Angela. When the sun rose, I dressed and went to class—as I had done the morning of my grandmother's death. I told my friends that my sister died and the response was almost invariably, "How could you go to class the day your sister died?" I could not answer. Honestly, I was asking myself the same question. At the time, I loved my sister and I hated myself for not breaking down. But I did not know how to express myself. I had spent my whole life reprogramming myself to be what I thought was a man. I could have blamed my father for teaching me to endure pain, or my mother for teaching me to be autonomous and strong. But the fact is, I will never have that moment back. That morning when I should have dropped everything to find my mother, cradle her, and share my fears and tears. Throughout the period, from my sister's death, to her burial, I only cried once—alone.

My sister's death was the first of a series of deaths that sharply impacted my father. It was my first year of college and all of a sudden, I became my father's son. The connection began so superficially, I am a little embarrassed to share. My father bought me a sports car for graduation. No, it was not the *plastic*, poignant moment, where I started to feel like my father loved me just because he spent money on me. It was more about the process of us going to dealerships together and him teaching me how to drive with standard transmission. My father was teaching me how to 'wheel and deal.'

On campus, I had the nicest car among Black freshmen, and everyone became curious about my background. The story became, "His dad is a psychologist with a successful private practice and he works with his dad to pay his car notes." There was so much more to our story, but for the first time in my life others perceived a strong bond between my father and me. It took me a few years to perceive the same connection. I did not take my job at my father's practice seriously. His employees quickly recognized me as the kid who collected a check for doing nothing. Eventually, my father found out that I, not only had a second job at the university, but my *other boss* adored me. But I spent so many years honoring my ability to function without my father, *needing* him to maintain car notes embarrassed me.

In college, I was a good student and great student worker, but an unmotivated son. On the job I was shiftless, and as a driver, I was irresponsible. I collected so many tickets that my father's insurance dropped us. Eventually, I wrecked the car. In addition, my father's employees were constantly complaining about my work performance. Ironically, I worked at a fast food joint and at my mother's daycare center throughout high school and never skirted a shift. Furthermore, I never received a ticket or had an accident in the raggedy car that I bought with my own cash in high school. I was indeed an unmotivated son.

But my father never gave up on me. He remained patient, yet became sterner. He demonstrated that he loved me unconditionally. He talked to me about his concerns with my behavior, and openly listened to my anxieties about college and grad school. He proofed my papers, attended my college functions, and gave me advice about social issues. My college friends and I became regulars at his annual Christmas Party and Labor Day Barbecues. He was my dad in every sense of the word.

With his help, I got accepted into grad school at Penn State. During the summer before grad school, he and I worked together to design a day treatment program for at-risk youth. This was the first time I demonstrated real leadership at his private practice. I was proud to be the boss's son, and I loved my father enough to give my heart to his company.

After I started grad school in counseling, I continued to build my relationship with my father—a building process that continues to this day. At the same time, in grad school, I started to introspect and understand my emotions. It took me 4 years to grieve my sister and grandmother's death in a way that satisfies my spirit. I wrote tributes to both of these wonderful women during my first year of grad school with a poetic touch that I inherited from my father.

Today, I am a man who is not afraid to cry, yet I do not cry as often as I should. I am a man who is not afraid to say I love you, yet I do not say it as often as I could. I am not afraid to be afraid, yet sometimes I am still too afraid to say. Luckily, I am a man who is still learning how to be a real man, and I thank God my father is leading the way.

PROUD MOMENTS

Notwithstanding many gaps in our relationships, my father attended most of my milestone events. My first time seeing my father and stepfather together at a festive occasion was at my college graduation celebration at the LSU African American Cultural Center. I sat in awe as I watched them casually chat. Only 5 years earlier, I felt void of a *real* father, but as a college graduate I had two.

Throughout college, my relationship with my father has grown in ways I never imagined. Earlier, my father mentioned that he began to see himself in me when he stopped trying to make me his clone. Likewise, I began to see myself in my father when I stopped trying to be like him. Ironically, many others saw my father in me before I noticed him in myself.

I joined the Black Culture Committee my first year at LSU. At my first meeting, I volunteered to pick up Na'im Akbar from his hotel for a speaking event. When I introduced myself to Dr. Akbar, he immediately associated my name with my father. He spoke of my father with great esteem, and told me that my father was lucky to have a son like me. Just becoming reacquainted with my father at the time, Dr. Akbar's words intrigued me. Without saying much, he told me something new about my father and sparked my desire to know my father on another level.

When I was a college senior, I completed a summer internship at Penn State. Dr. Harold Cheatham was the Counseling Psychology Department chair. Unknown and unsolicited, I made an appointment to meet him. I waited in his lobby on the day of my appointment, and when Dr. Cheatham entered, he looked past me. After I caught his attention he asked, "May I help you?" I told him, "I'm Ivory Toldson." He scratched his wits and asked, "Are you a *junior?*" I replied, "No sir, I'm a *senior.*" He focused his eyes and scrutinized, "You can't be a senior." After sorting through the confusion, we had a productive meeting, followed by great years in Penn State's counseling masters program.

My father started working on his book, *Stolen Innocence* (Toldson, 1997), when I was in grad school at Penn State. At the time, I worked at the Middleton Library reference desk at University Park. My father called me often to help him conduct research on child abuse. When he released his book, once again I was proud to see my name in the acknowledgments. And again, I got an autographed copy this time only stating, "Thanks son!" Oddly, the two words, "Thanks son!" said so much more to me than the crafty sentiments he wrote to me on his book, *Roots of Soul.* The message on *Roots of Soul* was a complicated message to a 9 year old, while the message on *Stolen Innocence* was a simple message to a 22 year old. It was 13 years later and my father learned that actions speak louder than words, and I learned that a man never outgrows the simple pleasure of receiving simple words from his father's heart.

I married a very beautiful woman in July 2002. My father traveled from Louisiana to New York City in an SUV to attend the ceremony with his wife and children from his second marriage. Interestingly, my 27-year-old first cousin on my mother's side, along with her daughter, hitched a ride with my father and his family. My cousin's daughter fell in love with my father, calling him grandpa and running to his arms throughout the wedding weekend. My father hosted the rehearsal dinner and my half-brother was one of my groomsmen. My father took more than 100 pictures with his digital camera, of which he only appeared in three.

My father continues to selflessly dedicate himself to me personally and professionally. He has become everything I could ask for in a father, and more. I enjoy submerging within his shadow, as I come into my own light. I share the same esteem for him as do thousands who admire him from afar, and a love for him that *only* a son could have for his father.

AUTHORS' NOTE

The authors made references to Ivory Achebe Toldson's maternal grandfather, Rev. John Henry Scott, and stepfather, Dr. Imari Obadele.

For more information about Rev. Scott, see: Scott, J. H., & Brown, C. (2003). *Witness to the truth: My struggle for human rights in Louisiana.* Columbia, SC: The University of South Carolina Press.

For more information about Dr. Obadele, see: Obadele, I. (1984). *Free the land.* Baton Rouge, LA: The Malcolm X Generation, c/o House of Songhay Commission for Positive Education.

REFERENCES

Achebe, C. (1958). *Things fall apart.* London: Longman.

Evans, M. (1975). *I look at me!* Chicago: Third World Press.

Gibran, K. (1973). *The prophet.* New York: Alfred A. Knopf.

Haley, A. (1976). *Roots.* New York: Dell.

LeVert, G., & LeVert, E. (1995). I got your back. Father and son [CD]. Los Angeles: Elektra/asylum.

LeVert, G., & LeVert, E. (1995). The apple don't fall. Father and son [CD]. Los Angeles: Elektra/asylum.

Muhammad, E. (1965). *Message to the Black man.* Chicago: Muhammad Mosque of Islam No. 2.

Pasteur, A., & Toldson, I. L. (1982). *Roots of soul.* Garden City, NY: Anchor Doubleday.

Shakur, T. (1994). Papa'z song. [LP Version]. Santa Monica, CA: Interscope.

Toldson, I. L. (1997). *Stolen innocence: Preventing, healing and recovering from child molestation (stories about children who live the blues).* Baton Rouge, LA: CPHC Press & Products.

Toldson, I. A. (in press). *Black sheep.* Baton Rouge, LA: The Malcolm X Generation, c/o House of Songhay Commission for Positive Education.

Toldson, I. A., & Toldson, I. L. (1999). Esoteric group therapy. Counseling African American adolescent males with conduct disorder. *Journal of African American Men, 4*(3), 73–88.

Toldson, I. L., & Toldson, I. A. (2001). Biomedical ethics: An African-centered psychological perspective. *Journal of Black Psychology, 27,* 401–423.

Welsing, F. (1991). *The Isis papers: The keys to the colors.* Chicago, IL: Third World Press.

X, Malcolm, & Haley, A. (1992/1965). *The autobiography of Malcolm X.* (AMX). (One World First Trade ed.). New York: Ballantine Books.

Zona, G. A. (1993). *The house of the heart is never full and other proverbs of Africa.* New York: Simon & Schuster.

Chapter 10

The Fatherless Father:
On Becoming Dad

Leon D. Caldwell
University of Nebraska, Lincoln

Le'Roy Reese*
Center for Disease Control and Prevention
National Center for Injury Prevention and Control

African American fatherhood is rarely discussed from the perspective of men anticipating fatherhood or the positive involvement of African American fathers in the parenting process. There are limited venues that allow for African American boys and men to discuss how their experiences of being fathered or not being fathered influenced their view of fatherhood and their desire to be fathers themselves. Although there is great diversity in fathering experiences, it is the absence of African American father that is most often discussed in the literature. Zinn and Eitzen (2005), for example, reported that 49% of African American children lived in a mother-headed household. Over the last several decades this trend has continued with increasing numbers of African American children residing only with their mother. Due to the social and economic realities of single-parent households, children from these households are reported to be at greater risk for academic, behavioral, and health problems (McLanahan & Booth, 1991; Spencer, 1990).

The analysis of the single-mother family structure has dominated the economic, educational, and prevention literature and discourse regarding African American families. Recently, some scant attention has been given

*The contributions of Le'Roy Reese were completed independent of his responsibilities and position with the Centers for Disease Control and Prevention (CDC) and thus do not represent the opinion or policy position of the CDC, the Department of Health and Human Services, of the federal government.

to the condition and challenges facing African American teenage fathers (e.g., Kiselica, 1999). Noticeably absent from the research literature are investigations of the resilience of African American families and the significant numbers of vocationally, academically, and personally successful individuals from single-parent households who succeed despite facing multiple challenges. Moreover, there is a paucity of theoretical explanations and empirical tests of those theories examining the impact of these family structures on the adult children of single-parent homes. Although this chapter does not specifically address this issue we offer insights into some of the potential consequences of single-parent mother-headed households, the son who becomes a father, whom we refer to as the fatherless father for the purposes of this volume. If the cycle and intergenerational transmission of father absence is to be broken, we argue that it is critical to create opportunities for dialogue about this issue by boys, young men, and men impacted directly as it relates to their future view of themselves as fathers.

This chapter is offered from the perspective of two African American men both reared absent their biological father and now themselves fathers. It would be misleading to suggest that "fathers" were not present and active in our development as boys and men. Even more misleading and irresponsible would be to suggest that an African American child from a single mother-headed household is synonymous with high risk and poor developmental outcomes. In fact, our experiences with surrogate fathers from our families and communities revealed to us the range and complexity of fatherhood in its various forms as well as African American masculinity and helped shaped our own views of African American fatherhood and masculinity. Acknowledging the presence and role of these surrogate fathers will deepen our understanding of how boys from single-parent mother-headed household make or avoid the commitments to be fathers themselves.

We acknowledge the various, positive and negative experiences of growing up in a single-parent home may allow some to carry "their story" as a badge of honor while for others, it represents a source of embarrassment. For example, it is not uncommon to be in the company of 30-something African American men where a majority was raised primarily by their mothers or other female caregivers. Notably, this observation is more common among African American men of the last two or three generations. In an attempt to explain the state of African American males during the 1980s and 1990s, this chapter focuses on the absence of fathers and not failing school systems as a primary reason for gang involvement, not issues of un- and underemployment as a reason for risky behavior, and not the proliferation of stereotypic negative media images that placed low social value on the life of Black male youth (Kunjufu, 2001; Madhubuti, 1991). Although this commentary on the analysis of the Black family isn't backed by empirical support, we see the restatement of the "Monihayn-esqu" indictment of African

American families in general, fathers and mothers in particular, which is often considered a major treatise on the condition of the African American family.

The successes or lack thereof for Black children from single-parent households ranges from the achievements of Ben Carson to the tragedies committed by John Malvo. Fatherlessness does not and should not equate to a jail sentence, poverty, or drug addiction no more than growing up in a "nuclear" family entitles you to a college degree, sobriety, or a middle-class lifestyle. Many, actually most fatherless children become productive members of their community, who later themselves become parents. To be clear, we are not suggesting that responsible fathers and caring and committed men are not necessary, if not critical, to the success of children. Instead, our goal is to counter the rhetoric prefabricating the life course of fatherless males by sharing the process of two fatherless men on their journey to becoming Dads.

EXPERIENCES OF THE FATHERLESS

All too often, the narrative stories of African American men begin with a discussion of being fatherless that often serves as the foundation for future brushes with the law, the mistreatment of women, and the subsequent creation of another generation of fatherless children (Franklin, 2004). The processes and challenges confronted by many African American men raised without the presence of their biological father who now find themselves blessed with the gift of a child are rarely captured in the context of a healthy adulthood. In particular, the developmental and psychological literature gives short shrift to the developmental experiences of fatherless children beyond characterizing such children as being at heightened risk for poor developmental outcomes due to the greater challenges these youth may experience when compared to those who benefit from the love, support, and guidance of two committed parents.

Many of us, African American adult males who grew up fatherless, find ourselves excited and terrified about the possibilities of parenting without the benefit of observing our own fathers and learning from their successes and failures as fathers, husbands, and men. As a result, we ask questions like, "Will we fail like our fathers failed us? Can we be the fathers we want to be in the absence of a real model? Am I supposed to shout or cry? And how do I ask for help when I don't know what I am doing?"

Our goals for this chapter include trying to help and support the many Brothers who, like us, grew up fatherless and have at different points in their life became fathers and had to work through adjusting our expectations, our plans, ideas, and ultimately our life in order to embrace the awesome and at times overwhelming responsibility of Black fatherhood. We feel this is an important chapter because it gives voice to the generation of

Brothers who both physically and emotionally lost their fathers to social castration (institutionalized racism), personal choices, or both. Here, we attempt to separate blame from responsibility by acknowledging that not all and, in fact, most Black men of the 1980s and 1990s fell victim or played victim to the social and economic constraints and abandoned their children in the face of personal, familial, community, and societal challenges. We acknowledge the role of the Vietnam War and Desert Storm, the most recent wave of corporate and "other" sponsored drug infiltration of Black urban America, and the effects of economic hardship nurtured by racism as contributing to the absence of many fathers. In this acknowledgment, we recognize that some men did not have the personal resolve and know-how of their enslaved and Jim Crowed great-great-grandparents, great-grandparents, grandparents, and parents to stand by their wives, girlfriends, or children through life's hardships. We acknowledge that not every "deadbeat" dad had the support, encouragement, or resources to change their station in life as fathers, partners, and men. We also acknowledge those African American males who defined manhood as "spreading seeds" without taking responsibility for the offspring created by that spreading. As a result, there are at least three generations of Black men, many themselves fathers, who grew up without the presence of biological fathers, who are seeking to understand and hungry for responsive and loving Black fatherhood.

This is the voice of many of us who went through disillusionment, disappointment, anger, contempt, acceptance, reconciliation, healing, and liberation with our absent fathers. The days of waiting on the steps, by the window, or after school hoping he would appear has deeply affected the way many of us define relationships, keep promises, think about families, and perhaps, most importantly, define ourselves. Due to the support of our communities in the form of churches, mosques, schools, athletics, surrogate fathers, therapy options, reconciling with our own biological fathers, or creating a network of teachers, healers, and mentors, many of us have been able to shake and heal from the traumas and disappointments of our childhood and commit to being better men and fathers. We hope this chapter gives voice, support, love, and encourages the collective healing to the still wounded and healing Brothers who, like us, seek personal reconciliation as we dedicate ourselves to becoming manifestations of the excellence of responsible Black fatherhood.

SEEKING AFRICAN AMERICAN FATHERHOOD WISDOM

Madhubuti (1991) stated in his book *Black Men, Obsolete, Single, Dangerous? The Afrikan American Family in Transition,* "These days most Black boys learn to be fathers by watching the wind (i.e., spaces reserved for missing fathers). Many of them also receive instruction in fathering from their mothers' discussions about absent 'dads' or whatever names these men are given" (p. 191). An important method that many humans learn to parent is by observation. Yet for the fatherless father, robbed of lessons from previous generations (for good or for bad), learning how to be a father is more often a vicarious process at best. As a result, many fatherless African American men lack the collective experience and wisdom of the previous generations of fathers (Franklin, 2004).

Seeking the knowledge base and developing critical parenting skills such as prioritizing the importance of quality time spent with children, nurturing the brilliance of children in what can and at times will be a hostile world, disciplining children with a focus of correction and teaching, communicating and modeling self-love, self-respect, and responsibility are among the many important attributes required of responsible Black fatherhood. Other important skills includes time management, negotiating competing parenting interests, balancing your romantic relationship, and satisfying obligations to extended family (e.g., grandparents) and the larger community regarding the raising of your child(ren). Although the acquisition of these skills and knowledge may rarely be explicitly discussed by fathers who are present, they are more often learned through observation and experience. Hutchinson's (1995) *Black Fatherhood: The Guide to Male Parenting*, for example, is one resource that provides practical information from a number of Black fathers who share their experiences and gleaned wisdom from their own fathering experiences. All parents and, in this case, fathers, should be encouraged and supported to admit areas in which they lack appropriate knowledge and skills and to ask questions about parenting from trusted friends, surrogate fathers, parents they respect, elders, and helping professionals. Perhaps our lack of knowledge is because we were "watching the wind" as Madhubuti suggests, but now that the "tornado" has passed we can learn how to be effective parents by seeking knowledge and advice from those "others" in our life that we see as models of responsible African American fatherhood. On this journey to responsible fatherhood, it is important that we are fair with ourselves, being sure to give ourselves some latitude for error as parenting is not an exact science and requires humility, being open to constant changes, and being willing to re-learn what we thought we knew.

IMAGES OF BLACK FATHERHOOD: CREATING AN IDEAL WITH VISION

In the absence of a father figure many men create images of the father ideal from tangible and vicarious father images. Tangible images are the men who make themselves available in the community as surrogate fathers.

These could be extended family members, fathers of peers, formal and informal mentors, teachers, coaches, and even gang members. Vicarious father images are those who are visible but who may be inaccessible to talk with or seek support from. For example, there have been a number of Black television fathers, viewed by millions, like Heathcliff Huxtable (*The Cosby Show*), James Evans (*Good Times*), Michael Kyle (*My Wife and Kids*), Bernie Mac (*The Bernie Mac Show*), Robert Townsend, and so forth, who have informed societal images of what should constitute Black fatherhood. The images of these men, their styles of fathering, their handling of parenting challenges, and how they manage the multiple relationships in their lives leave indelible images for not only Black men but more generally for the Black community. As an example, few in Black or White America would argue about the impact that Bill Cosby has had on the lexicon of family life in this country generally, let alone in the African American community.

However, a limitation of many of these media images is the rather myopic view they provide of Black fathers: Most are professional men (either persons with advanced degrees or business owners), with income levels that are middle class and usually higher, and who are married and homeowners. Thus, although positive images of Black fatherhood are needed, we also need other, more realistic, images that reflect the diversity and complexity of lifestyles Black men in family situations find themselves. Since we (Black men) use these images and role models to inform how we think about and understand the role of father and partner, we become frustrated when these images do not correspond to the realities of our lives. Indeed, many of us do not have advanced degrees, six-figure salaries, or own businesses even as we aspire to provide greater stability and comfort for our families. A number of us are not married and may not have positive relationships with the mother(s) of our children. We may work in the service industry or management, have had a child(ren) out of wedlock or be divorced, or have court-ordered child support or other "unofficial" arrangements for how our child(ren) are cared for. Our point here is that there are many challenges to responsible Black fatherhood, none that are insurmountable, but the images given to Black males about fatherhood and the visions we create for ourselves as fathers need to reflect "the real" in our lives even as we work toward creating something else.

Beyond the images of Black manhood and fatherhood we see or don't see in our schools, communities, in our homes and through various media outlets, a question that most men have to embrace regardless of their circumstances is how they see themselves as fathers (Franklin, 2004; Kunjufu, 2001). What is their vision? Under preferred circumstances the process of defining who you are as a father is somewhat proactive and planned and understood as a process that will unfold and change over time. In reality, the preferred option doesn't happen as frequently as we would like and we

(Black fathers) often end up playing catch up and creating on the fly who we are and want to be as fathers, assuming that we want(ed) to be fathers. Herein is one of the greatest challenges and disappointments for many Black men, especially those who themselves grew up fatherless and never healed from the injury that experience caused their spirit (Caldwell, 2000). Do you want to be a father? This question and, more importantly, its answer sets the framework for any vision or lack thereof that you create. The answer becomes a critical step in creating your own image of yourself as a Black father, because at the end of the day depending on your cultural socialization, your son or daughter will value the time you spend with them, your being at a school play or t-ball game, tucking them in bed at night with a story, or being there when they are adolescents and really need to talk with you about drugs, school, sex, and relationships.

It is easy enough as many of us know to become a father, at least biologically. However, the process of becoming father, dad, baba, papa, etc., emotionally, spiritually, and relationally is quite different. Becoming a father on these dimensions of the human experience requires choice, effort, commitment, vulnerability, humility, patience, love, and learning from failure to ensure future success. To varying degrees, our consideration and embracement of these issues is influenced by what our vision for fatherhood is, assuming that we have chosen fatherhood beyond the impregnation of a woman.

Beyond having a vision, there is the issue of "becoming" and "being" that vision, working to affect it every day and changing it so that you are constantly stretching yourself to become more and be more understanding, that as you grow and evolve so will your child(ren). The process of *becoming* and *being* has received little discussion in the dialogue about the quality of fathering. Contrary to popular thought it is not enough to just have a man in the house, around the house, or who comes by on weekends when it comes to our children (Beymer, 1991; Kunjufu, 2001). It is more important to have a father who spends quality time with his children. Toth and Xu (1999) in a national study found that African American and Latino fathers surpassed their White counterparts in such activities as monitoring, supervising behaviors, teaching their children skills, and responsibility. One of the questions that researchers need to answer is what are the characteristics of these fathers and, more importantly, what was the impact of these behaviors on the developmental outcomes expressed by their children.

ON BECOMING DAD: MAKE A PROMISE

Becoming a Dad (i.e., parenting) is a conscious choice to "rear" a child (see Madhubuti, 1991, pp. 191–192). It is a promise to dedicate one's life to nurturing and preparing the next generation of the African American community. Becoming a Dad is not synonymous with sperm donation; it is an active and positive engagement in the parenting process. Being involved in positive and loving ways and not just present in the lives of our children is what is needed to increase the number of healthy and fulfilled children in our communities (Beymer, 1995; Kunjufu, 2001).

Earlier we shared that many of us come to fatherhood via different paths and that is certainly true for us. I did not choose to become a father. I (Roy) am not married nor was I married at the time my son was conceived and born into this world. As an academic and practicing psychologist, I had read a great number of books and journal articles on fatherhood, seen many children in my practice who struggled with the absence of their own fathers, and counseled many Black men who struggled with being responsible Black fathers.

Leon and I met briefly in Accra, Ghana West Africa in 2000. We were there for the Association of Black Psychologists Annual Conference where I was directed to Leon by one of my elders and mentor's Linda James Myers who said because of our shared personal and professional interests that we would make good colleagues. Shortly after this conference, we began to email and talk regularly. Our relationship has grown to a place where we frequently plan our conference schedules together, vacation together, and have spent time with each other's family. Last, we have and continue to play integral roles in each other's life and assumed the position of uncle to the other's son.

Indeed, the brotherhood and love that Leon and I share is based in part on our common experience of trying to find our way in this world as Black men and now as Black fathers. I strongly suspect that our sons Aman and Kahlil will be life-long friends because of the bond we share and the ways that we model Black brotherhood and manhood.

Personally, I had struggled for many years with the abandonment and hurt I experienced in my youth and carried with me into adulthood because of the choice my own father had made to not participate in my life. I reconciled with my father at age 30 only to realize that all the anger, violence, and hatred I held toward him was really hurt and disappointment masked as anger. I realized that although an adult and professionally successful, that in forgiving my father I experienced a real liberation unlike any of my prior successes, although I still held him accountable for his choices. I have struggled with, supported, and been supported by my Black Brothers who like me had grown up fatherless or with fathers but who either way were trying to make their way in a place called America, a place where being Black, positive, productive, and a father at the same time can represent unique challenges. For all of this work and experience, I had not created a vision for myself as a father, let alone Daddy.

I intentionally use words like choice, commitment, humility, vulnerability, love, patience, learning, and sacrifice among others to talk about responsible Black fatherhood. I use these words because they have become part of the lexicon that give form to the vision I have created and that I'm working to effect for myself as a Black father. This section is aptly titled because becoming Dad is a process, it is the embodiment of the care, love, protection and assumption of responsibility that allows my son to know that Daddy will take care of him, that Daddy has his back, and that Daddy is there and will be there no matter what because Daddy (I) promised and Daddy doesn't break his promises. I did make a promise, first to myself and then to Aman. It was a promise inspired by my father, a commitment nurtured by my mother, and a work of love supported by a community of family, friends and like-minded Brothers.

To be clear, fatherhood is singularly the greatest blessing and challenge of my life, although from a place of peace I recognize God has been preparing me for this opportunity and responsibility for years. From watching my mother raise me, to my own struggles with defining my manhood by positive and productive attitudes and behaviors, to the confrontation, reconciliation, and then peace with my own father, to the supportive and challenging Brother's and Baba's God has placed in my life all of whom have been brothers and fathers to me. All this has been about my process of becoming Dad.

My father died when I was 35, five years after I made contact with him. It seemed to me that my father had made peace with God and me when he passed, he certainly had taught me a number of lessons about what type of father I wanted to be and, more importantly, what type of father I didn't want to be. Upon reflection, I don't think anyone else could have taught me those lessons but him and the most important lesson he taught/shared with me was about having regrets, humility, and forgiveness. For example, I have about as much formal education as a person can have but the graduation my father was most proud of was that I graduated from high school. I was a standout athlete in football and track throughout high school and college, yet he talked about missing watching his son grow up, not my athletic achievements. I have been fortunate through opportunity and hard work to be financially successful yet the first time I wanted to take my father to dinner, he refused and insisted he take me out to eat, we went to Shoney's. Last of the things I wish to share here, when my father died his sister (Aunt Barbara) asked if I wanted any of his things. I went to his apartment with her and found an old briefcase. When I opened it, it really took my breath away. Even though I didn't have a relationship with my father from the age of about 4 till I was 30, without my knowing it, my mother had periodically sent him clippings and announcements about my accomplishments. He had kept every one of them. Here I was at 35 looking at stuff from when I was a child and a teen, things I had not thought about myself for 20 or 25 years. He kept these things with his most important possessions, his birth certificate, discharge papers from the military, his gun, and pictures from his military service in Korea. I experienced an empathy and love for my father than I had never known. He loved me and had loved me for a long time but didn't know how to express that love in a way that would have allowed us to have a different type of relationship.

All the above have been and continue to be part of my process/journey on becoming Dad. My choice to participate in this process is, in fact, predicated on a promise. I promised myself that my son would never have to wonder if his Dad loved him, he would know it and experience it in a way that transcended words. I promised myself I would do everything I could not to have regrets. For me, that means that Aman has been and always will be the priority in my life. His school plays, t-ball and soccer games, school events and sicknesses take priority as does reading to him at night and the walks we take with the dog. I promised to be there when he has a blue (this isn't good) day at school, is injured, or wonders why things are the way they are in life. In short, Aman is the organizing principal in my life and making this choice and accepting it as a choice has simplified my life. I trip less about career, or the drama that accompanies dealing with racist people and institutions. I have a positive and responsible attitude regarding dating and relationships, and appreciate the blessing that healthy relationships can be. I have learned to lean on the positive and loving people God has placed in my life as I now understand that I don't have to do it by myself. Most importantly, I am learning to rely on God more and me less but this has been my process, my promise, and while many of us committed to responsible Black fatherhood will have a number of similarities in our process, each journey will be unique because it's your own. Last, my process has not been without disappointment and failures (I prefer to call them lessons from the school of hard knocks). There were more than a few Chicago-style potholes hit along the way and I have shed more than a few tears, had a few profanity-laced tirades, and doubted myself and my abilities. The beautiful thing for me is because this is a promise of love and commitment, I get over myself, and I'm learning to be okay with the imperfections and fragility of my humanity and increasingly recognize these challenges as opportunities to be and do Dad better.

Unlike Roy, my journey to fatherhood was planned; you'd have to know my wife to appreciate the precision of the planning. After two years of marriage Celika (my wife) and I initiated our plan to transition from husband and wife, to husband, wife, and child. The two years of prefatherhood was part preparation, part procrastination, and a whole lot of reflection on what and who I was going to be as a father. I was comfortable with the idea of becoming a father because I was married. This had been a major issue for me because I was in my early 30s, had completed graduate school, traveled extensively domestically and internationally and had "managed" to remain free of unplanned children until marriage.

Despite my "clean" slate I still had my own baggage to sort through regarding fatherhood. My baggage was related to not truly knowing who I was or would be as a father because I had been abandoned by my biological father. Complicating this struggle at the time was that my mother and I were embroiled in litigation with my father over his attempt to seek monetary compensation in the aftermath of the September 11th World Trade Center attack that claimed the life of my younger brother Kenny. So I am being stretched in a way I have never experienced before, mourning the loss of my brother while celebrating the beauty of his humanity (he was my Best Man), preparing for the blessings and responsibilities of fatherhood, while arrested by rage and disgust prompted by a man who had done little more than impregnate my mother, now seeking monetary gain. In particular, I was haunted by a heated exchange about his application to the Victim's Compensation Fund where he asserted: "I'm his father, I deserve something." The audacity of this man, whose name I share, to assert fatherhood after abandoning both his sons for more than 18 years. How could you claim to be a "father" when you emotionally and financially (the legal definition of fatherhood) abandon your children?

My father decided not to be involved with our family when I was about 4 years old. There were periods when he would re-surface with empty promises of picking up Kenny and me for visits and trips. Sometimes we wished he would break his promises because his presence was certain to bring shouting, tears, and in some instances physical violence between him and my mother. Visions of protecting my mother at the cost of my father's life have haunted me for years. In many ways I have been conflicted as his absence brought both relief (i.e., no fighting) and rejection (accepting that you weren't a priority in his life).

These formative experiences had prepared me for fatherhood in the "not gonna be" stance that unfortunately many young men facing fatherhood experience. I was "not gonna be" a man who hit women, abandoned his children, and effectively placed his family on the welfare rolls. Rejecting the image and actions of my biological father became my framework for fathering. Part of my journey to responsible fatherhood was realizing that I had the power through conscious choice to shape my fatherhood experience and more importantly the experiences of my child(ren). Prior to this, my idea of fatherhood had been shaped in reaction to not being fathered. However, this gave me a clean canvas to paint my own vision of fatherhood not from the stilted stale paint of my father, but with my own brush of life. I was free to create a vision of fatherhood free of the baggage and pain caused by broken promises, disappointment, and dishonesty. What was my image to look like?

While Celika was pregnant I began to think about what images of fatherhood I wanted to project and more importantly manifest. In a causal conversation with my neighbor Andy Bajc, I sat on his deck and marveled at how he code switched from an aircraft hangar manager to a compassionate caregiver to his toddler sons. Who would I be when I code switched? Could I even code switch? In these questions were the seeds of my apprehension about fatherhood. Void of living with or experiencing a responsible father daily or even sporadically, I had to acknowledge that most of my journey to responsible fatherhood would be truly exploratory. This acknowledgment opened the doors for the journey to begin.

I had to liberate myself to seize this opportunity to create a vision of fatherhood that was uniquely mine and not one that just contrasted who my father had been in my life. First I had to acknowledge my baggage. For example, my disdain for verbally making promises is a direct result of unresolved issues of wanting to avoid feelings of disappointing others. A feeling I knew all too well. Delaying marriage and starting a family is another example of how I lived my life in reaction to my father's failures. Failure was a tacit theme as I prepared to create something I had never seen nor experienced—responsible Black fatherhood.

My journey thus far can be summarized by the two weeks I took to paint Kahlil's room. I worked out my fear in the detail of each Adinkra symbol on his wall and the blue sky and clouds on the ceiling. As I painted and designed the room in preparation for his arrival, my vision of fatherhood was beginning to take shape. With each stroke, the room transformed and so did I. It was something about the creative energy in painting, the time in solitude, the small imperfections of painting two tones, and the occasional wipes of paint drips from the molding. This paint job was far from perfect but it was my creation for Kahlil. His room became the metaphor for my journey toward fatherhood, imperfect but constantly changing and growing. And like most journeys, there was a twist, Kahlil arrived three weeks early. Welcome to fatherhood, where plans and schedules are there to be changed while the need for love and commitment are your constants.

TOOLS FOR THE FATHERLESS FATHER

The commitment process of Fatherless Fathers benefits from guidance, considering that many of us have limited previous experience observing and experiencing responsible commitment by Black fathers. The process of observation and experience is a form of social learning but not our *only* learning. Fatherhood must be highlighted and a central aspect included in the range of male African American experiences. Contrary to claims regarding its invisibility, Franklin (2004) reminds us that responsible fatherhood does exist in African American communities. Indeed, there is a legacy of responsible Black fatherhood during our time in the Americas and on the African Continent, thus our work is not entirely about re-defining but reclaiming fatherhood. The charge to African American men is clear; we must re-create and promote cultural definitions and demonstrations of responsible and loving fatherhood. The experience of being Fatherless and then becoming a Father can no longer be accepted for being less than what your child(ren) deserve from their father—instead, it should serve as motivation for becoming Dad.

In this section we talk about the need for opportunities and venues that support responsible fatherhood (i.e., mentoring, intergenerational dialogue, reading) and creating opportunities for new and not so "new" fathers to talk about their dreams, hopes, fears, and challenges for themselves, their children, and families. What are the tools that Black men, especially those who themselves were fatherless can and should use as they seek to create a vision for themselves as responsible Black fathers.

Creating Intergenerational Dialogue

We suggest intergenerational dialogue as an African American male intervention (Caldwell & White, 2001). Creating opportunities for fatherless men to talk with men who could be their friends, fathers, uncles, or older brothers gives them access to information and opportunities to share concerns and aspirations as they consider fatherhood. What we mean here is that there is real learning and change that can occur when men relate to one another about the substantive issues in their life and the men involved in that process are seen as having social currency with other members of the group. The other thing that occurs out of these natural support networks is not only is there support for creating your vision and plan for effecting that vision, there are also men who will hold you accountable as they support and challenge you. This process is a replication of an Afrikan custom of men's societies whereby the goals of the group were to promote the health, productivity, and leadership of participants as husbands, fathers, and civic leaders.

The need for local conversations among African American men to discuss parenting and fatherhood is critical and must go beyond notions of "baby Momma Drama." A positive is that many of the structures for these conversations already exist as evidenced by in the uses of barber shops, sports bars, gymnasiums, basketball courts, churches, barbecues, and jail yards. There is a belief among some prevention specialists and health promotion experts that large sums of money have to be spent and that effective "interventions" must take place in structured environments. However, help and support can happen in multiple settings, some semistructured and some spontaneous. The challenge facing us is to have this dialogue become constructive and solution-oriented. These dialogues must also involve Black males across multiple generations as one way to understand and learn about fatherhood for young and old alike as they share differing perspectives about their shared common concerns.

Reading

We also suggest the use of reading materials (some included in this book) as there are a number of helpful and informative books that range from telling stories about fathers to preparing for fatherhood. These readings can provide a stimulus for dialogue, although we submit that dialogue is only part of the process. For starters we recommend the following authors: Na'im Akbar, Asa Hillard, Mychal Wynn, Raymond A. Winbush, Carter G. Woodson, William Cosby, Courtland C. Lee, Haki Madhubuti, and Earl Ofari Hutchinson, to name just a few. Many of these scholar–activists have written books that are readable, moderately priced, and geared to the range of fathering experiences. While we encourage anyone looking to understand responsible Black fatherhood to be critical in what they digest, there are also some decent resources available on the internet.

The Baby Shower

The tradition of having a baby shower is usually considered a maternal activity. I (Leon) had the pleasure of having a baby shower as the community of men who surround me celebrated my becoming a father for the first time by creating a social event that mimicked my wife's concurrent shower at another location. Between the good spirited contest of drinking beer from a baby bottle, bathing and clothing a doll baby, and a duct tape diaper-wrapping speed contest, I received lessons about fatherhood from this multigenerational gathering of men, some new fathers themselves and others, grandparents.

Consistent in all their advice were stories of sleepless nights, which turned into days of endless play, which later turned into sleepless nights of worry as their children moved from adolescence to young adulthood. Eric Lee and Dominic Witherspoon would recount the excitement and anxiety the first time they held their child(ren) and the first time they were left alone overnight as the primary caretaker. Dave Jefferson and John Reed spoke of each stage of their parenting, and now grandparenting, and how they now watch their own children negotiate parenthood. We all listened as the two grandparents told their humorous stories of having the first conversation about sex with their sons and daughters. Vaughn Robertson and Willie Banks gave me advice about how to adjust to my wife's new status as a mother, how to cope and manage my occasional feelings of isolation and helplessness, and to expect a change in our relationship. Jason Wagner offered stories about how challenging it can be to discipline his teenage son; as others chimed in about how they thought it was necessary to establish a baseline of behavioral expectations and household values.

These men, some old enough to be my father, in their own way did their part in preparing me for the most important role in my life—Dad. Dave also warned me how I would change as my priorities shifted. My hectic travel schedule would become emotionally draining as I would miss my son and wife in a way different than before. They spoke of how I would have to reorganize my daily calendar and spend more time planning my hobbies like golf and the gym. They were preparing me for successful fatherhood. My community of fathers gathered to share stories of their failures, an effort to prepare me for the inevitable time I would question my parenting skills. Each of these men, in their sharing, would also learn about parenting from each other in a way that I believe made all of us better.

In many ways this was my rite of passage into responsible Black fatherhood. The baby shower was a re-creation of an old custom where the elders of a village would take the pubescent boy away to prepare him for manhood. It was also a statement of support as these "brothers" and "fathers" were telling me they had my back and that I was not alone. I felt then and now, supported, encouraged, prepared, and special that they would take a Saturday afternoon to be my fathers and brothers and that they continue to support me as such. These are the types of activities that need to be highlighted and replicated as we create our own support and helping networks. Needless to say that parenting in the 21st century is different and requires new tools in order to succeed in raising and rearing healthy, happy, and productive children.

Many of us, fatherless fathers, are around men all the time who have stories to tell about being a father and parenting. Not all the stories are good or have happy endings but each has a lesson. We encourage and invite our Brothers, African American men, to share their fatherhood experiences, to seek opportunities to talk to each other about the blessings and challenges of parenting. We encourage Black fathers to admit to themselves and trusted others what they are feeling and ask for the help we need. We encourage Black fathers to find and/or create an image or ideal and aspire to meet that vision for yourself. We encourage Black fathers to commit to the next generation of African American families and children the creation of a loving, supportive, disciplined experience with us—Dad. We choose to focus on father presence with the understanding that each of us may choose to create different legacies for our children.

Create an Extended Family

We think it is important that new fathers create their own extended family. We suggest finding those surrogate fathers and mothers, those you refer to as Baba, Papa, Nana, and Big Mamas who you can go to for advice, support, some good old-fashioned direction and who will listen to you and to whom you will listen. We also suggest that you call on your peer group for support and accountability by making them "Aunties," "aunts," "unks," "uncles," etc. and their children become "nieces," "nephews," and "play cousins" for your children. Creating a healthy and loving village around you and the child(ren) is invaluable. The relationship that you engender with your trusted friends will help create a sense of security around you and your children. We, like many others, support that rearing a child is not an individual task and that it really does take a village. We also acknowledge that the natural villages in our communities have been distorted but not destroyed; therefore we must look to re-create extended families.

Make the Commitment

For many of us fatherhood comes as a mixed bag. On one hand we are ecstatic about the potential and possibility of having a "mini-me." We are full of the "I can't wait . . ." statements or daydreams about playing ball together, curling up and reading the nighttime story, cooking breakfast before school, applauding loud at the school recital, or passing on our favorite hobby. We think of all these wonderful things that we wished someone had done with and for us or that were done for us and that we want to repeat for our children. Our longing for a responsible and loving fathering relationship becomes the basis for our commitment. We suggest that this commitment be overt, that your environment symbolize your commitment to fatherhood with pictures, signs, and symbols of the importance of fatherhood and your vision for successful fatherhood.

To support fathers everywhere in the commitment process, we suggest Madhubuti's (1991) Afrikan American Father's Pledge in the form of a plaque as daily remainder to our commitment and striving to become Dads:

Madhubuti's Father Commitments

1. I will work to be the best father I can be. Fathering is a daily mission, and there are no substitutes for good fathers. Since I have not been taught to be a father, in order to make my "on the job" training easier, I will study, listen, observe and learn from my mistakes.
2. I will openly display love and caring for my wife and children. I will listen to my wife and children. I will hug and kiss my children often. I will be

supportive of the mother of my children and spend quality time with my children.

3. I will teach by example. I will try to introduce myself and my family to something new and developmental each week. I will help my children with their homework and encourage them to be involved in extracurricular activities.

4. I will read to or with my children as often as possible. I will provide opportunities for my children to develop creatively in the arts: music, dance, drama, literature, and visual arts. I will challenge my children to do their best.

5. I will encourage and organize frequent family activities for the home and away from home. I will try to make life a positive adventure and make my children aware of their extended family.

6. I will never be intoxicated or "high" in the presence of my children, nor will I use language unbecoming for an intelligent and serious father.

7. I will be nonviolent in my relationships with my wife and children. As a father, my role will be to stimulate and encourage my children rather than carry the "big stick."

8. I will maintain a home that is culturally in tune with the best of African American history, struggle and future. This will be done in part, by developing a library, record/disc, video and visual art collections that reflect the developmental aspects of Afrikan people worldwide. There will be order and predictability in our home.

9. I will teach my children to be responsible, disciplined, fair, and honest. I will teach them the value of hard work and fruitful production. I will teach them the importance of family, community, politics and economics. I will teach them the importance of the Nguzo Saba (Black value system) and the role that ownership of property and businesses plays in our struggle.

10. As a father, I will attempt to provide my family with an atmosphere of love and security to aid them in their development into sane, loving, productive, spiritual, hardworking, creative Afrikan Americans who realize they have a responsibility to do well and help the less fortunate of this world. I will teach my children to be activists and to think for themselves.

SUMMARY

The reader of this chapter should be encouraged to know that the cycle of father presence begins with being able to talk honestly about our experiences as fatherless children, our lack of knowledge about parenting, constructing new and positive images of fatherhood, making a commitment not to repeat the cycle, and seeking and creating intergenerational networks of fathers to support you. We suggest that future research investigating the lives of the fatherless African American is a critical act in the future development and success of the African American community. How would they describe their childhood experiences being fatherless? What are the parental experiences of those boys who grew up without a father? What are their successes, fears, and failures? What guidance can they give the next generation of fathers who lost their fathers to the war on drugs, predatory criminal justice systems, HIV/AIDS, and a failing educational system?

Despite the social constraints placed on African American men we hold that responsible fatherhood is a choice, a choice that only a Black father can make. The examination of this topic is timely and critical because of the deleterious impact the cycle of father absence has had on developing healthy African American children and communities (Darity & Myers, 1995). Our enslaved ancestors were brought to America in inhumane conditions and no material resources, yet somehow they managed to protect "their" children and build families with woman the best they could despite the pathological terrorism exacted on them. It is imperative that we never forget their fortitude, commitment, and the life-sustaining choices they made by drawing strength from their example as we seek to represent the excellence that is responsible Black fatherhood and advance the state and condition of the "village."

REFERENCES

Beymer, L. (1995). *Meeting the guidance and counseling needs of boys*. Alexandria, VA: American Counseling Association.

Caldwell, L. D. (2000). Psychology of Black men. In L. Jones (Ed.), *Brothers of the Academy: Up and coming Black scholars earning our way in higher education*. Sterling, VA: Stylus.

Caldwell, L. D., & White, J. L. (2001). African-centered therapeutic and counseling interventions for African-American males. In G. Brooks & G. Good (Eds.), *A new handbook of counseling and psychotherapy approaches for men*. San Francisco, CA: Jossey-Bass.

Darity, W. A., & Myers, S. L. (1995). Family Structure and the marginalization of Black men: Policy Implications. In M. B. Tucker & C. Mitchell-Kernan (Eds.), *The decline in marriage among African Americans* (pp. 263–308). New York: Russell Sage Foundation.

Franklin, A. J. (2004). *From brotherhood to manhood: How Black men rescue their relationships and dreams from the invisibility syndrome*. Hoboken, NJ: Wiley.

Kiselica, M. S. (1999). Culturally sensitive interventions with African American teenage fathers. In L. Davis (Ed.), *Working with African males: A guide to practice*. Thousand Oaks, CA: Sage.

Kunjufu, J. (2001). *State of emergency: We must save African American males*. Chicago, IL: African American Images.

McLanahan, S., & Booth, K. (1991). Mother only families. In A. Booth (Ed.), *Contemporary families: Looking forward, looking back*. Minneapolis, MN: National Council on Family Relations.

Madhubuti, H. R. (1991). *Black men obsolete, single, dangerous? The Afrikan American family in transition*. Chicago, IL: Third World Press.

Spencer, M. B. (1990). Parental values transmission: Implications for the development of African American children. In H. E. Cheatham & J. B. Stewart (Eds.), *Black families: Interdisciplinary perspectives* (pp. 111–130). New Brunswick, NJ: Transaction.

Toth, J. F., & Xu, X. (1999). Ethnic and cultural diversity in fathers' involvement: A racial/ethnic comparison of African Americans, Hispanics, and White fathers. *Youth & Society, 31,* 76–99.

Zinn, M. B., & Eitzen, D. S. (2005). *Diversity in families* (7th ed.). Boston, MA: Allyn & Bacon.

Chapter 11

A Letter to My Dad

Nnamdi Pole[1]
University of Michigan

Dear Dad,

I have been invited to write a chapter for a book about African American fathers. Not surprisingly, you came to mind. For a moment, I had the urge to pick up the phone to call you, to ask for your philosophies or observations about fatherhood. Then I remembered that we don't have that kind of relationship. We haven't had that kind of relationship for a long time now. As you know, we haven't spoken a word to each other in almost four years.

So, I am left with a dilemma. The intent of the book is to highlight the bright side of African American fatherhood. Yet, much of what I have to say about you is far from upbeat. And you know what they say, "If you can't say something nice . . ." On the other hand, perhaps our story, the story of how our relationship went terribly awry, could be an important addition to a book aimed at elevating and inspiring Black fathers. Maybe others could learn from our mistakes. Maybe sharing this letter with others and revealing the pain that it contains will underscore the importance of getting it right.

What happened to us dad? I know that at one point you really cared about being a good father—but then something went radically wrong. I think that it was something inside of you, something that led to a disintegration of your relationship with mom, with me, and ultimately with yourself. But the truth is that I don't know what happened. So I'll do what I often do

---

[1]This chapter is dedicated to my mother, Delores Carter Pole.

as a psychotherapist listening to other people's problems. I'll look at the facts and fill in the blanks. Maybe some day you'll read this and let me know how close I got. Then again maybe you won't.

On the day I was born you became a father for the second time. I don't know why you didn't marry the mother of your first child. Did you feel guilty about leaving him behind in the Virgin Islands when you married mom and moved to Brooklyn? Did that guilt light a slow burning fuse on the bomb that would later explode in our family? After your first un-planned foray into fatherhood, what was going through your mind when I arrived on the scene?

I am told that you were overjoyed. They say that you used to rush home from work to take me for stroller-rides through Prospect Park before the sunset. I am sorry that I don't remember anything about those rides or the things that you said to me. Those may have been our best conversations. Did you have hopes for our future? Did you have any idea that we could come to this?

My earliest memory of you is a violent one, watching you pummel mom with your fists while she tried to block your blows with her elbows and fore-arms. You were clearly bigger and stronger than she was. Yet, you pressed your advantage by pinning her down on the couch. I don't how exactly how old I was but I know that I too small and too weak to stop you. But I tried anyway. After rummaging through my room for my red leather belt, I raced back into the living room and hit you with it as hard as I could. My "spank-ing" didn't seem to hurt you but at least it got your attention. You stopped. Unfortunately, it would neither be the last time that I would watch you bru-talize her nor the last time that I would intervene to stop you. But thank-fully, in the beginning, these violent episodes were rare.

In fact, I mostly remember a childhood full of play. You bought me great toys. My favorite was the pedal-powered blue aluminum car that I used to "drive" in our yard. You stenciled my name on the hood. I always liked that detail, your personal touch. You seemed sincerely interested in being a good father in those days. You even invested in the obligatory baseball glove and bat despite the fact that neither you nor I seemed very interested in baseball.

Boxing was your sport. At least you liked watching it. You tried to get me to watch it with you but I wouldn't come near it. Looking back now, I won-der if that hurt your feelings, if you felt rejected by my lack of interest in your favorite sport. Maybe you were right. Maybe I was rejecting the part of you that identified with beating the crap out of another human being.

But if I resisted your efforts to lure me to the ringside, I tried to make up for it by "hitting" the books. You and mom both emphasized education from the very beginning. You both seemed determined that I learn how to read, write, and do arithmetic before I started school. I was lucky to have a stay-at-home mom. Especially one, who like many African American mothers, devoted herself entirely to providing a better life for her children than the life that she had (and the life she was having). Her unconditional love and unselfish presence during my childhood contributed to the confidence and self-esteem that has been a building block of all of my later achievements. In fairness to you, I know that it was only possible for me to have her at home because you were working hard to put food on the table and a roof over our heads. Mom worked hard too. In addition to cooking, cleaning, and keeping house, she also ran our home schooling curriculum. On weekends, you ran the class. You encouraged me to learn to read aloud from *The New York Times.* Thanks to you, I was the only kid in kindergarten who could do that trick.

It may have been through my readings of *The Times* at age four or five that I came to learn about the Watergate scandal. All I remember is that, at your urging, I used to do mocking impersonations of Richard Nixon to amuse your friends. With V-shaped fingers pointed in the air and my baby fat cheeks wobbling, I'd happily repeat, "I am not a crook . . . I am not a crook." That used to crack you up! What you probably didn't realize is that you were teaching me an important lesson: *Any person who abuses his power should expect consequences, even the President of the United States, even my own father.*

Among my favorite childhood memories were the times that you took me to work with you in Manhattan. The city seemed huge to me back then, the buildings seemed impossibly tall, like Jack's beanstalk. Yet, I always felt safe with you. I remember being amazed that you knew your way through the subway system and city streets. I remember the thrill of the elevator ride up to your engineering firm and my awe of your view of Rockefeller Center. I was delighted to spend my days in a nearby cubicle, with some blank paper, some of your drafting tools, and the biggest assortment of colored pencils that I had ever seen. I was never bored.

On the way home from your office, we'd usually pass by a cigar shop and you would put the cherry on the top of my day by buying me a few comic books. I loved comic books, especially the superheroes. I think that you encouraged it because you realized that they motivated me to read. What you may not have realized is that the comic books were teaching me lessons too. Superhero stories inspired me to work to the limits of my potential. They also taught me about the importance of standing up for what is right and against what is wrong *even if it costs me dearly.*

I think that things really began to deteriorate for us when mom pressured you to move to the New Jersey suburbs. Though I was not quite ten at the time, I remember your reluctance. You made no secret of it. At times, you cursed and shouted so loud that most of the neighborhood knew what was on your mind. Though I don't remember in detail, I am fairly certain that mom took a few body blows for her trouble. What I don't understand is where the protest was coming from? You knew that our neighborhood in Brooklyn was dangerous. You had been threatened by youth gangs numerous times. It was so bad that you wouldn't let me play outside. Yet, you treated mom terribly as she tried to get you to act in your own best interest (and mine).

It seems that improving the quality of our lives was always mom's idea and it was always your role to insist that she was reaching beyond our means. She was the one with vision. Vision was not your strong suit. To be fair, you were the one carrying the bulk of the financial burden, working overtime and weekends to make ends meet. I suppose the prospect of moving to a nicer home with a bigger mortgage must have been intimidating and stressful. I don't fault you for that. I do wish, however, that you had considered working with mom instead of against her. I wish that you had been able to recognize that she brought strengths to your relationship in areas where you needed help. It seems like the thought of getting help from her never occurred to you even though, as I see it, she would have helped you to do more and be more than you could do and be on your own.

You seemed to get worse after we moved to New Jersey. I wonder if the move to a predominantly White neighborhood had some something to do with it? After all, you grew up on a predominantly Black island, and from what you told me about your experiences, Whites had not always been good to you. I was especially saddened when you told me that your White teachers discouraged you from a biomedical career and steered you toward a "trade" because they claimed that Blacks "couldn't" become doctors. It must have been deeply demoralizing to be blocked from actualizing your potential because of something as irrelevant as the color of your skin.

That is part of the reason why I have a hard time understanding why you were so opposed to mom going back to school. After giving birth to me at age 18 and my brother and sister shortly thereafter, she had totally devoted herself to full-time mothering for years. It seemed only reasonable that now, as her children were entering adolescence, she would want more out of her life. You hated the idea! Frankly, it seemed to me, even then, that you were worried that you would lose some of your power over her, the power that came from having her completely financially dependent on you. I know that many men of your generation suffered from such sexism but that is hardly an excuse. You should have known better. You knew what it was like to have your race used against you. You should never have used mom's gender to justify blocking her from her goals. I expected better from you.

Despite your lack of support and outright abuse, mom went back to college and earned an associates degree. I am glad that she did. I would never have known what a stellar student she was if I hadn't seen it with my own eyes. It was not until she returned to school that I discovered that I inherited my scholarly side from her. I recently found out that, as a child, she was skipped ahead two grades! Did you know that? In college, she excelled at physiology and the other biological sciences and began to get excited about pursuing a career in physical therapy. Predictably, you staunchly opposed her plans out of some fairly paranoid idea that she was seeking to elevate herself above you. At least that is what I gleaned from the loud arguments that kept me up half the night.

By the time I was in high school, mom settled for a secretary job to bring in some extra dollars. You took to staying out late and coming home drunk. The drinking was a new and disturbing dimension to your deteriorating behavior. At the time, I had the impression that you were staying out and drinking to avoid coming home and fighting. Maybe it made sense to you but it turned out be a very ineffective plan.

You usually came home after everyone had gone to bed not only drunk but also hungry. Your first order of business was to warm your dinner, the dinner that mom dutifully prepared for you even though you almost never ate with the rest of us. Your second order of business was usually to pass out on the couch with your dinner warming under a low flame. I woke up several times to the smell of burned metal only to rush downstairs and find the kitchen stove on fire and you soundly asleep! After the third or fourth time that I had to put out one of your fires, I just got into the habit of staying awake until after you had finished eating and gone to bed (often at 2 or 3 AM, shortly before I had to be awake for school at 7 AM).

In the beginning, I used to worry about whether you would make it home. Later on, I dreaded your arrival because you invariably provoked arguments with mom that often escalated into shocking profanity, threats, and all too often physical abuse. On several occasions I had to intervene by literally pulling you off of her, always running the risk that your flailing fists would one day connect with me.

Your behavior was horrific at a lot of levels. But for me the worst part of it was your insistence upon being "wrong and strong." You were an absolute tyrant demanding absolute control while at the same time you were clearly way out of control. I repeatedly pleaded with you to seek some help, if not for yourself, for the sake of our family. You arrogantly denied that you needed any help and continued to drive our family off of the cliff. That was an abuse of power.

I have wanted to see another side to the story, one that puts you in a better light. I have tried hard to understand how mom could have contributed to your rage episodes but I think that even you would agree that you deserve the lion's share of the blame. Mom was a gentle and loyal wife. You could hardly claim that she provoked you. The truth is you didn't need provoking. You just got angry all by yourself. I am not saying that mom didn't have faults but I think that one of the few things that we can agree on is that her biggest fault was loving you unconditionally and continuing to forgive you. Maybe if she'd shown you some true consequences to your abominable actions you might have been able to stop.

You joined Club 8, a local African American social club named after a famous piece of "black" sporting equipment, the eight ball. Despite (or maybe because of) the fact that the club was located in a dilapidated old bar, you certainly seemed to like it there. You spent more time with them than with your family. I learned a lot about you by watching you in that club. On the surface there were a lot of positive things. You engaged in fund-raisers and events that were presumably aimed at improving the quality of life for Blacks in the surrounding community. Yet, there was something puzzling about your club. It appeared to reinforce your sense of alienation from the Blacks who were closest to you, your family. Somehow, you only felt at home in your club if you downplayed your own achievements and the achievements of your children. No one could tell from watching you in your club that you had a good paying job and an upper middle-class life. You seemed to want to be mistaken for a custodian or a blue-collar worker. Though there is nothing wrong with custodians or blue-collar workers, there is something wrong with pretending to be one when you are not. You seemed utterly ashamed of the status that you had achieved in life, like you were suffering survivor guilt for the entire race. As I began to excel in school and win national academic awards, you went so far as to disavow any role in helping me to grow into the man that I was becoming. Nothing could be further from the truth. Even at your worst, you influenced the man that I was becoming, if only by showing me clearly what *not* to be and what *not* to do.

I'll always remember the look on your face when I told you that I would not be following in your career path. You seemed disappointed but you shouldn't have been surprised. At that point, the last thing I wanted to do was to be like you when I grew up. No, I knew that my best shot at not re-enacting the horror movies that you directed and enacted in our home was to choose a path where I would learn how to exorcise the kind of demons that were driving you. I chose to be a psychologist, the kind that not only helps women who have been victimized by people like you but also the kind that helps victimizers when they decide that they want to change. I hoped to be able to save both my mother and my father.

So I headed off to college to become a psychologist. Though you would never say so, I could feel you beaming with pride as we sat together in the Rutgers College gymnasium listening to the Dean of the College telling a room full of parents how lucky they were that their children beat the fierce competition and gained admission to Rutgers. I know that it also gave you some satisfaction to know that thanks to my scholarships, my education wouldn't cost you a cent.

I remember the day that you and mom moved me into my first college dorm room. Though it was a mere thirty-minute car ride from home, I felt homesick as soon as we arrived. I was eager to get out of the war zone and to try the independence of living away from home but it was more painful than I expected to separate from the two of you. Nonetheless, I managed to adjust. I saw you guys on holidays and during the summer breaks. However, my fantasies of family reunion were frustrated by the fact that you were more and more emotionally distant. Your center of gravity was clearly elsewhere. I tried several times to reach out to you. I started many conversations with you that you refused to continue with me. I tried to invite you for a Father's Day lunch once in order to make yet another plea for you to make some changes in your life. You must have known what I had in mind. You never showed up, you never called, and you never spoke of it again.

In the meantime, I continued to succeed in my studies and managed to put myself in the position where I had my choice of graduate schools throughout the country. I felt a natural affinity for the University of California, Berkeley, perhaps, in part, because I had been living on a type of "fault line" in my own family for so long. But after feeling homesick 30 miles from home, could I move 3,000 miles further? Our increasingly acrimonious household made leaving an attractive prospect. Yet, I felt a sense of dread that it would all fall apart in my absence. Then I thought of something worse, that it might all fall apart *in my presence.*

As expected, California provided somewhat of an escape for me. I was far enough away and busy enough to put you and mom and your troubles out of my mind. Coming home for the holidays was a chore not only because things seemed to keep getting worse but also because I felt so responsible to do something about it. So I kept coming home with new plans to persuade you to try to change. Sometimes I found the courage to talk to you. Sometimes I didn't. By this point the physical abuse seemed to stop but you were almost never home at night. So I set up regular meetings with you at your favorite bar to watch your favorite local singer. You never seemed willing to have actual conversations about anything significant during these outings but I kept doing it because it was my only shot at communicating with you. My method was to request songs that expressed some of what I was trying to get through to you. I hoped that you would get the message.

Then a ray of hope sprung from tragedy. Your uncle died. You and your siblings went for a long car ride together to attend the funeral. It was probably the first time in decades that you had all spent so much time together. I was surprised to hear that you went with them at all. It always seemed like you couldn't stand them. I don't know what happened at that funeral or what you talked about in the car but you seemed to come back a changed person. You had a restored interest in your family. You seemed to develop a sense of spirituality and for the first time in my memory an interest in foster-ing connectedness through our extended family. You even edited a family newsletter and asked me to write an article offering my "professional opin-ion" on grieving. It felt good to be having healthy dialogue with you and to be contributing to something that mattered to you. I became hopeful.

Ironically, just as you were showing improvements in mental health, mom's physical health began to take a disturbing turn. She was very vague and private about it. She simply asked for our prayers for her eyes and her lungs. Somehow, despite my fancy education, I remained mostly ignorant about the seriousness of her condition. I suppose that I wanted to be. But after a while, her deterioration was too dramatic to ignore. Every time I vis-ited she seemed to spend more and more time in bed until it got to the point that she only got up to work and cook. She became emaciated. At first, she said that it was because she was on a diet but after a while it was clear that it wasn't what she was eating but rather what was eating her. And the coughing, she never seemed to stop coughing. To this day, I still hate to hear a woman coughing.

As mom continued on her downward slide, for reasons that are still un-clear to me, you returned to your old tricks. The ray of hope was en-shrouded in dark clouds once more. On the rare occasions when you were home, you seemed to be looking for a fight so that you could have an ex-cuse to leave again. I couldn't understand your total failure to even try to help. I took you out to lunch to try to draw you into taking some kind of leadership to help the situation, to offer mom a fraction of the support that she had given to you throughout your marriage. Nothing could have been further from your mind. In fact, it wouldn't be too much longer before you would decide to just leave . . . without a word.

You went back to the Virgin Islands. You later claimed that you went to help care for your ailing father but we both know that isn't true. Your mother told me that she rarely saw you. The truth is that you went to re-sume your relationship with the mother of your first son. Or maybe more clearly put, you went hoping to escape, to start over. Fair enough, but, with all due respect, your timing was lousy. You left your wife, my mother, on the brink of death. As far as I am concerned, when you made that move, you went too far.

There were many difficult aspects to mom's end of life. One of the hard-est was deciding when to stop her life support. I felt slapped in the face by God when I discovered that I would have to make that decision on Mother's Day. The lung cancer had found its way into her brain. She was unconscious and incapable of breathing on her own. There was very little left in my power other than to offer her some relief from the pain, the pain that had been a seeming constant companion in her life from the time that her par-ents named her "Dolores," after the Spanish word for pain. If I could do one thing for this woman who had done so much for me, it was to find the courage to finally stop the pain. So, with the support of my brother and sister, I released her from it one month before her 51st birthday.

After you got word of mom's death, you sent a well-written, sympathetic condolence letter peppered with hollow platitudes about your undying love for her. I am not sure who you thought you were fooling except maybe yourself. Did you forget that I was there? I saw what you did and what you failed to do. Your actions spoke louder than your words. Your letter ended with an absurd excuse about your own health difficulties preventing you from traveling back to New Jersey to attend her funeral. That was a wise move. You wouldn't have liked what I had to say about you during her eulogy.

I saw you one month later in the Virgin Islands at another funeral, her mother's funeral, undoubtedly accelerated by the crushing news that she had outlived her own daughter. When I saw you at grandma's funeral, you seemed utterly surprised that I refused to talk to you. Maybe you thought that you were dealing with someone like my mother, someone who was willing to forgive and forget no matter what you had done. And in a sense you are right, you are dealing with someone who is 50% my mother, a living record of all of the injustices that you committed against her. But you are also dealing with someone who is 50% you, capable of the same coldness that you showed mom, only much more selective about who I share that part of myself with. How does it feel to be on the receiving end?

So yes, I freely admit that this "silent treatment" between us has been *my* prescription to treat the chronic illness that our relationship has become. I didn't want it to come to this but even after all that has happened you still refuse to discuss your abuses of power, your wrongful actions against my mother, your role in making a mess of my upbringing, and ultimately your failures as a father. Instead, you have asked me to forget the past and move on. I won't do that. Some would say (and have said), that I must forgive you because you are my father. I say that you won't have my forgiveness until you find the decency to ask for it.

Simply forgiving you would be bad for me. It would imply that I accept your behavior. If I accept your behavior then I am on the slippery slope to repeating it. To paraphrase Joseph Heller, every culprit is a victim, every victim is a culprit and someone has to end that cycle somewhere. I decided that the buck stops here with me. I must not perpetuate your misdeeds into another generation. So I have chosen to cut you out of my life and consequently out of me. I would have preferred to handle things differently. I would have preferred to reject your behavior and accept you as a person but, as of yet, you have offered me no way to understand your behavior, and thus no way of separating you from it. This may be your greatest failure as a father. Yet, there is still time for you to remedy this shortcoming. I wonder if you ever will?

And there are other reasons why I will not speak to you until you are willing to talk about our past, reasons that go beyond my obvious anger and disappointment with you, reasons that have to do with my love for you. You are
not happy with where your life has taken you. Yet, you continue to move
steadily toward your own annihilation. It is your prerogative to self-destruct
but if that is the course that you've set for yourself then don't ask me to walk
that course with you. I'd rather be out of your life. If, on the other hand,
you don't want to self-destruct then it is imperative that you get really honest with yourself about the destructive force that lives within you. A good
way to begin would be to get honest with me. You have a son who is a
trained and licensed psychologist. I may know a thing or two about how to
help you to overcome problems that you have been unable to overcome on
your own.

I recently found and read one of mom's diaries written during the worst
part of her illness, after you had abandoned her. Do you know what is in it?
Mostly prayers and wishes for her children, her brothers and sisters, and
even for you. Can you imagine that? Even while she was dying, even while
you were dishonoring the most sacred of your wedding vows, you know the
part about "in sickness . . . ," she was praying for you to be healed, to find a
path to salvation. Perhaps, in a way, this letter is mom's final gift to you, her
final attempt to help you to become a better man.

That is basically all that I have to say to you. The only question that remains in my mind is whether I have written something worthy of inclusion
in a book on Black fathers? I have offered a case study. Like all case studies,
mine cannot be assumed to be generalizable. Nonetheless it may be informative. I wonder what lessons emerge from our story for readers seeking to
learn about Black fatherhood?

Well, one of the points of the book is to challenge stereotypes of African
American fathers. Though you were tyrannical you were certainly not stereotypical. You were technically present in the home, custodial, married to
mom, financially responsible most of the time, and seemingly interested in
parenting. In fact, I think that it is not inconsequential that despite your
record of spousal abuse, I never doubted your love of me. You also contributed importantly to my moral development, which ironically has set the
foundation of this difficult choice that I have had to make to exclude you
from my life.

Your terrible performance as a husband raises other lessons. Black fathers and Black men in general would be wise to work harder to respect
their women, their mothers, sisters, and wives. We should respect them because they've earned it—often the hard way. We should remember that our
typically larger size and greater strength carries with it the responsibility to
never, ever, strike them. Hitting a woman is one of the greatest acts of cow-

ardice a man can commit, and therefore one of the least "manly" things that we can do. Finally, in our marriages and other co-parenting relationships we must strive to *be good partners*. I want my Black male readers to remember, "There is more at stake than you." Most mothers know this intuitively. Some fathers never seem to learn this at all.

Black fathers must also learn how to maintain open lines of communication with their children. You seemed to have virtually no capacity to communicate about yourself or to carry on a meaningful conversation with me. This cost us not only essential relationship building but also opportunities for mutual understanding. As I have documented in this letter, I tried repeatedly to reach out to you with no avail. It is ironic that we have come to this place were I am now enforcing a rule of no communication with you. Maybe I am trying to give you a taste of what it has been like for me for the last 25 years.

I don't know whether these lessons will make a difference for the readers of this letter but I know that they have made a difference for me. The difficult times between us have made me more attentive to my own fathering potential. Though I do not yet have biological children, I have devoted myself to the surrogate fathering role of mentoring the next generation of psychologists. Many of my students have been ethnic minorities and/or women. I strive to offer them a positive, supportive, and constructive relationship with an African American male "father figure." I also work to be sensitive to the special challenges that they face because of their gender and ethnocultural backgrounds. Where you were dictatorial and closed, I work to be egalitarian and open. Though I will always have more work to do, I am deeply proud of the fact that the American Psychological Association of Graduate Students awarded me with the Kenneth and Mamie Clark Prize in recognition of these efforts. I know that mom would be proud. I think that you would too.

My only concern about publishing this letter is that it may lead some to the false conclusion that our relationship is somehow representative of fathers and sons in Black America. I am hopeful that readers will realize that one does not need to be Black to have an estranged relationship with one's father. For example, the Czech author, Franz Kafka, wrote and published a monograph entitled *Letter to Father*[2] to document his own struggles to connect with his father. His letter ended as follows, "Naturally, in reality things cannot fit together the way the evidence does in my letter, life is more than a jigsaw puzzle; but . . . in my opinion something so very near the truth has been achieved that it can calm us both a little and make our living and dying easier."

---

[2]Kafka, F. (1919/1999). *Letter to father*. Vitalis: Czech Republic.

So, I close this letter and share it with the world. I hope that by telling the truth, by showing where bad choices can lead, I can inspire someone to make different choices than you did, and ultimately to be a better father than you have been able to be so far.

Your Son,
Nnamdi

Part IV

STRENGTHENING THE ROLE
OF BLACK FATHERS

Sunrise to Sunset
(a typical day in Berkeley)

morning time . . .
i must protect the child within
notice colors in the morning light and that
love without jealousy will move me gently through life
but despite the fact that i can't find my house keys anywhere
i feel absolutely alive

noon time . . .
i walk to the corner of haste and telegraph
waiting for a lunch date
observing the strut of a Black man
10 paces in front of the white Woman
who has mothered his child
he pretends to be alone in hopes to attract
while his Woman looks around with indifference
'jazz' duet plays melodies almost n'sync
as a Latino brotha noooooooods to a different beat
all of the sudden two young cats approach me
figuring i must want company
i politely with positivity let them know i'm just chillin'
and the larger of the two out of the blue calls me a bitch
i guess his size was supposed to intimidate me
but instead it infuriates me

within 30 seconds of a greeting i have to deal with this shit
young cat tells me to stop trippin' because it's a dick thang, baby
except you don't know me well enough to call me baby
and as for your dick . . .

at that moment my lunch date appears
saving these boys from a serious read
and i shake off the negativity
to keep the break light and airy
further down the Ave we pass these same two brothas
kickin' supposed game to yet another

evening time . . .
sunset swirls in the twilight
as age begins to blend in the corner of my eyes
i soak in the last ray of the setting sun
precisely as boldness steps in to inform me
that my man looks good and i'd better watch out
gurrl please . . . i ain't got nothing to worry about
because he takes me to a place where
Oshun greets Yemaya and i bathe all day
i watch beautiful Nubians pass by and i hope
the sista peacocks catch their eye

    early morning mantras
    give way to late night realities.

                           —Malia, June 10, 1997

Chapter 12

Shane Price: Father
to Four Generations

Julie Landsman
Independent Consultant, Minneapolis, MN

Perhaps all that went into the making of Shane Price culminated in the summer of 2002 as he walked the streets on a steamy evening in North Minneapolis calming neighborhood residents after yet another police shooting. All his training in conflict resolution, his work with the Native Community on building Healing Circles of Trust, his reaching out for years to the youth on Minneapolis street corners and in classrooms, served him well as tensions rose. On that night, and subsequent nights, Shane Price, along with other African American men and women, some his mentors from childhood, kept violence from building to a point where it could have claimed a life. While allowing for the expression of pain and anger, he and others in the community—ministers, activists, business leaders—also asked for peace. Gradually tempers cooled and talks began.

Much of what has gone into the making of Brother Shane Price has also culminated in the African American Men Project and his leadership of that project over the last 2 years. Yet one could also say Shane's work with Bob Cross with the Highland Park Presbyterian Church, a church that was dying, defines him most closely. After working to acquire the building, they spent more than 3 years recreating this church into the Kwanzaa Presbyterian Community Church. In 3 to 4 years the building went from one that had served an older White population and was almost abandoned to become one that served a primarily Black congregation, which is very much alive.

Or maybe it was the Wellness Center Shane Price founded, with its massage, counseling, and spiritual aspects that typifies his work. Yet there is also the mediation he has done and the mentoring he continues to do each day. Knowing all this, we are reminded that no one event or action can encapsulate an entire life or illustrate a philosophy. It takes the whole story, to do that. It takes an understanding of the circular nature of our lives: how we arrive back at the same place we started and "know that place for the first time." This is especially true when learning about Brother Shane Price, because his story is one that has taken him all over the country, from high to low places, in his journey toward where he has arrived, now in the 21st century.

Shane Price's story starts at a real place, a real address; 1131 Lyndale Avenue North in Minneapolis. Minnesota, in 1954. Here lived Jean and Eula DuBois: Jean a Pullman Porter for the railroad, Eula or Ma Dearie as Shane called her, a cleaning woman, homeowner, and inveterate gambler. These were Shane's grandparents who raised him up from an infant. Shane's mother dropped in occasionally but was involved in the street life much of his early days. She named him though, after seeing the western movie *Shane,* starring Alan Ladd. In African culture, Shane says, names were said to reveal God's destiny for the child passed down through the mother's bones. This name, based on a character who was a gunslinger and a slickster trying to change his life, turned out to be prophetic.

Shane had some sense of his father, Louis Robinson, a hustler who ran nightclubs on the Chitlun Circuit on Olson Memorial Highway and provided Black entertainment and restaurants for Black audiences. These clubs also were there to bring music to European Americans who wanted to come to them to appreciate jazz.

Yet Shane will say unequivocally that it was Eula and Jean who taught him what it meant to be a Black man in this country. In their house he witnessed many "wanton acts of kindness." Those who needed a meal, or just wanted a safe place and good conversation, showed up in Ma Dearie's dining room on Sunday afternoons after church for one of Eula's fine soulful meals. During the week, Jean DuBois gave Shane one of those gifts we rarely acknowledge: patient time. Jean was never in too much of a hurry to stop or explain or demonstrate to Shane how to live his life. Shane watched him shave, dress for work and, in the evening, dress for going out. He got to know the intimate details of manliness: the smell of shaving cream, the sound of the shower running, the sight of Jean DuBois' strong arms in the mirror as he wearily removed his porter uniform and the smooth texture of his skin as Shane touched his grandfather's face. Shane learned what it meant to do "man things" just by being in the presence of his grandfather who was never in the "same hurry as you are" but could stop and simply "be" with his grandson. Shane will tell you that this patient pace was hardwired into his brain and stands him in good stead in his community work today.

During this time he was never hungry, had the latest toys, and rode around in Jean's hard earned Cadillac when the elder was off work. Shane was raised by Jean to believe in the value of hard work, the benefits of a strong labor union, and the importance of sharing what one learned and earned with others in the African American community. Jean brought home what he learned along the Soo Line Railroad where the Pullman Porters talked about issues in the larger world. He shared this information with those who lived in North Minneapolis and who came to Ma Dearie's breakfasts. Jean also provided a role model for Shane, of a Black man who worked hard, treated his wife like royalty, and who worked side by side with her to make a fine home.

He was also a stylish man. Shane says to this day that his love of hats came from watching his grandfather dress, his hat seeming to say: "Treat Me Like a Man." He combined strength and compassion, with an ability to love and care for those in his community including Shane, his mother, and his wife.

Some days Jean and Shane went to the pool hall together. Jean was a fine shooter of pool and passed along this skill to his grandson. Here in the male bastion of the hall, Shane got to be where Black men gathered, talked together, laughed often, and told stories. Whenever he could, Jean also took Eula and Shane on train trips, making sure he ate with great ceremony in the dining car. Shane considered this early childhood exposure to elegance a sheltered existence: living in a big mansion-like house on Lyndale Avenue with so many rooms and traveling on trains in style. Eula let out rooms on the top floor of their home to make a little money.

As he grew, this existence became more tenuous. Jean DuBois was seriously injured on a train and his grandmother had to work more often and more intentionally. They had to move out of the house when Shane was 8 years old, and knowing what we know about the importance of consistency of place—in a child's early life—this was a major upheaval in Shane's existence. One consistent fact remained, however, from the time Shane spent with Jean for the first years of his life: Even though things got bad and Black removal was at its height, even though their income dropped precipitously, Jean DuBois never resorted to drinking or abusing his family.

Even though Shane would go through a time when he strayed from Jean's value system, he never forgot or lost the importance of being kind, something his grandfather imparted to him. Jean also taught Shane how to be a bridge for his people, to each other, and even to the White community. All this Shane kept with him, no matter how he might part from Jean's ways in his later years.

As he explored further and further from home, Shane found important friends and mentors in other places. He can name them, even now: Sylvester Davis, Mahmoud El Kati, and Spike Moss. In 1967, Syl Davis, then the executive director of The Way Community Center Unlimited, Inc., gave him a safe place to experiment with his identity as an athlete, as a young man, and as an African American in the city. At The Way, Shane along with his best friends Malcolm Smith, Michael Reese, and Steve Burston played sports, fought, talked, and "loved on each other." It was here, at 10 to 14 years of age, where Shane learned to speak of the events of his life quickly and concisely. He was able, in 15 minutes, to fill his brothers in on all that was happening to him, day by day, week by week. He got to tell his story. The Way, with its presence of old and young African American men, was key to Shane's early identity, an identity that would eventually survive a decade of tough years and misdirected experiences. It was at The Way, as well as with his grandmother and grandfather, that Shane received an intergenerational learning that was so important in building the foundation for his hard values that would serve him later.

About Mahmoud El Kati Shane tells this story:

I thought of myself as "Negro American" until Professor Milton Williams of the University of Minnesota (now El Kati, of Macalaster College) came along. El Kati asked me if I believed that there were German Americans, or French Americans. I responded that yes, of course, there were those who came from France and Germany to settle in the United States. Next El Kati asked me to point on a map to the countries from which these men and women had emigrated. I went up to the world map in the classroom at The Way and pointed to France and Germany. Then El Kati looked at me and said, "Now, go to the map and point to Negroland." When I could not do this, El Kati spoke to me of Africa, a whole continent, and then of its separate and rich collection of countries and cultures where I had my place of natural origin. Before this I had no desire to be connected with Africa, a country the European American media depicted as full of men and women partially clothed, or dancing in strange costumes, or as cowering, frightened and submissive in Tarzan movies. Even National Geographic, the Bible of what was going on in the world at that time, did not picture Africa in a realistic or flattering light. I had internalized all these negative images of Africa. After studying with El Kati however, I gained a respect not only for the important parts of my own culture that came from Africa, but a respect for what had been lost when Africans were kidnapped and brought to the shores of the Americas, the great damage done. In an instant my mind and heart changed with respect to Africa.

In Spike Moss, an African American activist who still works sometimes hand-in-hand with Shane on the Streets of Minneapolis and in the African American Men project, Shane saw someone who was a straight shooter who worked and loved his community. He witnessed a man who walked the talk, stayed true, remained disciplined and guided his life in the right direction, no matter the hardships and setbacks that inevitably arose.

This was the 1960s, early 1970s. In a melodious aside Shane will stop the story of his life and reflect an old Beatles phrase, snatches of that time gone by:

All we are saying, is give peace a chance,

He will tell you that the work he witnessed in these years was "more connected with heartspace." The work around Peace, done by Blacks along with those Whites who "got it" was work of universal love and connectedness. For awhile, in those days, Shane Price felt hope.

During this time he found himself clashing with Jean over what he wanted to call himself (African American) and over his increasing militancy. However, there was never any question that these two, the boy and his grandfather from such different generations, loved each other despite the hot arguments, the disagreements over activism and hard work. "Boy, you gonna miss me when I'm gone" was Jean's refrain through the last years of his life and Shane, in his heart, knew this to be true.

The combination of Jean's hard work ethic, his kind and open heart, and the more radical leaders of the Black power movement, influenced by W. E. B. DuBois, contributed to the complex background of Shane Price. His grandfather believed, ultimately, that hard work, in the manner of Booker T. Washington, was what would save African American people. Shane believed this, and also believed that it was time to become activist in demanding a change in the laws and institutions that had kept African Americans out of the mainstream of education and work for its entire history. As early as middle school he organized fellow students to demand Black history classes in his junior high.

Finally, with the death of Jean and the change in the political scene, despair set in for Shane Price. And so, despite the advice and nurturing from Black men, from his grandfather and the community leaders, Shane began to drift from their influence. Many things coalesced to pull him away. By 1969, when Jean died, many of Shane's national idols, and the idols of many others had been shot down: John Kennedy, Martin Luther King, Malcom X, Medgar Evers, Robert Kennedy, Freddie Hampton, and more. Like all of us, he witnessed these events on television. He also witnessed not only Blacks, but even White young people protesting the Vietnam War, gunned down at Kent State, a scene no African American believed would ever take place.

He, like many others then and today, looked for role models on TV and the big screen and found athletes. For a while he dreamed of playing basketball and baseball, as did many young Black men in the 1970s. However, he was physically small during his early adolescent years and his friends outgrew him. Although he was coordinated and fast, because of his height he was not played. He sat on the bench; this killed his desire to go on with athletics. Without sports, which he saw as one of the most viable ways to become prominent, and without *hope in change* as he watched so many important leaders die, Shane was drawn to the street life.

He had a brief respite from the temptation of the streets and disillusionment from the destruction of his heroes, in the ninth grade. Shane's mother, who had by then, turned her own life around, helped Shane take advantage of an opportunity to attend a school in New England called Sterling Academy. His own quick intelligence and personality helped him gain admittance to the ABC (A Better Chance) program, a program that placed young men and women from tough neighborhoods into excellent schools in towns and rural areas all over the country. With a scholarship and with money from savings bonds his mother cashed in, he was able to attend this exclusive Ivy League institution. His mother sensed that getting him away from the streets might be the only way to keep him on an educational track.

At first Shane failed miserably in academics. However, because he was a competitive young man, nurtured in this competition by his friends and mentors in the community centers and playgrounds of his community, Shane was ready to fight and to win. He also had Jean's work ethic and belief that Black men could make it if they just worked hard enough. Thus, as he spent months in the idyllic campus of green and gardens that was Sterling, he figured out certain things he had to do to succeed in this new environment. These included: the necessity to go to class, a respect for his own intuitive intelligence, the necessity to seek help with assignments, and the importance of etiquette. These are some of the behaviors Shane tries to instill in young men today as part of his work in the African American Men Project. Thus he is passing along what he learned from Jean as well as others later in his life.

By the time he left Sterling Academy, a year and a half later, he had made the honor roll, completed a solo survival experience in the wilderness as part of an Outward Bound Program, and had developed what he describes as a "can do" attitude. He had also experienced the ways of the White Power structure, the culture of White males who came from and would most surely be, in positions of great authority in his future.

Shane learned something even more personal when he was in this ivy covered New England space far from the streets of the North side of Minneapolis: he became aware of his own strength and charisma. White kids wanted to hang around him and emulate him. Ironically, in this distance from home and community, he became acutely aware of the fact that Black culture has great power in its innate rhythmic beauty, style, and spirituality.

Upon returning to Minneapolis he resumed studies at North High school and, while he admits he had good teachers and eventually graduated with his class, he also resumed his infatuation with the street life. Crucial to this time in his life was one single movie that was so compelling and so brilliant in its imagery and attraction, it changed how some African American men saw themselves—especially young, high school-age Blacks desperately looking for self definition. *Superfly* was a movie that portrayed dope pushing and prostitution as a job opportunity while defiling and defaming women as a way of being macho and important.

As Shane puts it:

> African American women went from being black and beautiful to bitches, hos and dope fiends almost overnight. The model for black success went from brothers working together to brothers competing, hustling, shooting and killing each other. An ethos of hate combined with an emphasis on the present moment, pushed those of us who were influenced by this movie and others like it, to suppress our earlier belief systems. We began to deny the values that nurtured us and began living solely in the NOW.

In this way, he strayed from his grandfather's teaching, denying the goodness Jean had encouraged. Much of Shane's next years would be spent in inner conflict, living the life of drugs, while knowing all along the strong values of work, compassion, and consideration he learned in his earliest years.

Many of these young men were raised and encouraged by "old heads" to know the right way to live. Yet, because adolescence can be a time of extremes, a time of living impulsively, a time to defy and test parental and elder guidance, many young Black men experimented with rebellion by mimicking Black men in *Superfly* and other movies that imitated it.

We know now that there is no more powerful influence than the peer group for young men and women who are between the ages of 16 and 20. As Professor Joseph White describes it, in his book *Black Man Emerging*, "The peer group acts as a stage on which the adolescent can present or project himself" (p. 214). While he was still influenced by his mother, grandmother, his grandfather's memory, and other men who came along sporadically in his life, Shane too became caught up in a street life identity. He is what Dr. Joseph White describes as one of the "bright, sensitive young men who turn into aggressive macho types who engage in predatory sex and [sometimes] violence" (p. 221).

Yet even in this life, he made important connections that would have an impact on his life when he emerged from his time on the streets. One woman, whom he robbed, felt great compassion for Shane even as he was being charged in front of her.

"She looked at me as a mother looks, seeing her own son," Shane says.

This look broke through the tough image he was projecting and he felt ashamed. There was evidence linking him to the robbery and he was convicted. Shane served 2 years in St. Cloud Reformatory. During this time he wrote to the woman and her husband whom he had robbed. They not only forgave Shane, they also ended up sending him money without his asking and kept in touch with him as he went on his way after leaving prison. Recently, Shane spoke at this gentleman's funeral at the request of his wife. Shane still speaks of this couple as loving and forgiving people who exerted an important influence over his own life, demonstrating to him, in a visceral way, the kindness and connection that can be had between and among different people working together in a spirit of hope and change.

Yet Shane went back out onto the streets. He will tell you that, in a sense, he went to sleep to the cultural values he had learned, in 1972 and woke 14 years later. During those 14 years he became a player, big time. He separated from his community, home, and church. He got involved in seeking material objects and built his life as an *individual* instead of living a *collective and cooperative* life as African Americans and Native Americans had taught him. *Things* became his life. He became the antihero, stopped believing in the WE, but focused in the ME. He went from being a person who reflected proud Black Nationalism, from love for Black people and all people, to being driven by looks and appearances. He suppressed much of what he learned from Jean and this is what caused such inner conflict in him all this time.

He will say at this time the pain of living such a self-destructive, valueless life was so great that he had to numb his senses to keep going. He self-medicated with cocaine, alcohol, and at times heroin. Because he had grown up knowing a righteous way to live, as taught to him in his earliest years by Jean DuBois, and other role models from The Way, he kept himself high in order to continue to do what he was doing out in the world, knowing the whole time it was against his earliest teachings, against the way he was raised up by his grandfather.

During this time Shane Price learned much of what he would need to know about the lure of this life for young Black men today and about the structures and substructures that contribute to it. He worked against his own community with no thought for his kinsmen. He describes it as being in the "I place." He was using his "street muscle," able to live a hustler's life to perfection with fine clothes, fine car, and a big house.

During this time he had sent his youngest daughter, LaShayne, on home to Minneapolis to be raised by his grandmother Ma Dearie.

In 1985, Ma Dearie called Shane home: in more ways than one. Shane's brother Floyd told him he thought Ma Dearie was going to die and wanted Shane with her. There were very few people at that time in his life who could have reached down into Shane's soul at this time and drawn him out of his preoccupations. Ma Dearie was one of them. So he returned from Alaska where he had been living, helped his grandmother get up on her feet for a while longer, and remained in his home, a cold city on the prairie. He can say now that although he defamed the Northside of Minneapolis, he longed for it. His grandparents had raised him in great compassion and kindness to fight for righteousness and freedom and he had kept that in his heart all the years he lived the high life around the country.

He came home to LaShayne and began to take responsibility for her life, providing for her a nurturing environment. He did this with the help of a woman, 11 years older than himself, named Judy Baker. She became a very important force for good in Shane's life over the next years.

In 1986 Shane's life changed, again, literally overnight. The story of this change is central to his current success as a mentor and community activist. He will tell you now: "I am a righteous man," and in the next breath, he will say, his hazel eyes flashing, "And I have to work at that all the time." In the spring of 1986, he was taking his 2-year-old daughter to a face-painting party at the Phyllis Wheatley Community Center in North Minneapolis. As they walked along, in the new warmth of Minnesota spring streets, he heard a young Latino Evangelist ask "Is there anybody who wants to be free of drugs or alcohol here?" This man had formed a circle of people around him and Shane stepped into it, raising his hand. He will tell you now that his hand was raised in anger and even cynicism. It was a challenge to this Religious preacher; "Prove it to me! Get me rid of drugs and alcohol, go on now and do it!"

The man prayed over him as he stood in the circle holding his daughter's hand. Awhile later, after wandering from booth to booth, buying his daughter ice cream and helping her with the games she wanted to try, Shane took her home and lit up his crack pipe. Yet he could not smoke it. A man came by who owed him money. This man wanted to give Shane payment in drugs. Shane tried to get high again with this man, but could not. A few hours later, for the first time in years, he simply went to sleep without any dope or alcohol.

He will also tell you this about the next morning: "When I woke up, I heard a bird singing. Clear. Like I had never really heard before. I went to the window and could not see it, yet I heard it singing clear."

For weeks after this, his old crew kept coming around, calling and wanting to get high, go in pursuit of some dope. But now, Shane put them off. He had no desire to do any drugs or alcohol any longer. He simply stopped.

It has been 16 years. Now, Shane says: "The Spirit of God came, and so I went to the Bible." When he went to his studies, and to the Bible, he stopped living in the NOW and instead focused his efforts toward the future for those around him, for those beyond him. With the help of Judy Baker he learned how to nurture and raise a child, how to look at his life and organize his years toward becoming a leader. He gives Ms. Baker much credit and true affection for supporting him during the crucial 10 years after his conversion. He likens it to Paul's conversion story in the Bible, Shane says: "As Saul became Paul, Shane became Brother Shane. My whole body took on that name." With the help of others, and in those long Minnesota winter nights studying while the wind blew with its arctic chill at his window, Brother Shane was developing his "Faith Muscle."

He came home not only to the Church, but also to those who had kept on fighting for justice all the while he had disappeared. Mahmoud El Kati and Spike Moss were still working in the city, and his old friends from The Way were still nearby. Even more important, the spirit of his Grandfather, the love of his Grandmother, continued to be present along with this new faith muscle to raise him up and keep him there. He was no longer in conflict with Jean's views and felt his influence in his life every day without fighting it.

And as, in some of the deepest ways, our children raise us, LaShayne provided her father with the purpose he needed to help him reshape his own life. Over these years Judy Baker saw who he was, and whom he was becoming. So, she, along with LaShayne, provided high expectations for Brother Shane by being with him, day by day. Every Sunday he met with Judy and her family, went to church each day, and, with time began to remake his identity as an African American male. And now, as he works with young Black fathers, Shane talks about the importance of being physically present in their children's lives, about the importance of family for African Americans, and about putting family and community above self in their lives. In this way he urges Black men to think about the future, about their children's future, instead of focusing solely on momentary pleasures.

One of the most important events that provided stability and even hope to Brother Shane came when he was able, through working two jobs in the mainstream job market, to buy a large duplex. Now he could move his grandmother in downstairs, and he and LaShayne could be upstairs. He had come full circle, from the large home he was raised in by his grandmother on Lyndale Avenue, to a home where he provided for this same grandmother, now on Bryant Avenue North. The spirit of that elegant Pullman Porter, Jean DuBois, was now accompanying Shane in his every day hard working life.

It was also, as a result of owning this house, that Brother Shane brought his organizing skills back into play. This new place was right in the middle of what was called "hooker's row." Each day, Shane would watch the kids go to school. However, he could not help but see that these children were afraid to stand at the assigned bus stop because of the men who pulled up near them, the women who walked by them, and the drug transactions going on right there in front of them in early morning and later afternoon daylight. With help from his old connections in the activist community, and with the organizing skills and daring of Spike Moss, Shane and the rest of the Northside Hawthorn and Jordan communities, took back eight blocks. By video taping license plates of the "Johns" who were using the prostitutes, and sending letters to the owners of the cars bearing these plates, they often reached the wives of these men. It turned out that women were often the owners of the cars and they were the ones to whom the letters were addressed. It became too uncomfortable for men to frequent the block on Bryant Avenue, so the drug and prostitution traffic ceased. Eventually the kids could go and return from school in safety. He cites this action and its success as an example of what his early activism and work with Black men in his teen years helped him to accomplish much later in his life. He also uses this as an example of what Black men can do for their families and for their neighborhoods. Again he was returning to grandfather Jean's concern for community and neighborhood, a generosity of spirit that Shane had inherited from his earliest years.

It is not lost on Brother Shane, or on this author, that his experience in the prostitution trade combined with his activism made Shane Price the perfect person to take on this situation, but now from the other side of the block, so to speak. Time and again, Brother Shane's past intersects with his present to make him the street smart, compassionate, warm, charismatic, and devoted leader his community needs.

At the same time, Shane has also gone through many of the hoops mainstream White culture demands to get to where he is today. He says that his new "faith muscle" prepared him to look forward. It gave him a sense of the future as a distinct reality. He went to college, where he learned the clinical model for treating those in trouble with drugs and alcohol. He is a licensed addiction counselor. He believes that his spiritual training has prepared him to speak the message of hope and change in his work with addicts, and that if this does not succeed entirely, he can combine this spiritual guidance with all that he learned of the clinical model in his higher education training. He has graduated as a new minister from the Didasco Institute in Robbinsdale and is continuing his theological studies at Northwestern Bible College.

Over these years Shane has developed a working relationship with many in the political and governmental mainstream, including the late Senator Paul Wellstone and his wife Sheila. His belief in taking what mainstream America has to offer, working with those Whites who want to bridge the divide between cultures in this country, are what allow him to continue to work in corporate America as well as in community centers to accomplish change for African American men. He counsels those who come to him and in his organization to do just that, to maintain necessary contacts in White America, while not giving up their identity as Black men.

Yet to be with Brother Shane is not to be with a man who wants to talk about paper accomplishments, degrees granted, certificates earned. It is to be with a man who wants to talk about redemption, faith, and hope. He has let go of any bitterness in order to be in the place he is today: an inspiration for many African American and White men and women who want to go well in this world.

Brother Shane has reconnected with his five children over these years. Shaunetta, born when he was 16 years old, is now 31. He has assisted her in getting a job and has supported and counseled her through tough times. Brother Shane is very clear that his home is his children's home. He can be reached any time and he will help financially when he can. He has earned the respect and trust from his older daughters he needed to earn because he was not with them during their growing up. Now they know it is all right to trust him and to care for him. He is in touch with these young women and they believe that they can come to him anytime they may need to, or want to.

He realizes there is resentment because, except for LaShayne, his presence was not always a part of their early years. Yet raising up LaShayne, seeing the hard work such parenting entails, has galvanized Brother Shane to do what he can to make up for his absence in his older children's lives. He understands that healing is a process and that it will take time for these things to be worked out. And now he has time, all the time in the world. The tribe, the clan, the community, the family are where his heart is now. He has lived a life with a focus on his own personal needs. He knows its seductions. Now he has come home truly, to be an integral part of his children's lives. Thus he advises young men to reconnect with their children, make space and time for them, no matter how long it has been. He reminds them of the obligations of fatherhood.

One of those children, his son, is a source of real pain for Brother Shane. When Shane came back into his life, Akwanza was in deep trouble. He had witnessed the murder of his own mother when he was 6 years old, a mother who had shrouded him in her love. Akwanza did not have a strong Black man in his life as Shane did in his grandfather. Brother Shane will tell you now that a young Black child needs a man to set parameters and standards of behavior, to stand up and say no or yes with love and conviction. Akwanza had lived without Shane most of his growing up. On April 23rd, 2000, Shane's son was arrested in the shooting of a Liberian shop owner in Minneapolis. At one point in a healing circle, the mother of the dead man absolved Brother Shane from guilt for his son's crime. Yet he found the pain he saw in her eyes almost unbearable.

Out of this time he learned about what he calls true intuitive communication. He learned that you are not completely defined by the things you say, but by a deeper form of communication and knowledge etched in your psyche and in your bones: called your *emotional* IQ. The intelligence of our hearts is real and it communicates through sound and vibration, much quicker than oratory. Brother Shane survived this difficult time because he sensed this mother's forgiveness, not through her words but through her wordlessness, her pain, and her sound.

Brother Shane still struggles with his son. Akwanza went with a plea bargain. In prison he is developing artistic skills, legal abilities, and even cooking talents.

Seeing what his own son lacked because he did not have the consistent presence of a father, and the consequences it has brought on him, has made Brother Shane a strong advocate and leader for young Black men and the importance of their role as fathers through the African American Men project. Shane goes into churches, barbershops, schools, prisons, and community centers to find young men, to connect them up with mentors, or to mentor them himself. He speaks with them about making sure they do not let anyone come in the way of their dreams. He counsels them frankly, emphasizes the importance of men and women coming together as whole human beings, each 100% their own person. He urges them to go beyond concern for only themselves, but to take into their lives a real activism with their families, their community, and their spirituality.

Shane now counsels young Black men how to take an active role with their sons and daughters. He talks about his own grandfather and even his father whom he came to know as he grew older, and their influence on his life. They were African American men who worked every day, bought houses and left their wives and children with a small insurance and legacy. Shane explains to them how the image of the smart Black man has changed over the years to one generated by media today: the cool streetwise Black man is the one into drugs, jewelry, and hustling. He talks to the men he mentors, to the students he meets with, to the groups he leads, about the importance of countering such images and providing *real* role models for their own children: the model of the working man he received from Jean, the mentor and model he found in Mahmoud El Kati. He emphasizes the need for older men to fill in the gap for young men who have no active fathers in their lives. He stresses the importance of encouraging young Black men to provide for their children, not only in monetary terms but in their constant presence every day. It is when children see their fathers day and night, on weekends and in school conferences, church services, that the values of work, and commitment, consistency, and caring become imprinted on young people's brains and hearts. He knows this is a crucial time for African American families and works to support men in their desire to become active fathers in their children's lives through his mentoring programs, his own example now with his new family, and his day-to-day discussions with men about what it means to be a good father and husband.

Now, in Minneapolis, a mother might say to her co-workers, "my son is going to do alright, he is working with Brother Shane." And her co-workers will smile. Brother Shane works with each young man and each mentor whom he trains to make sure they understand the importance of finding a place in the world of work, in the family, and in the wider community. What he is doing in the project and in all his work is trying to instill responsibility in each young man who comes before him: responsibility for earning a livelihood, not only for himself but for those around him. He emphasizes the importance of being in their children's lives as a nurturing adult, as a leader. He urges them to be for their families and communities what Jean was for him.

What does Shane draw on to go on? The answer is in the Black churchs' spirituality. He also finds it inside himself and, too, in the faces of the children. Brother Shane feel strength in a reconnection with the joys and pains of his African American community. His relationship with "old heads"— men from days gone by who are still a part of his support and trust group: Mahmoud El Kati, Spike Moss, and Dr. Joseph White, (one of the editors of this book who has mentored Shane these last years)—sustains him. Brother Shane draws on memories and experiences of the love of his grandfather and grandmother, even though they are no longer present in this world. He draws on "peace which passes all understanding" from his faith and the profound lyrical expressiveness of his friends in the Native and African American communities.

The story in the Bible of the Wayward son, the phrases from scripture that echo for Brother Shane: "Teach him young in the ways of God, so when he is older he shall not depart from You"—these are what keep him stable in a troubled world. Brother Shane does not give up his identity to make change and progress. This in itself provides an important model to young men who are searching for a way to be identified as African American and yet who want to participate in a broader world. He makes it clear when counseling young men that you can work in the mainstream without surrendering your own culture. You can embrace White folks who are also working for a just community, and can work with them without having to sacrifice your deepest sense of your African American manhood.

And Brother Shane also counsels the importance of reconciliation. As an example of this he has come to know his own mother. He understands that this woman who left him in his early years did the right and just thing for him and his growing up. She knew the gifts his grandparents would give him and he appreciates her today for her decision to place him in Eula and Jean's loving home. Eventually Cherie Price Lovelace went to college and became a Diversity specialist in corporate America. She worked for Control Data, traveling the country in the service of the hearing impaired. Now they communicate frequently and Shane appreciates the network she is able to help him negotiate in the corporate world. She, in turn, relishes their dialogue.

LaShayne recently called her father to tell him she voted for the first time at age 18 in the senatorial election. This was an important moment for both of them. He had raised up a young woman who was not afraid, was not too cynical, was not without hope, to claim her rightful place in the city and state and country. He had raised up a strong African American woman who participates in the system without giving up her identity.

Brother Shane devotes much of his life to helping young men believe they can achieve what his daughter has achieved: a stance of hope, a willingness to struggle, and a belief in the power of the African American Community in her life.

This story, the one that forms the portrait of this leader and organizer of the African American Men project, is a story of resilience. It is, as professor White describes, "more than stoicism or a return to the status quo; it involves going beyond healing and recovery. The goal in moving successfully through tragedy is to become stronger in the broken places, to keep moving toward revitalization and psychological renewal" (White & Cones, 1999, p. 49).

Walk down any street on the Northside of Minneapolis, and watch the young people heading home from school. Stop. Listen to them call out, "Hello Brother Shane!" Or "There is Brother Shane. Hello there, Brother." What Shane Price has done is to take the elements that made up his unique story and used them in the service of young people in their community. He has the admiration for hard work and the compassionate heart he experienced living with his grandfather, Jean DuBois. He has the respect for his African roots he learned from Professor Mahmoud El Kati, the knowledge of the often impersonal system of power he learned at the exclusive Sterling School, the understanding of the lure of the life of possessions, drugs, and sex he learned from living on the streets. He comes with an experience of working with and contemplation of White folks who "get it" and who are involved with social justice. Combined with these experiences is the spirituality and support he receives from his religion.

Over the last 14 years, Shane's resumé reflects his gifts. As part of the Department of Children and Family Services he helped create a community-based social service site known as "Village" Social Services. He is also the director and cofounder of the Social Justice and Cultural Wellness Center, providing leadership on proactive, community-based, socially responsive activism for neighborhood change. Brother Shane conducts peacemaking circle trainings in Minneapolis and around the country, provides educational presentations on topics of racism and White privilege, and often speaks to young people at the middle, high school and college levels. Shane trained in the Canadian Yukon as a circle keeper. He is a qualified neutral registered with the Minnesota State Supreme Court, a trained mediator and has mediated conflict resolution on university campuses, in marriage disillusionment and in severe instances of grief and loss. He is directly responsible for sharing the gift of circle through trainings with countless individuals in the Twin Cities area and around the country. In the cadences with which he speaks and the passion for justice and forgiveness he expresses, it is clear to those who listen to him that his position as guest minister and motivational speaker come from a deep commitment to do good in a difficult world.

When he brings his story and his message to young men and women in our high schools and middle schools, he speaks eloquently of the journey he has taken from drug dealing to leadership. When he finishes speaking, before the hands shoot up with questions, there is a respectful silence, the kind of silence one finds in churches and ceremonies. This is a pause in the mind—an entrance into a psychological state that can bring about powerful reflection before the chatter and busyness of the world resumes and intrudes again.

He centers much of his work with young people, with all people on two questions:

What do you believe? and What are you going to do about it? He insists that we look inside ourselves and our communities to find the answers. To do this we have to separate our internal reality from the external existence often defined by *systems*, government, education, European history, and media images.

Shane's work with young people, especially young Black men, involves inviting them to look at the way the system shapes them: the way television is relentless in its parade of things they do *not* have, in the way African Americans are perceived, in the false impressions it gives of what is important in the world and who values it. He mentors youngsters by a combination of preaching, reasoning, mediating, and reconciliation. He admits that, like many White folks, many African Americans see success as defined by possessions. Shane tries to bring to young people a way of seeing the world his grandfather taught him, to value family, children, work, education as well as material possessions.

"Life exists in between the beats for African Americans," he says. "Europeans control the beat and African Americans live in between, with their passion, their concept of self, their knowledge of *the circle*."

Brother Shane points out that theirs is a people who have survived pain, death, threats, and oppression. Today, young Black men feel unconsciously encouraged to mimic their oppressors in the demand for more stuff, in the belief that there is never enough. Shane asks these young people to rethink their quest for possessions at any cost. African Americans have often closed ranks to protect each other in tough times. "Now, is one of those times," Shane says. He tells them that this is not a time for separation and competition with each other, but is rather a time for unity and for understanding the power of love.

For African Americans it will come down to: how deeply are you socialized? How much to do you buy the vision of success as defined by TV radio and the Internet? Brother Shane Price aims to create a system by which African Americans can get what they want and need without having to be co-opted. It is clear, through statistics and predictions, that soon European Americans will be a minority in this country. Brother Shane believes that White people who "get it" understand this, and are already working, side by side with Blacks and Latinos, Asian and Native Americans, for the common good.

Brother Shane will tell you that out of oppression came, among many things, the Blues, Jazz, theater, lyricism, brilliance, and an uncanny ability to feel the pain of others. He aims to take such strengths and bring them into congruence with opportunity for all African Americans. He means to do no less than to combine the blues and strong fathers, jazz and great providers, hip hop and Black male protectors. His hope is to transcend culture in some ways and to integrate it in others. In his work as head of the African American Men Project, he aims to find and nurture the power of the elders, the men from the community, who will participate, help, execute, be gentle, work, share, enrich mentor serve, grow, and lead.

As Brother Shane defines him, the enlightened Black male can see the box that surrounds his life, the external rules and regulations set up to define life as a Black man. Black men are going to have to see beyond such a box, deeper into themselves, connecting the communal joy and music, dance and African American brotherhood and fatherhood with the spirit of a unified circle that embodies everybody.

When I asked Shane where he gets his hope, he told me the story of his life. By sharing this story with me and with others, by being honest about his past, his desires, and his constant need for guidance, he demonstrates to African American men who call out to him, "Brother Shane!" that no matter what your age or history, your past misdeeds or your present status, you can re emerge on a path of value to your community, your family and growth in your own spiritual health. By encouraging those in the neighborhoods and city streets in this way, Shane is also following in the path of his hardworking grandfather, a man with a generous heart and great compassion for all those around him.

To be with Shane is to become part of his circle and his history, and while there, to find the hope he has in the resiliency of his beloved community.

REFERENCES

White, J. L., & Cones, J. H., III. (1999). *Black man emerging: Facing the past and seizing a future in America.* New York: W. H. Freeman.

Chapter 13

A Visible Future: The African American Men Project and the Restoration of Community

Gary L. Cunningham
Northpoint Health and Wellness Center
Minneapolis African American Men Project
Minneapolis, Minnesota

> *I'm not blaming anyone for this state of affairs, mind you; nor merely crying* mea culpa. *The fact is that you carry part of your sickness within you, at least I do as an invisible man. I carried my sickness and though for a long time I tried to place it in the outside world, the attempt to write it down shows me that at least half of it lay within me.*
>
> —Ralph Ellison, *Invisible Man* (1952)

THE YOUNG BLACK MEN ON THE CORNER

Everyone sees them. They are a part of virtually every large and midsize urban community in America. Yet, as Ralph Ellison so eloquently wrote two generations ago in *Invisible Man*, "I am invisible, understand, simply because people refuse to see me." Today, throughout the United States, many people refuse to see the young African American men who hang out on street corners; most of us are busy working, running errands, doing chores, and raising families.

Young African American men have been largely overlooked in public policy discussions, as well as in most efforts to strengthen low-income Black families. They tend to become visible only in discussions of urban pathology—that is, in terms of incarceration, school failure, dropout rates, unemployment, absent fatherhood, drug dealing, community violence, and a host of illnesses often leading to disability or early death.

North Minneapolis, where many of Minnesota's poorest African Americans live, has been no exception. In 1999, as newly elected Hennepin County Commissioner Mark Stenglein drove around his district trying to determine how he could best represent it, a simple question kept bothering him: "Why are all these young African American men standing around on street corners during the day?" It made no sense to him that in a county suffering a structural labor shortage—where the unemployment rate was between 2% and 3% and businesses were crying out for trainable employees—so many young men should be living outside the economic mainstream. Meanwhile, the majority of inmates in the Hennepin County jail were young African American men; the county's emergency homeless shelters were full of young African American women, trying to raise children who received little or no financial support from their fathers, and only 23% of young Black men in Minneapolis were graduating high school in 4 years.[1]

While Commissioner Stenglein was pondering this question I was starting my new job as Hennepin County's new Director of Planning and Development (OPD). As the person in charge of policy research for one of America's largest and most prosperous counties, I was entrusted with providing Mark Stenglein and the other commissioners with objective research, policy analysis, and recommendations for policy solutions. Soon after I arrived at OPD, Stenglein and I met and he asked me why I thought so many young Black men were populating street corners instead of earning money and raising families.

My initial internal response was *why does this White commissioner care about these young Black men? Is his question a backhanded attempt to reinforce the old stereotypes and suppositions?*[2] As we initially discussed his question, tension filled the room—as it often does in discussions about race in America.[3]

Quickly, however, I found our conversation to be fundamentally different; the tension we originally felt seemed to dissipate. We both agreed to suspend our assumptions and viewpoints and recognize that we didn't know the answer. We also agreed we really didn't know much about who these men were, how engaged or disengaged they were with their families

---

[1]Source: Minnesota Department of Children, Families and Learning, 2000. Also see: African American Men Project, Crossroads: Choosing a New Direction, Research Compendium, 2002a: *The Education of African American Boys, Kindergarten through grade 12*, p. 125.

[2]In fact, at the time I first met with Commissioner Stenglein, I had just finished reading Michael Levin's very disturbing book, *Why Race Matters: Race Differences and What They Mean* (Praeger, 1997), which attempts to demonstrate, largely through statistical analysis, that Blacks are genetically inferior to Whites.

[3]In *A Dream Deferred* (HarperCollins, 1998), Shelby Steele describes this tension as one in which Whites declare their innocence and attempt to assuage their guilt for centuries of slavery, segregation, and injustice, while Blacks take a position of moral indignation and self-righteousness, claiming a right to victimization. Throughout my life I have never found such sterile, self-protective conversations helpful.

and community, and even whether they were truly a problem. By the end of our talk, I had agreed to develop an outline for researching Commissioner Stenglein's question. This became the basic framework for the African American Men Project.

LAYING THE GROUNDWORK

Over the following weeks, Commissioner Stenglein and Commissioner Peter McLaughlin coauthored a county board resolution creating the African American Men Project (AAMP). The resolution was approved and my staff, the two commissioners and I, began to have discussions with community leaders. At first we were met with both reticence and mistrust. Why was the county conducting a research project to study young Black men? What was the county's ulterior motive? I vividly recall our first meeting with a group of clergy—all of them African American men—who wondered why we needed to study the issue at all. "Haven't we been studied to death?" they asked me. For some of them, and for many other Black leaders, such as Cornel West, the problem was abundantly clear. "The fundamental crisis in black America is twofold: too much poverty and too little self-love. The urgent problem of Black poverty is primarily due to the distribution of wealth, power, and income—a distribution influenced by the racial caste system that denied opportunities to most 'qualified' Black people until two decades ago."[4] For some Black leaders the answer was also clear: support public policy and other activities in service of social justice and wealth redistribution. Although this point of view has some merit, I knew from my own background in public policy research that most efforts in that direction had not borne much fruit in recent years. Indeed, the very existence of the African American Men Project was an acknowledgment that more of what had been done in the past would be insufficient.

As we spoke with the ministers and as trust grew among us, the tenor of our discussion slowly changed, accentuated by one clergyman's forceful statement: "This is not someone else's problem. This is our problem. We are the only ones who can address it. We need a new approach." Everyone in the room emphatically agreed.

Over the next few months my colleagues at OPD and I convinced some of these ministers and many other community leaders to cosponsor the AAMP. That I had worked in the community for many years helped. In addition, I, like many of the leaders themselves, had once been a fatherless young Black boy hanging out on the street, who watched his friends get into drugs, go to jail, and get killed.

---

[4]West, Cornel. *Race Matters*, Vintage, 1994, pp. 93–95.

Understandably, African American leaders responded to us at first with trepidation and caution. Initially, they would often launch into disquisitions about racism, the disenfranchisement of African Americans, and the disdain and disinterest they felt from Whites. But after some venting, almost all of them responded the same way: "How can I help?" In addition to requesting their leadership and guidance, we asked them to do what Commissioner Stenglein and I had done: to put aside their apprehension and worries and to simply look and listen for a time. The great majority agreed to do so.

NEW EYES, NEW DIRECTIONS

In 2000, the African American Men Steering Committee was formed. This group was made up of 40 community leaders—male and female, Black and White—including Sharon Sayles Belton, then mayor of Minneapolis; Samuel L. Myers, Jr., Director of the University of Minnesota's Roy Wilkins Center; John Powell, Director of the University of Minnesota's Institute on Race and Poverty; John Turnipseed, Director of Urban Venture's Center for Fathering; and three county commissioners. Herman Milligan, Jr., Assistant Vice President for Market Research at Wells Fargo and Company, served as committee chair.

In the months that followed, dozens of other community organizations, businesses, churches, and community leaders signed on as partners, researchers, and advisors. Some of the many organizations that partnered with AAMP included the city of Minneapolis, the Minneapolis Public Schools, the University of Minnesota, the Minnesota State University and College System, the Greater Twin Cities United Way, the Council on Crime and Justice, The Twin Cites Ministerial Alliance, and the Minneapolis Council of Churches.

From the beginning, the approach AAMP took was not to tell the same old stories of disparities and inequalities, but to look at the issues of race, class, and gender with new eyes. We acknowledged several things from the outset:

- Simply throwing money at the problem would not do much good.
- Until public policy and/or the prevailing social contract are modified we would continue to get the same results.
- Our social service systems have been somewhat successful in providing people with a safety net, but they have not done very well in encouraging self-determination.
- The social and economic situation of many young African American men does not stem from a single cause, but from a multitude of inter-

related ones—what researcher George Galster (updating the earlier work of Gunnar Myrdal) called a "web of mutually-reinforcing connections that serve both as causes and effects."[5]

- No single initiative, cause, or program can have the systemic impact needed to change the social and economic conditions for these men.

We understood that no singular entity can alone significantly improve the situations of young African American men. The government cannot accomplish this alone, the police and criminal justice system cannot do this alone either, and certainly, young African American men cannot do this alone. In short, this was not *someone's* problem; this was *our* problem to address as a community.

WHO WE ARE

The African American Men Project began by taking a long, honest, detailed look at young African American men in Hennepin County, and at the nonprofit and public sector organizations that seek to assist them. We also examined the forces behind poverty, crime, poor health, and isolation that surround many of these men. With qualitative and quantitative studies, focus groups, and community forums, here is some of what we discovered (which can be found in the AAMP's final report and research compendium, Crossroads: Choosing a New Direction, 2002):

- 49% of young African American men 18 to 30 years of age in Hennepin County live in one of Minneapolis's five poorest and least safe neighborhoods.
- In Hennepin County, homicide is the most common cause of death for 18- to 30-year-old African American men.
- Over 44% of the entire population of 18- to 30-year-old African American men in Hennepin County are arrested each year—a higher percentage than were arrested in South Africa at the height of Apartheid.
- Young African American men in Hennepin County are 27 times more likely to go to jail than young White men and twice as likely to die.
- Hennepin County spent almost $219 million per year in policing and criminal justice costs in relation to young African American men.
- The county spent more than $26 million per year supporting fatherless African American children in out-of-home placement programs.

---

[5]Galster, George. *The Metropolis in Black and White*, CUPR Press, 1992.

- 54% of African American children in Hennepin County are raised in single-parent households.
- In a study of 11 metropolitan areas—Atlanta, Baltimore, Cleveland, Denver, Miami, Minneapolis, Phoenix, Portland (Oregon), St. Louis, San Diego, and Seattle—the disparities between Whites and African Americans were by far the greatest in the Minneapolis metro area.
- Our systems of justice, education, social services, and health care are highly fragmented and difficult to access and use. Furthermore, these efforts are typically too disjointed and uncoordinated to be effective.

When we talked to hundreds of young African American men in focus groups we found that most had hopes and dreams—of careers, families, home ownership, and belonging to a community. Many were looking for a path to safety, security, good families, good jobs, good educations, and legacies they could leave for their children. Yet we also learned that without fundamental changes in the institutional arrangements that maintain the status quo, the county would not be able to assist many of these young men in any appreciable way.

ASKING THE RIGHT QUESTIONS; FINDING THE WINNING ARGUMENT

As we reviewed much of the prior research on African American men and on Black men and women in America, in general, it became evident that much of this research:

- Viewed young African American men as inherently dysfunctional people who need to be fixed by other, wiser folks (i.e., government bureaucrats).
- Framed the situation as a sickness to be healed; any conceptual map of the situation would thus get drawn around needs, problems, and limitations.
- Looked at young African American men in isolation, as if their lives are not organized around relationships and connections.
- Viewed the remainder of the community (in this case, Hennepin County) in isolation (i.e., ignored how other people and groups stand to benefit from the success of young African American men, as well as what they stand to lose when these men do poorly).
- Ignored the contributions that can be made by existing community groups, businesses, and faith communities.

After a year of work, a pivotal point in the process came when the Steering Committee conducted a stakeholders' mapping analysis with the help of John Bryson of the University of Minnesota's Humphrey Institute of Public Affairs.[6] The stakeholder analysis revealed that the question we had been asking—"How can we help young African American men in Hennepin County succeed?"—was the wrong one. In fact, framing the issue in this way only aided in defining young African American men as inherently deficient and flawed, and posited various programs and organizations as the vehicles through which those flaws or deficiencies might be corrected.

Asking the question in this way limits the range of possible answers, as well as the types of relationships among the parties involved. This approach only continues to make young African American men into outsiders who are too weak or marginalized to act on their own behalf. Rather than encouraging these men to build full lives, the question we had been asking focused on how their lives would be acted upon by the county.

We discovered that the question we needed to ask instead had to be built around personal and collective responsibility, proactivity, and mutual assistance. This question quickly emerged: "How can young African American men and Hennepin County help each other succeed?" This question views each party as having assets to bring to the relationship, rather than one party having needs that must be filled by the other. This question also acknowledges the need for young African American men, like all men and women, to accept the necessary and unavoidable challenges of individual and community responsibility. Furthermore, this new question no longer defined "help" as the alleviation of some deficiency or the removal of some barrier. Rather, help was positive support toward a positive end.

We had at last defined the situation appropriately, in win–win terms. We understood that what is good for young African American men is good for the county—and that this had always been the case. (For example: When the local economy thrives, the unemployment rate among this group drops dramatically.)

In particular, what is good for these young men is good for families. A father who is employed and economically stable is much more likely to get married, stay married, and provide for his children than a father who is poor or unemployed. Indeed, a large body of research has taught us that one of the most effective ways to raise the standard of living for a single-parent family is to add a working father or stepfather to it.

---

[6]For details, see Bryson, Cunningham, and Lokkesmoe, "What to Do When Stakeholders Matter: The Case of *Problem* Formation for the African American Men Project of Hennepin County, Minnesota," *Public Administration Review*, September–October 2002, Vol. 62, No. 5.

FATHERS AND SONS

Several AAMP studies, including one focus group, focused on fathering and families. Participants in this focus group corroborated what many earlier studies on families (most notably those of psychologists Ann Masten and J. Douglas Coatsworth) had already revealed: For many children, the key to success is the regular presence of a competent, caring adult who serves as a mentor.

Focus group participants whose fathers played a strong role in their lives said that they wanted to emulate their fathers in raising their own children. Those who had grown up with absent fathers grieved their losses and expressed a yearning to be different. As one man explained, "I don't want to miss all that with my son."

Yet, 58% of all African American children in Minneapolis are raised by single mothers.[7] Many young African American men grow up without a father, a father figure, good male role models, or an intact family.

The young men in our focus groups were often fathers themselves, though many were unconnected to their own children. Nevertheless, many focus group participants believed that fathers, mentors, and role models are important to young African American men and that they desired such figures in their own lives and wanted to be good fathers to their own children. However, most of these men had no clear idea how to achieve their goals or get what they needed to be good parents.

After looking at young African American men in numerous ways, we kept coming back to the same simple insight: A young African American man (like any young person) needs a father or father figure who loves and cares for him. And this in turn, naturally benefits the father or father figure. Our research continued to show that a young African American man will have worse outcomes in his life, socially and economically, without a strong, present, caring father or father figure.

GROWING UP UNCONVENTIONAL BUT HEALTHY

My own childhood closely fit the pattern of many African American boys. I had no visible father, no stable home, and no strong male role models I was close to. By the time I turned 13, I was on track to spend most of my life in jail and, to varying degrees, my four siblings were on the same track. At that young age I dabbled in drug dealing and stealing; I was a part of a small street

---

[7]Source: AAMP's Crossroads: Choosing a New Direction, research compendium, 2002: *African American Families*, 185.

gang, and I was a truant. I met lots of men at home, but they were typically heroin addicts passed out on the couch or shooting up in the bathroom.

But shortly before my 13th birthday two good things happened: I ran away from home and a few weeks later my uncle Moe offered to take me in.

Moe was a Marxist, a Black Panther leader, and a revolutionary. All kinds of intriguing people showed up at his home—university professors, community organizers, activists, philosophers, writers.

Moe had a reputation as a troublemaker, but his home was a very stable place, and he and his friends all treated me with care and respect. They would stay up late talking about culture, politics, philosophy, and the future of the world, and after a while I wanted to be part of those discussions. "If you want to join in, fine," my uncle would say. "But you'll need to read this book first." Then he'd hand me Mao Zedong's *The Little Red Book*, or Fidel Castro's *History Will Absolve Me*, or a treatise on dialectical materialism.

I dropped all my old buddies and started hanging out with these older men and women and tried to be like them. They taught me to become a serious reader and writer. They also taught me to play the game of Go, which taught me discipline, strategy, tactics, and pattern recognition. Most of all, the men and women who mentored me taught me about a bigger world beyond the street corners and alleys I had known. Through a variety of community projects, they also taught me that I could do many things well and that I could make a difference. They created an environment that fostered learning, experimentation, and creativity.

For a time we traveled around the country, living in communes in New Mexico and California and rural Wisconsin. Getting up at sunrise and working all day on the communes taught me how to work hard and get along with others. We returned to Minneapolis in time for me to graduate (in advance of the rest of my class) from high school. Soon afterward I opened a cooperative grocery store for low-income people. I was 18 and knew how to be an adult.

It took me a while longer to grow out of the dogmatism of Marxism but that didn't really matter, because I had the skills and self-confidence I needed to make my way in the world. This period also set the direction for my future career in public administration.

What made the difference for me was precisely what so many young African American men lack: a stable home, a caring, respectful father figure or mentor, a group of respected peers who challenged and supported my intellectual and emotional development, and the ability to make a positive difference in other people's lives.

My uncle Moe caught me at the right age. Before my life with Moe, I was just another hopeless, clueless, fatherless young African American boy on the street corner.

CALL AND RESPONSE

In 2002, after 2 years of research, community forums, and relationship building with community organizations, businesses, and communities of faith, AAMP issued a final report entitled *Crossroads: Choosing a New Direction*. This report marked the end of the research phase of the African American Men Project and the beginning of significant efforts to transform relationships among young African American men, county government, and the community at large. Simultaneously, AAMP also published a *Research Compendium*, which contained many of the studies that supported the conclusions and recommendations of the final report. Both documents can be accessed online at www.aamp_mn.org/publish.htm

Here are some of the key insights in *Crossroads*:

- The situation cannot be addressed with quick fixes and no single initiative will do the job. There needs to be an aligned and coordinated response—one involving multiple stakeholders and multiple strategies.
- Traditional economic and social service approaches have not worked. A complete rethinking of what we do and how we do it is necessary.
- Mutual accountability is essential. Young African American men, community groups, county government, and all other stakeholders need to hold themselves and each other, responsible for better outcomes.
- Lasting change comes from within communities; it cannot be superimposed from the outside (except in undesirable ways, such as conquest and colonization). Thus, the building of partnerships with and among community-based organizations is critical.
- More significantly, the coordination of programs, resources, and initiatives must be taken out of the county bureaucracy and restored to the community.
- Without a critical mass of successful young men to serve as mentors and role models, the prospects for many young African American men will remain dismal. One goal of future efforts should be to create such a critical mass.
- Hennepin County government should not take the lead in creating a structure through which young African American men and Hennepin County can help each other succeed. The county's mission is to serve its citizens, not direct their lives. As part of a democracy, it must respond to the will of the people rather than impress its will upon them. Furthermore, creating such a structure within county government would only repeat past mistakes, and add yet another head to the hydra of ineffective bureaucracy.

- However, the county is ideally suited to support and assist change efforts by providing the right infrastructure.

- The county already has many worthwhile mechanisms in place that can benefit many or all Hennepin County stakeholders—and young African American men in particular. Yet many of these resources and programs are being underused and each one is typically presented in a vacuum. Better coordination and greater accessibility can make many of these mechanisms far more effective.

- The county needs to move away from a model of social services and incarceration and toward a model of community building and individual self-determination. The county needs to rethink and redesign its policies so they support people, families, communities, and economic growth, rather than contribute to (or fail to address) dependence, labor shortages, economic recession, and multigenerational poverty. This means being willing to realign, and in some cases redesign, a variety of institutional arrangements—including priorities, strategies, what is funded, and how funding should be guided. This means building and encouraging partnerships among all kinds of organizations and individuals that can serve young African American men and Hennepin County. This means replacing competition among service organizations with collaboration and coordination. This means pairing new and vital approaches with the best of what already works. And, this means no longer operating in ways that continue to deliver poor results.

- None of this should be read as "let's turn away" or "let's push these men off the dock and force them to either swim or drown." The county and its present and future partners must be active and committed participants.

Most significantly, *Crossroads* put out a call for leaders—seasoned and new, old and young, traditional and atypical—to step forward. The report suggested that many, but by no means all, of these leaders would be young African American men. The report also put out a call to rediscover citizenship and public work: "sustained, visible, serious effort by a diverse mix of ordinary people that creates things of lasting civic or public significance. . . . It changes the community, the larger world, and the people involved."[8]

That call was answered in a variety of ways and as of this writing in January 2005, the insights outlined above have been the basis for a wide range of new partnerships and initiatives, almost all of which are qualitatively differ-

---

[8]Source: AAMP's Crossroads: Choosing a New Direction, Final Report, 2002b, pp. 49–50.

ent from what has been done in the past. Most of these are outlined in what follows.

In the fall of 2002, AAMP sponsored a conference on African American men at the University of Minnesota's Humphrey Institute of Public Affairs. This conference, which drew over 800 participants, featured talks, seminars, presentations, and a wide range of opportunities for networking, partnership building, and the exchange of ideas. The keynote speaker was educational consultant Jawanza Kunjufu, author of *State of Emergency: We Must Save African American Males* and *Countering the Conspiracy to Destroy Black Boys.* At the conference, Kunjufu challenged African American men to become better fathers. "One of the biggest issues affecting our youth, especially males, isn't racism," Kunjufu said. "It's not even economics, per se. It's the disease called fatherlessness. We need brothers to be accountable and responsible." At the same time, Kunjufu challenged Hennepin County commissioners to maintain their commitment to AAMP and to young African American men. "We need to go from theory to practice," he said. "We need to get serious."

Other speakers at the conference included Floyd Blair, special assistant to the White House for faith-based and community initiatives, and psychologist Dr. Joseph White, coauthor of *Black Man Emerging* and an editor of this volume.

The AAMP conference focused and inspired a huge amount of energy and commitment, which transformed into concerted action over the next 2 years. Indeed, many of the following initiatives are direct or indirect results of this conference.

In late 2002, the African American Men Steering Committee, which had directed the research portion of the project, was dissolved. A new coordinator, Shane Price, was chosen to manage the project, although I remained as its director. In December of that year, more than 130 citizens were sworn in as members of a commission that has directed AAMP's efforts since then. During this period AAMP was given a new focus: to reach out to potential partners—from individuals to businesses to community-service organizations to faith communities to educational institutions—and encourage them to step forward and take leadership roles in assisting young African American men and Hennepin County.

In early 2005, AAMP has established partnerships with more than 120 Quality Partners: groups and organizations in the areas of education, health, housing, economic empowerment, community and civic involvement, family, communications, fundraising, and criminal justice. These range from the American Cancer Society to the Minneapolis *StarTribune* to Big Brothers/Big Sisters of the Twin Cities to the Minnesota Association of Black Psychologists to the Metropolitan Economic Development Association.

As of January 2005, these partnerships have resulted in the following on-going programs and initiatives, virtually all of them unique or unconventional:

- Emerge!, a weekly support group for African American men.
- Black Men Reading, a weekly book discussion group.
- "Street Soldiers," a weekly radio show on KMOJ 89.9 that focuses on violence prevention, gangs, crime, drugs, teenage pregnancy, and other community issues. This show includes a regular call-in segment.
- The Men of Color Clinic opened in North Minneapolis to address the specific health care concerns of African American men.
- Call to Mentorship, a campaign to recruit and train 200 mentors to work with African American boys and young men.
- *Black Man Emerging: A New Direction for African American Men and Their Families*, a weekly cable television show.
- Housing Consortium, a group of African American landlords and AAMP staff who work together to provide housing for young African American men.
- "Men Emerging," a monthly column in the *Minneapolis Spokesman*, a widely read newspaper with a Black focus.
- A partnership with Central Minnesota Legal Services to provide legal services for young African American men.
- A partnership with Northwestern College's Urban Institute, which offers short courses in people skills, personal responsibility, and successful marriage specifically for African American men.
- Educational partnerships to provide scholarships, mentoring, and programming to young African American men. One such partnership, with The Fathering Project, helps young African American men study for and pass the GED exam.
- Partnerships to train African American guardian *ad litems* to represent the best interests of African American children involved in the court system.

A variety of short-term partnerships has also been established, such as a house-building project with Habitat for Humanity; Black and Blue, a day-long conference on depression and anxiety in African Americans; and a street outreach partnership with NorthPoint Health & Wellness Center, which encourages young African American men to get health checkups and provide them with information on HIV/AIDS.

A partnership with the Fourth Judicial District Court and a variety of city, county, nonprofit, neighborhood, corporate, and faith-based groups organized two Restorative Justice days, one in 2003 and one in 2004. On each day, people with outstanding misdemeanor warrants or minor driving citations were given the chance to have their fines waived or significantly reduced by appearing before a judge and agreeing to perform community service. People with small fines were given tasks such as a few hours of cleaning up intersections or registering voters; those who owed hundreds or thousands of dollars in fines were given "sentences" of dozens of hours of community service. More than 2,400 Hennepin County residents—most of them young Black men—appeared before judges on these two days, collectively saving hundreds of thousands of dollars in fines and providing the county with many thousands of hours of service. In the process, many residents were able to quickly get square with the law and those with revoked driver's licenses had them reinstated. For many of the young men who participated, the event was literally a life-changing experience: They suddenly transformed from minor criminals into regular citizens and valued volunteers. The two Restorative Justice days also saved Hennepin County around $800,000 in court costs, an amount far exceeding the total fines waived. Both Restorative Justice days proved so successful that their principles have been incorporated into the county's regular Traffic Court calendar. In addition, two suburban Minneapolis counties, Washington County and Dakota County, have copied the initiative, and a third is considering doing the same.

The great majority of AAMP partnerships move the focus out of county government and back into the community—which is, after all, where all of us live. However, the county provides partial support for these partnerships through money, training, and/or skilled people. Some of these partnerships involve faith-based organizations, though none discriminate on the basis of religion.

RIGHT TURN

The centerpiece of AAMP's efforts has been the Right Turn initiative. This is a community partnership with two faith-based nonprofits, Urban Ventures in South Minneapolis and Holding Forth the Word of Life Church in North Minneapolis, both headquartered in heavily African-American areas.

Right Turn provides free services to African American men ages 18 to 35 from throughout Hennepin County. Many of these men are referred to Right Turn by county organizations, community organizations, the Minneapolis Police Department, M.A.D. D.A.D.S. (a volunteer platoon of men and women who patrol the streets of Minneapolis, finding and referring delinquent fathers), and other forms of street outreach. Other young men simply walk in, or call one of the two anchor sites to schedule an appointment.

Through hard work, charismatic leadership, and a panoply of services, these anchors have established neighborhood roots that allow them to succeed (and give them credibility and accessibility) in ways that government agencies can never achieve.

Everything Right Turn does is community based. The rationale is that if young African American men are to be restored to the community—and if a sense of community is to be restored to them—then they must begin restoration in the community, rather than through the county bureaucracy.

Right Turn realigns both the use of the existing resources and how young African American men interact with those resources, and the same with the government. Participants are no longer on an assembly line in a governmental factory—whether it's the welfare factory or the health care factory or the criminal justice factory. Instead, once a young man has signed on with Right Turn, he immediately begins two relationships: a central personal relationship with a single advocate, called a Systems Navigator, and a central relationship with a faith-based organization that is already part of the community. This is a radical departure from the typical bureaucratic approach, in which citizens get in many different lines in order to receive uncoordinated services from many different impersonal government programs.

At the initial meeting between a young man and his Systems Navigator, the Navigator asks him about his present situation. Does he have a job? Does he have any legal issues that need to be addressed? Does he have a wife, a partner, and/or a child? Does he owe money for child support? Does he have a safe and stable place to live? Does he have health insurance? Does he hope to get further education or job training? What are his occupational goals? What are his hopes and dreams for his future? The Navigator then assesses the young man's needs regarding education, housing, employment, health, social and emotional support, chemical dependency issues, and/or legal issues. Next, the Navigator guides each young man through the complete range of available services and programs, in a process specifically designed to cut through bureaucratic red tape.

Most importantly, however, over a series of meetings the Navigator helps the young man create a realistic, step-by-step plan for turning his life around. If the young man has a child, then the Navigator encourages him to formally declare paternity (if he has not already done so), to begin reconnecting with his son or daughter, and to provide financial support for his child as soon as he is able to. If the young man is in minor trouble with the law, then the Navigator works with the criminal justice system to have the charges dropped or reduced, provided that the young man follows his life plan, stays out of trouble, and in some cases, fulfills a specific community service requirement. He may also be required to discuss the impact of his past behavior with a neighborhood panel. (Chronic offenders, and men facing felony charges, do not qualify for this option.)

Each Systems Navigator is familiar with all the different county, community, and faith-based resources, and designs for each young man the package of services that will be most beneficial and most appropriate for him. This saves the young man time, trouble, and confusion, while also saving the county money.

The Navigator also assigns each young man a mentor who provides further support, guidance, encouragement, and oversight. As appropriate, the young man might also be referred to a tutor, a training or educational program, and/or other people, programs, and organizations that can help.

Right Turn actively recruits community members to serve as mentors. These are not necessarily community leaders. Many are African American men who quietly, without fanfare, do the good work necessary to be successful employees, responsible family members, and good neighbors. These mentors listen to the young men, coach them, and accompany them to various appointments and activities. In a very real sense, they become the father figures and role models that many of the young men never had.

Although any African American man in Hennepin County who is 18 to 35 years old can sign up with Right Turn, some men are referred to it by the police after being arrested for livability crimes—that is, minor nonviolent crimes such as loitering, trespassing, drinking alcohol in public, disorderly conduct, or driving with a suspended license. Rather than simply set a court date, the Minneapolis Police Department offers these young men a choice: They can go to court, or they can sign up for Right Turn within the next 48 hours.

In part, Right Turn targets young men who have not done anything seriously wrong, but who have few or no prospects for doing things right, no high-school diploma, and no skills for making an honest living. These men are on track to committing more serious crimes—and to cost the county and the community dearly in both dollars and reduced quality of life.

Right Turn is thus intended to simultaneously help young men turn their lives around, reduce crime, reduce the county's costs, and improve the quality of life for all of citizens. In the process, it also helps to restore hope to many young African American men. As Systems Navigator Greg Bauldwin explained, "If a man leaves our office without hope, then we haven't done our job."

A thorough evaluation of Right Turn will be done in late 2005. However, the results so far are generally positive. In particular, its community-based approach and its System Navigator concept hold great promise for use with other populations and in other situations. Indeed, the day may come when most Hennepin County citizens turn not to county bureaucracies, but to neighborhood-based sites and System Navigators, to get what they need. The county may also save millions of dollars as a result.

WALKING THE NEW ROAD

The next phase of the African American Men Project, which will begin in late 2005, will include the following initiatives:

- A strategic and operational plan to create a sustainable economic model for the continuation of AAMP's work.
- The expansion of Right Turn beyond the boundaries of Minneapolis, into Brooklyn Park and Brooklyn Center—two suburbs where large numbers of young African American men live in poverty.
- The creation of Right Step, a parallel program to Right Turn, for African American boys ages 12 to 17. This will be a partnership between AAMP, Hennepin County Community Corrections, District Court judges, and the Minneapolis Police Department.
- Building support for the creation of a business incubator in Near North Minneapolis.
- Continued partnership-building efforts with other organizations, especially faith-based groups and other county units and departments.
- The reconfiguration of AAMP as a freestanding nonprofit organization. Although some of AAMP's current funding comes from outside organizations (the Minneapolis Foundation, for example, recently awarded AAMP a $200,000 grant), most funding continues to come from Hennepin County. Nonprofit status should greatly increase contributions from outside organizations.
- Fundraising for this nonprofit.
- A conclave where prominent African American academics and elected officials from around the country can meet, network, and share ideas.
- A thorough evaluation of AAMP work to date. This will help us to learn from both our successes and our failures.

Our goals for this phase are to create a model for partnerships for the future, both for Hennepin County and other communities; to help young African American men to move off the criminal justice track and onto a track of self-reliance; and to assist the people and businesses of Hennepin County by helping a steadily increasing number of young African American men build regular lives.

A HOUSE DIVIDED AND REUNITED

I never knew my father, or anything about him. As both a child and an adult, whenever I asked my mother about him, she would close up and refuse to talk. I was in my 40s before I even got her to reveal his name. When she did divulge it, I was disappointed that it was not a name I remembered. I was equally disappointed to learn that he had moved to Jackson, Mississippi three decades ago, and that he was probably dead. (He was born in 1924, and few African American men live to be 80.)

But at age 46, a year or so after I had first learned my father's name, I looked him up in the online phone directory, and, to my surprise, found his phone number and address. I wrote him a letter in which I introduced myself, told him what I knew about him, and asked if he was indeed my father.

A week later he called me. "Yes," he said, "I believe I'm your dad. I had an affair with your mother for about a year back in the 1950s. But when we broke up I didn't know she was pregnant. We never ran into each other after we split and she never got in touch and told me a child was involved."

I said to this man, whose first name was Robert, "I'd like to come and see you." At first he hesitated, because he had 10 other children, all of whom he'd surely have to tell about me. But after we talked for an hour or so, he agreed to meet.

Two months later I drove to Jackson, Mississippi, and he and his wife Linnie came to my hotel. At first Robert and I sat there for a long time, looking at each other. Both of us thought we didn't look much alike. "Your nose seems big." "What size shoe do you wear?" Still, it didn't take long before the three of us were exchanging stories, filling one another in, laughing together, and revisiting our separate pasts through one another. We talked until late in the evening.

Over the course of that night, Robert told me about his 10 other children, every one of whom has built a successful career. One is an ophthalmologist, another an accountant, another an electrical engineer. This stunned me. I had always been the surprise success in the family—going to Harvard, building a career as a county administrator, becoming a University of Minnesota research fellow, taking the job of director of planning and development, and today working as the CEO of a large urban health and human service agency. But now, suddenly—at least in terms of career—I fit right in.

Before I left Jackson, Robert and I took a DNA test, to determine beyond a reasonable doubt that I was in fact his son. The results took several days to arrive, however, so I was already back in Minneapolis when Robert called and said, "Looks like you're in the family."

Meeting Robert and Linnie provided some wonderful closure for me. I felt like I finally knew quite literally, who I was. Yet I felt another door opening at the same time. It was a quest fulfilled—my own personal version of Joseph Campbell's Monomyth, the hero's journey that climaxes in personal transformation and ends back home with family.[9]

---

[9]Joseph Campbell, the late autodidact known for his work on mythology and comparative religion. In his book, *Hero with a Thousand Faces* (Princeton University Press, 1949), he discusses the "monomyth cycle" of the hero's journey.

A few days after I learned the test results, I got a call from my new sister, the ophthalmologist. "I'm so happy to have a new brother," she said. She was coming up to Minneapolis for a wedding and wanted to meet me. We agreed to have lunch at the Mall of America.

When I arrived at the restaurant, to my surprise, a grand homecoming of sorts welcomed me. Unbeknownst to me, my new sister had invited several other local relatives—even my new niece and nephew. Our lunch became a celebration in which I was welcomed into the family. I also discovered that the neighborhood man I saw when I walked my dog every morning was my brother. For the past few years he had lived only four blocks away.

I told my own children—both in their 20s, both actively building solid careers—about my new connections with my new/old family. They were both pleased. "Can I meet them?" they each asked. I showed them and my wife a picture of Robert. All of them said immediately, "He looks just like you."

Robert and I have talked on the phone several times over the last few months. More recently, he invited me and my wife and children to a huge family reunion. I've now met or talked with most of my new siblings, and every one of them has been wonderful: enthusiastic, delighted to meet me, and as welcoming as a sister or brother can be. And every one of them has told me, "Gary, we're so glad to get to know you. We want you to be part of us."

At age 47, I have been restored to my family.

Meeting my father was a spiritual awakening for me. For the first time, I could clearly see parts of myself that had been invisible, and understood internal voices that, until then, I was unable to explain. In connecting with my father, I discovered both who I am and who I have always been. Yet this very discovery has itself been transforming, helping me to become more authentically myself, and reinforcing my place in my family and my community.

THE SECOND HALF OF THE STORY

For more than 40 years I was isolated from half of my biological family. Its blood was in me well before my birth and I belonged to it from the day I was born. Each of my family members only knew half the story—the official, public half—about our own family. It was a big relief—and a bigger blessing—to finally meet my lost family members, to discover all that we had in common, and to be welcomed into the group that, paradoxically, I had been a part of all my life.

Many young African American men live with a similar paradox. They seem isolated from their communities and from mainstream culture, hanging out on the street corner while much of the rest of the world hurries past and disapproves. Yet what appears to be isolation is, in fact, a form of collective blindness. Neighbors see these men as problems. City and county governments see them as users of our social service and criminal justice systems. And many of these men see themselves as destined to remain outside the mainstream of American life.

But all of this is simply the result of knowing only half the story—the half that focuses on failure instead of success, and on delivering government services instead of building community, personal power, and responsibility.

The African American Men Project began by helping Hennepin County, a community of over a million residents, to finally meet its lost members, and to discover what all of us have in common—including a big stake in each other's success. Today, through a combination of partnerships, mentoring, personal advocacy, support from community-based groups, and a group of tightly focused initiatives, AAMP is welcoming young African American men back into their—i.e., our—community. At the same time, a sense of community, mutual purpose, and support, is being restored to them.

In a parallel development, some of these men who have been absent fathers are reuniting with their own children. They are formally declaring their paternity, offering financial and emotional support to their children, and working hard to reclaim a place in family and community, both for themselves and for their daughters and sons.

I hope that in the future other communities will adopt, adapt, and improve on the AAMP model, so this great community we call America will someday welcome—and be welcomed by—all its sons and daughters.

These developments will of course be good for our communities, for young African American men, and for these men's partners and children. But they can yield more than just health and financial benefits. In many cases, personal or spiritual transformations occur: Men discover who they are and what they are capable of becoming. They begin to see a place for themselves in the world—in some cases, for the first time. And the larger world begins, at last, to see and acknowledge them.

The future of young African American men and the future of America itself are intimately bound together. We cannot create a successful future by blaming any group or institution or by merely crying *mea culpa*. Nor will a successful future emerge from a single effort or initiative; rather, it will be built from a multitude of interrelated ones—a web of mutually reinforcing connections that both spring from and support our communities. We can begin by making visible these connections, the people and groups they connect with and the ways in which we can help one another succeed.

We—as individuals and as communities—carry our potential for success inside us. Let us put aside for a time what we feel and believe, and just look and listen. What has been invisible or obscured can then become visible; what has been silent or buried in noise can be heard. We can then roll up our sleeves and build success together.

REFERENCES

Bryson, J. M., Cunningham, G. L., & Lokkesmoe, K. L. (2002). What to do when stakeholders matter: The case of problem formation for the African American Men Project of Hennepin County, Minnesota. *Public Administration Review, 62*(5), 568–584.

Campbell, J. (1949). *The hero with a thousand faces.* Princeton, NJ: Princeton University Press.

Ellison, R. (1952). *Invisible man.* New York: Vintage.

Galster, G., & Hill, E. W. (Eds.). (1992). *The metropolis in black and white.* New Brunswick, NJ: CUPR Press.

Hennepin County. Office of Planning and Development. (2002a). *Crossroads: Choosing a new direction, African American Men Project research compendium.* Minneapolis, MN: Office of Planning and Development.

Hennepin County. Office of Planning and Development. (2002b). *Crossroads: Choosing a new direction, African American Men Project final report.* Minneapolis, MN: Office of Planning and Development.

Levin, M. (1997). *Why race matters: Race differences and what they mean.* Westport, CT: Praeger.

Steele, S. (1998). *A dream deferred: The second betrayal of black freedom in America.* New York: HarperCollins.

West, C. (1994). *Race matters.* New York: Vintage.

Chapter 14

Fatherhood Training:
The Concordia Project

Clarence Jones
Southside Community Health Services
Minneapolis, Minnesota

> *I am an invisible man. No, I am not a spook like those who haunted Edgar Allan Poe; nor am I one of your Hollywood-movie ectoplasm. I am a man of substance, of flesh and bone, fiber and liquids—and I might be said to possess a mind. I am invisible, understand, simply because people refuse to see me. Like the bodiless heads you sometimes see in circus sideshows, it is as though I have been surrounded by mirrors of hard, distorting glass. When they approach me they only see my surroundings, themselves or figments of their imagination—indeed, everything and anything except me.*
>
> —Ralph Ellison (1947)

We find Ellison's invisible man in the "fragile families" forged by unwed parents and their children. These men are a challenge to our community. Their actions are exaggerated, dismissed, or considered unimportant. Black men in general, but especially those in fragile families, continue to be stereotyped as unresponsive to the needs of their children and community. Regardless of their effort, they are portrayed as either unwilling or unable to provide for their families, and often ostracized when judged deficient.

This is judgment based on what? Until McLanahan et al. presented their baseline study of Fragile Families and Child Wellbeing in 1998, there was very little research on the role of the unwed low-income father in the family. Their study examined unwed parents, their backgrounds, their attitude toward having children, their potential as caretakers, and the societal impact on these families. It looked at both parents—fathers as well as mothers—and their behavior patterns.

This judgment of men in fragile families has been the source of much of my work in Minnesota's social service arena. This judgment has led me to question how we meet the needs of men and how we value—or under-value—their contributions. This judgment eventually led me to the development of the Concordia Project—a training program for family practitioners in Minnesota.

Waldo Johnson (1995) believes these men want to be good fathers, but social barriers prevent them from fulfilling that role. He observed men with normative paternal role expectations but reflected inadequate paternal role performance. Perhaps, as a result of the lack of social expectations, they fell short of their idealized paternal position.

Until recently it appeared that through the federal welfare program Aid to Families with Dependant Children (AFDC), the government wanted to take over the role of "daddy" in fragile families. Programs were created that would provide most of the necessities of life for the children, supplanting the father. This assumed responsibility drove American welfare policies until the passage of the Personal Responsibility and Work Reconciliation Act of 1996 (PRWORA, PL-104-193 Sec.103 [a] 401 [2]), which replaced the old AFDC system of assistance. Because the government no longer wants the role, draconian public policies have been enacted to bring alienated fathers back into their children's lives by making these men financially responsible for their children. These policies, which equate money with fatherhood, make them only "paper dads," and have driven many men from subsistence employment into an underground economy, perpetuating the perception of invisible fathers within the families.

PRWORA called for social programming to reduce pregnancies and encourage the formation and maintenance of two-parent families. Therefore this program, which serves the Temporary Assistance for Needy Families (TANF) population, was also required to provide services for fathers. In addition, funding was made available for programs that service noncustodial fathers whose children receive public assistance. Many of those affected are from low-income families. In many cases, they are unmarried teen-age parents who's children will likely have their own children as they become young adults and continue the cycle. The research indicates that children born to teen and unwed mothers will frequently grow up without a consistent relationship with their father, will most likely be poor, and end up on welfare (Blankenhorn, 1995).

Very little attention is paid to the social or environmental conditions that exacerbate the situations of nonengagement for fathers. The lack of a quality education, access to resources, emotional or physical constraints, health issues, public policy, criminal convictions, lack of parenting skills, or parental role models stymie expectations.

Low-income fathers who cannot provide child support payments are labeled "deadbeat" even when they are "dead broke." A report by the National Conference of State Legislatures (1999) found that, for this population:

- The average wage was $6.70 per hour;
- 51% had child support payment arrears of less than $2,000;
- 70% had been arrested;
- 60% had no high-school diploma or GED; and
- 54% had not lived with their own father.

It is obvious that a man without resources struggles to be a good parent.

DEFINING FATHERHOOD: ROLES FOR BLACK MEN

When we examine the current picture of the fragile family as presented by sociologists, family practitioners, governmental entities, and the Black community, there are several disturbing questions to be raised:

- Where are the fathers?
- What role does the father play? What role can he play?
- Are there other positive male figures available? Is there a place for positive men in the conversation concerning fragile families?

I contend that within society's current social family paradigm, the true role of the father and male parenting contributions have been minimized, if not demonized.

James Levine and Edward Pitt (1995) made an important delineation of what it means for any man to be a responsible father. They wrote that a man who behaves responsibly toward his children does the following things:

- He waits until he is emotionally and financially ready to have a child.
- He establishes legal paternity if and when he has a child.
- He actively shares with the mother the ongoing emotional and physical care of the child from the pregnancy forward.
- He shares with the mother financially, from the pregnancy onward.

Many of the current perceptions regarding Black fatherhood have lingered from the institution of slavery. During arguably the most significant era in his American history, the Black man was used to breed with women, forced to have children he could neither claim as family nor provide for, and expected to watch his children being sold as property. The Black father enslaved was helpless and required to accept his fate without resistance or concern. It is arguable that centuries of this patterning have helped render him invisible today.

But even under duress, he found ways to be a father. Fictive kinships are the caregiving and mutual-aid relationships among nonrelated people that exist because of their common ancestry, history, and social plight (Martin &

Martin, 1985). These relationships have long been a hallmark of the Black community, and allow families to find African American male role models beyond direct paternity. Even now it is not uncommon for a man to claim children from his partner's previous relationships as his own.

In 1999, the National Conference of State Legislatures found that:

- 80% of low-income fathers are cohabiting or romantically involved with the mother at the time their child is born. More than half intend to get married.
- 90% of the new fathers provided financial support to the mother during pregnancy and indicated their intent to provide continuous support for their children.
- Among women not romantically involved with the father of their children, 90% reported wanting the father to be involved.

Clearly, the *desire* for present, active fatherhood is not the problem.

The majority of women reported a man's ability to be a loving and committed father is more important than his ability to provide financially. If the majority of men and women having children indicate that they want to be cooperative in the rearing of their children, what disconnects their desire and the statistical data on the Black family from our perception of these fathers and their contributions to the family? What are the social barriers preventing some from being responsible fathers?

Many young fathers don't see themselves in the picture of the family because they are not welcomed in the family. Many times they assume, and have been made to feel, that their only contribution to the family is supplying the seed and then financial support, and if something else were expected from them, what they might supply could never be enough. Sometimes extended family of the mother act as gatekeepers, preventing these fathers from being involved (Allen & Doherty, 1996; Wattenberg, 1993).

An article by the National Network for Health cites Allen-Mears' (1984) research concluding that four barriers hinder fathers' involvement in their children's lives:

1. The negative attitude of the grandparents;
2. The mother's rejection of the father's involvement;
3. Institutional rejection of the father's involvement; and
4. The father's lack of knowledge about child care and lack of money.

CHANGING HIS IMAGE

If we do not have the true impression of Black fathers or father figures in fragile families as I propose, how then do we tell their story? How do we change the picture? If these men are engaged in their children's lives, and are positively engaged with the mother of their children, how then do we change their reputation for negligence? What resources do they need to become better fathers, and how do we provide them? How do we change our language so that when we speak of fatherhood and fathering, the community, the mother, and the father all understand the meaning of the term in the same general manner?

The increase in divorces, numbers of never married parents, rates of teen-age pregnancies, and other family social issues has brought the subject of fatherhood forcefully to the American consciousness. Social scientists have been documenting the progressing phenomena of fatherless children in America for more than 50 years. According to Horn and Sawhill (2001), 14 million more children are fatherless today than in 1960. Sixty percent of all children born in the 1990s will spend a significant portion of their youth in homes without fathers.

More and more children are being born without the benefit of having both parents involved positively in their lives. Fatherhood and the role of fathers in the lives of their children have become an emerging part of the American social conversation. Because fathers are not as involved in their children's lives, social scientists are citing this as a significant, if not primary, factor in the increase of socioeconomic problems in our society. We must be able and willing to provide services to *both* parents who desire to be a part of their children's lives.

The role of the father has evolved from that of principal provider and disciplinarian to one more responsible for nurturing and care-giving to the children in the family (Griswold, 1993). If this is an emerging role for fathers, how do family practitioners help men to be more engaged in their families? Current fatherhood research is looking at the ways fathers contribute to the well being of the family. See Bradley and Corwyn (2000) for a discussion of the socioemotional investment of fathers in their children.

OUTREACH AND RESOURCES

There are several programs that support fathers in Minnesota, but their participation is usually limited by age, income, and other restrictions. Many social service agencies are not equipped to work with men. They have an unwelcoming environment, and staff can sometimes make the man feel uncomfortable for seeking services since it is not "macho" behavior to solicit help. Many times the staff is not trained to work with fathers, and may feel threatened by their presence.

Furthermore, many social service providers who seek to serve low-income populations have little or no experience in working with fathers. There is difficulty identifying who these fathers are and what services they need. Social service providers traditionally described the low-income family as the mother and child only, excluding the father.

Garrison (2000) referred to the barriers confronting agencies that have traditionally worked with mothers and children and are now trying to include fathers. "The people who run fatherhood programs come from a variety of backgrounds: social work, child services, early childhood education, mental health and social activism. They bring passion and enthusiasm and, in many cases, the pain of growing up without a father in their own lives. Their training is diverse and sometimes only peripherally related to the challenges they face in this field. Very often, they are on their own in a female-dominated work environment." Garrison further stated that "social service agencies are unprepared to work with fathers and their changing roles in the family." He speaks of the importance of investing in training for practitioners and continuing education for staff development.

Many programs, often when a male is assigned to run them, are staffed with peers of the participants, demographically, educationally, and socially. This similarity can make it difficult to represent the client in a holistic manner with other agencies. Because of inexperience, lack of direction from their supervisors, and a poor understanding of how the systems operate, they often do not meet the program standards established by funders, and their work is perceived as having failed to produce expected outcomes.

Many agencies sincerely desire training to learn how to include fathers and men in their service delivery population. They seek information to overcome fear of dealing with this population. Because so many social service agencies are female run and staffed, the issue of safety is certainly a primary concern. Many groups still struggle with having noncustodial fathers involved in programming that might bring them in contact—and therefore in conflict—with the custodial parent. Attention must be given to conflict resolution and mediation skills for practitioners.

From the research done on families, the next step appears to concern academic training regarding learning to work with fathers. This focused training should provide necessary skills and experiences for practitioners to work with fathers within the context of family.

"There is a need for individual and innovative client-centered family therapies aimed at strengthening the unwed, nonresidential fathers' capacity for relationship building and improved parenting experiences," said Waldo Johnson (1995) in a paper entitled "Paternal involvement in fragile African American families: Implementation for clinical social work practice." In representing low-income fathers, it is important that practitioners have training that enables them to feel comfortable and competent developing programs in an environment known for excluding males. The traditional definition of "family" as a wedded man and woman and their children must be expanded to include those who have not been married, cohabiting, same sex partners as well as other descriptions, and might include extended family members.

With all of the systemic barriers and issues their clients face, it is important practitioners be prepared to understand how to collaborate with other agencies to deliver services. They must also be sensitized to the importance of documentation, which, left undone or incomplete, could eliminate their program from future funding consideration. Programming has to be designed to take into account ethnic differences, social status, and culturally sensitive strategies in order to effectively serve this population and its community.

With appropriate training, peers are the most effective practitioners for young Black men. Because they often have common experiences and common backgrounds they can effectively relate, articulate the needs, aspirations, and hopes of these young men.

However, because they also have similar challenges and may still be struggling with their own fatherhood issues, one of the first questions faced is "What are your credentials?" This question is usually designed to assess whether this person has the academic credibility or has earned the right to speak or to be heard on this topic. When education is found lacking, the professional is marginalized and dismissed as charismatic characters, no different than the people that they represent.

In reality, these are not very effective practitioners with few or inadequate tools to move the men toward self-sufficiency. They can provide encouragement, minimal supportive services, and employment resources, but in the political, social, and economic system in which we exist, credibility is a crucial element of representing this population.

In spite of our righteous indignation at the minimization of these credible representatives of these fathers, we must acknowledge that education is many times used as a value sorter in our society. The development of an accredited Family Study program with a focus on fatherhood is necessary for addressing some of the training needs of practitioners. They would be skilled in core components of fatherhood as well as program development. Counselors could be trained in community outreach, parenting education, career development, education, and school strategies for fathers.

THE UNIVERSITY OF HARD KNOCKS AND HIGHER LEARNING

The program that ultimately became the Concordia Project began in 1996 with the title "The University of Hard Knocks and Higher Learning." Young fathers in our program expressed a desire to attend different social events to gain new experiences and develop their social confidence. They wanted to complete their GED or high school diploma, attend theater and other activities to expose themselves and their children to the "other" world. These were young men who described their world as being "ten square blocks." They wanted to experience mainstream American opportunities without losing their connection to home and community. It was important for them to do these activities and still "remain Black."

We named the project "The University of Hard Knocks and Higher Learning" because many participants had been involved in the streets since an early age and knew that the term *school of hard knocks* spoke to the belief that some learning and maturation had been obtained from urban life experience. To them, this was a positive term and they felt comfortable identifying with it.

We started The University with many creative activities and some enthusiastic fathers. We were, however, unable to fully implement a program that engaged a large group of fathers in community learning activities. But creating a place of higher learning for these young fathers continued to be a burning desire in my mind.

Our work with fathers created a different paradigm than the one often shared by many researchers. The University provided services to primarily low-income, noncustodial fathers between the ages of 16 to 28. Our goal was to prepare these men to be positively engaged in their children's lives and to respect the children's mother, whether they liked her or not. We provided case management, transportation, employment, other support services, and peer and parenting groups. Although we were not funded to help those outside these age parameters, we would not turn away any father or fathering figure that sought help to be positively engaged in the lives of their children.

We realized early that the picture of the father in our community had a different definition than generally held by the greater society. These most fragile fathers typically did not have a high school diploma or a GED, may have had a criminal record, were living with friends or with another girl friend, and were usually working in temporary employment. Many fathers were deeply in debt due to arrears owed on their child support order. In spite of these issues, many self-reported spending some time with their children within the previous month.

Often, we would work with an uncle who heard we provided parenting classes. These men were acting as role models for their nieces and nephews, and needed skills to cope with their new role. In other cases, we had young men providing parenting to their own brothers and sisters when their parents died. On several occasions, grandfathers would arrive with their sons in tow to enroll them in the class; the grandfather was involved in the child's life, and felt that his son needed additional support in his parenting role.

We would not work with men unless they self-identified a desire to be positively engaged in their children's lives. The old adage is true: A mind that's changed against its will is of the same opinion still. We wanted to work with men who understood and were willing to make the choice to connect with their children and work cooperatively with the mother.

Success from the perspective of many of the participants often revolved around performing traditional male roles, and being able to work with computers. Many of the fathers spoke about getting a record deal, knowing a producer, becoming a producer, being in a group or having some kind of connection with the music industry. This, along with the desire to become professional athletes, is common among urban youth with few skills but aspirations of social status and financial security. Rarely was there any conversation about college or higher education unless it concerned vocational school, internships, or getting into the labor unions.

These men wanted more than anything else to be a good father, to provide for their children, to make up for the absence of their own fathers by being an active, present parent, and to do so in a safe and healthy way. The men were often concerned about the virtue of their young daughters, especially if there was another man living with the children's mother. They talked about how bright and well behaved their children were, and how they were doing in school. Many of these men tried to take an active part in their children's lives by taking jobs that allowed them to take them to school in the morning, and be home when they completed the school day. They would sometimes go to school and check on their children, an act that was occasionally met with resistance from the administration in deference to the custodial parent.

In some cases, the men were living with a woman who had children of her own; they would often express how they were trying to be a good father to these kids. It often proved extremely hard for these men to provide for another man's children while not having access to their own.

Some of our participants would share that they had grown up in a two-parent home. Their father worked and they had a good childhood. They would report they had graduated from high school, and in some cases these young men had even attended college, but they had become entangled in a series of relationships that had created a lot of stress in their lives. They were involved in what many describe as "baby mamma drama," in which the mother of their children makes demands that they feel are unreasonable, unfair, or unobtainable. The men in turn would act unreasonable and set off a powder keg of problems that would result in limiting their access to the children.

The men in our program saw themselves as the protectors of their children and material providers, even when they are not providing much to the family. In spite of their limited resources, they still claimed the responsibility. They wanted to nurture their children and often spoke of the pain they felt when the mother denied them visitation or access. The denial was usually a result of a failure to give her some money, pay the child support, or not being responsive to other expectations of the mother. Many times they felt compelled to do something because their manhood had been challenged. This is a tough area, because on one hand they realize the consequences of their actions and what may occur, yet they want to save face and not be considered irresponsible.

Most of the men spoke with great affection about the struggle of Black people and their accomplishments. Most were able to name Malcolm X, Dr. Martin Luther King, and a few other current Black Americans of distinction, but were really unable to relate to them other than the fact they were Black and inspired a general sense of pride. They were generally unaware of the history of the struggle these pioneers endured to establish their place in society. They also wanted to be major contributors to their community but expressed their frustration at a system that they felt would not let them enter or accept their contributions. Most of these men don't see themselves in the picture of the community.

Many talked about having a sense of Black consciousness and when pressed further to talk about their feelings, would usually describe wanting a community that was able to work together to create a better environment for their children. They had a growing awareness of the larger picture of the world. They were aware of the changing demographics and shifting populations in Minnesota. They stated they were uncomfortable with this transformation, and unsure of where they fit into the changing picture. African Americans are no longer the largest group of people of color in this country. Where does that leave these men who feel they have never truly been part of the mainstream American experience? They are unsure how this will impact their children and most conversations were usually negative regarding their outcomes for the future. Conversations around politics were focused on the importance of voting, but strained by questions about whether their vote really mattered.

Many young men were recruited to our program by word of mouth from other participants and came with the intent of obtaining permanent employment in efforts to take better care of their children. Almost without exception, they would talk about their children or children in their care and the deep desire they had to provide for them. They would speak lovingly of these youngsters and of their intelligence, how much joy they brought into their lives and what they wanted these children to become. In most cases, when asking the participants about their own fathers, they would express the desire to do things differently from how they grew up. They did not want their children to experience the pain and frustration of not having their father present in their lives.

Many of the men struggled with car wash, janitorial, or other minimum wage jobs to make ends meet. Sometimes they had two and even three jobs in order to survive. They were not afraid of working, but many lacked the education, employment experiences, or money management skills to truly get ahead.

During conversations they often referred to themselves as real men. A real man to them was defined as someone who was responsible and attempted to take care of his family. A real man was someone who was available for his children and wanted to provide the best for his children. They often talked about buying popular brand-name items so that their children would not suffer from low self-esteem. When challenged concerning their desire to spend money on expensive pop culture trends rather than focusing on the child's basic needs with affordable quality products, they gave the impression that "cheap" items would not be acceptable to the children's mother. Two factors are at play here: They wanted their children to be successful and, in these cases, success was defined by appearances, and they believed that distance must be made up for with extravagance.

CONCORDIA

As the fatherhood program developed and we continued to undertake more innovative projects, my own lack of educational credentials became a difficult point for me. Many times, I felt unprepared and ill equipped to represent the issues of my participants. I recognized that many of the practitioners in this field had only a high-school diploma and were not recommending the young fathers to seek higher education than a GED or high-school diploma. You have only to look at the dismal record of high-school completions and college entries from the African American Men's Project Report to understand the need for an enhanced effort to get young men to finish school. But it is very difficult for many to advocate for someone else's higher education when that experience eluded them. I resolved to complete my education and went on to obtain my master's degree.

During my master's program I began work to match young Black men interested in supporting African American fathers with the credentials to do so. I knew many of the young men who worked with fathers wanted to go to college, and would go if they had an opportunity to succeed. Through Concordia, the National Practitioner Network for Fathers and Families (NPNFF), and the Saint Paul Urban League a collaborative was born. We wanted to provide training for family practitioners that instilled the importance of actively including fathers in the family. We wanted to increase the number of young fatherhood practitioners eligible to enter the university system and earn a degree.

The Concordia Project provides training to men looking to help facilitate the inclusion of both parents in the lives of their children. It focuses on a model of information, education, and training that allows family practitioners to develop the skills and knowledge to effectively work with fathers of color and low income. From this model, a specific curriculum emerges that includes accredited academic certification allowing practitioners to develop and maintain fatherhood programs that meet the requirements of participants, communities, and funding sources. Training that is accredited, research based, and practitioner driven provides the optimum learning environment. From this training come the best practices for working with this specific clientele.

The program continues to be a work in progress, but it continues. We constantly seek ways to engage our young men in activities that will position them for a place in mainstream America. Our young men are more than a cash crop to be picked and stored in correctional institutions and to be used in, as one speaker said, the last "chattel" system. Education continues to be the way for upward mobility for our families; we must be vigilant in cutting paths for our people.

REFERENCES

Allen, W. D., & Doherty, W. J. (1996). The responsibility of fatherhood as perceived by African American teenage fathers. Families in Society: *The Journal of Contemporary Human Services, 77*, 142–155.

Allen-Mears, P. (1984). Adolescent pregnancy and parenting: The forgotten adolescent father and his parents. *Journal of Social Work, 3*, 27–38.

Blankenhorn, D. (1995). *Fatherless America: Confronting our most urgent problem.* New York: Basic Books.

Bradley, R. H., & Corwyn, R. F. (2000). Fathers socioemotional investment in their children. *The Journal of Men's Studies* [online] Vol. 8, p. 133. Retrieved August 26, 2000, from http://Infotrac.galegroup.com!. Item A620865 52

Ellison, R. (1947). *The invisible man.* New York: Random House.

Garrison, P. (2000). Doing more than just inviting dads. *Children and Family.* Head Start Association. Brochure.

Griswold, R. L. (1993). *Fatherhood in America: A history.* New York: Basic Books.

Horn, W. F. (1998). *Father facts* (3rd ed.). Gaithersburg, MD: The National Fatherhood Initiative.

Horn, W. F., & Sawhill, I. V. (2001). Making room for daddy: Fathers, marriage and welfare reform. In R. M. Blank & R. Haskins (Eds.), *The new world of welfare* (pp. 221–241). Washington, DC: Brookings Institution Press.

Johnson, W. E. (1995). *Paternal identity among urban adolescent males.* University of Michigan, Institute of Social Research.

Levine, J. A., & Pitt, E. W. (1995). *New expectations: Community strategies for responsible fatherhood.* New York: Families and Work Institute.

Martin, J. M., & Martin, E. P. (1985). *The helping tradition in the Black family and community.* National Association of Social Workers, Silver Spring, MD.

McLanahan, S., Garfinkel, I., Reichman, N., Teitler, J., Carlson, M., & Audigier, C. N. (2003). *The Fragile Families and Child Wellbeing Study.* Baseline National Report. A joint study by the Center for Research on Child Wellbeing (Princeton University) and the Social Indications Survey Center (Columbia University).

Wattenberg, E. (1993). Paternity actions and young fathers. In R. I. Lermans & T. J, Ooms (Eds.), *Young unwed fathers: Changing roles and emerging policies.* Philadelphia: Temple University Press.

Chapter 15

Walking the Walk: Community Programs That Work

Michael E. Connor
Emeritus, California State University, Long Beach

> *Deeply imbedded in the mind of all men is the desire to serve, to nurture, to take care, to protect. We work untiringly with each father to create environments that bring out the very best. Their response is always positive.*
> —Charles Ballard, President for Responsible Fatherhood and Family Revitalization (Levine & Pitt, 1995, p. 115)

The chapter is dedicated to the memory of the late Reverend Ronald Francis Johnson, founder to the "Rites of Passage Program." Brother Ron passed on January 16, 2002 in Los Angeles where his fathers training program was based. A native of Brooklyn, Ron came to Southern California in 1985, and I had the occasion to meet him shortly thereafter. We first interacted at a local conference dealing with issues impacting young African American males. I had written a university level course dealing with fathers-fathering issues and Ron was developing his "Rites" program in the public schools. He asked me to visit his program on the campus of Hawthorne High School, and I invited him to come to the Cal State Long Beach campus and share his thoughts with my students. I am thankful for the exposure to this articulate, dynamic, thoughtful, engaging, and charismatic gentleman. My students and I were enthralled with his message, with his delivery style, and with him. Thus began a relationship that continued until his untimely death. Ron Johnson blessed my students and me on numerous subsequent occasions with an overview of his very successful program to aid young males in making the transition from youth to young adulthood. With each interaction, I learned more about life, about myself, and about the population I was attempting to serve. I am truly fortunate in having the opportunity to know Brother Ron Johnson, a man who certainly walked the walk. Those interested in learning more about Reverend Johnson's work are encouraged to read *Visions*, a State of California's Department of Education's book focusing on developing a plan for success in life for Black males.

NATIONAL INSTITUTE FOR RESPONSIBLE FATHERHOOD AND FAMILY REVITALIZATION (NIRFFR)

Charles Ballard, an African American Social Worker established the National Institute for Responsible Fatherhood (now the Institute for Responsible Fatherhood and Family Revitalization—NIRFFR) in Cleveland, Ohio in 1982. He was concerned about teenage boys who were fathers not having the necessary skills to positively impact their young children and families. Mr. Ballard knows of which he speaks because he was a teenage father. Charles grew up in Alabama without a positive adult male role model. At seventeen, he impregnated a young woman and became a father. Like many young(er) males, he had no notion as to the impact his actions would have on himself, on the mother of his child, or on his child. Charles dropped out of school, joined the army, and shortly thereafter went to jail for an assault. While in jail, he experienced a rebirth as an African-American man. He became aware of his spirituality and set about to reclaim his life. Upon his release from jail, Mr. Ballard gained custody of his child; completed his high-school training (earned his GED); went on to college and then to graduate school, earning a masters degree in social work. While working in Cleveland, Ohio he noticed too many young mothers without the fathers of their babies taking an active role in the lives of their families.

Mr. Ballard's observations and belief that men/fathers are the key to keeping families together spurred him toward developing a program that would attempt to bring fathers back to their families. Thus, the National Institute for Responsible Fatherhood was created. Initially the program served teen fathers, but soon men across ages were involved. One important tenant of the program is that fathers are often the solution to ending dysfunctional families.

Charles Ballard's program grew from a teen fathers training model trying to connect young fathers with their children in Cleveland, Ohio to a broader based program that works with men and families in distress across the nation. Although the target population includes teen fathers, high-school drop outs, those with limited work experience, many who are illiterate, those with criminal records, those with low self-worth, those from dysfunctional relationships (including dysfunctional families) and those with substance abuse problems, the program is not limited to teenage fathers. There are NIRFFR programs in Nashville, Milwaukee, Yonkers, New York, San Diego, and Washington, D.C. (the site of the national office). Blue-collar workers, professional men, and businessmen are recruited to work as mentors and counselors to serve the participants. Graduates from the program, in turn, are trained to be role models and peer counselors. The NIRFFR's program focuses on five areas of service:

- Teaching respect;
- Parenting skills;
- Involvement of the mothers;
- Educational enhancement and support; and,
- Commitment to the workplace.

A major focus is to help fathers develop a sense of self-control, self-awareness, self-worth, and to be in good mental health. Thus, teaching respect, respect for oneself, for one's child(ren), and for the mother of one's child(ren) is important. The model suggests that as one learns about oneself, learns to respect and value oneself, the person can and will make changes. A one-on-one approach is used to help emotionally connect dads with their children. Mr. Ballard believes that his trainees (referred to a protégés) want to do right by their children. They are encouraged to find themselves an acceptable role model for fatherhood, and follow the lessons they learn. Protégés are asked to visualize what they can be through these successful models. "How you treat people brings out the best in them" (Levine, 1995, p. 110). The clients first learn to take responsibility for their own behavior and then learn to help their neighbors. Thus, they learn responsibilities to themselves to their families and to their communities.

The second area of service deals with the development of parenting skills. The men learn to diaper, feed, hold, and bathe their child. Initially, the men were not asked to establish paternity, but they chose to do so on their own. Currently, the fathers are encouraged to legitimize their children. It is recognized that being a father goes beyond financial support— men must become good nurturers and be present in the lives of their children. Ballard believes fathers need their children as much as children need their fathers. To learn about fathering, the men work closely with others who have been successful fathers. In this context, they can observe (and learn about) feeding and diapering, communication, time management, and learn to make family decisions.

Third, the mothers of the men's children are included in the training. It is important that mothers learn what fathers can and should be doing with their children. Much of Ballard's work seems to evolve around his belief in and support of the institution of marriage. Married couples are encouraged to model the tenants of the program so that others may observe how couples "work." Additionally, committed married couples are hired to run the programs. They must live and work in the community they serve—thus a "reseeding" of the community. Families that model love, compassion, understanding, problem solving, and so forth are a tremendous learning and teaching tool. In short, family supports family in a positive manner.

Fourth, educational enhancement and support is offered. The protégés are encouraged to complete their high-school diplomas; dropouts are encouraged to return to school and earn their GED, thus learning the importance of education for themselves and for their children. Too many African American males allow themselves to be "pushed" from the educational arena, effectively eliminating many career options. Too late, many come to understand and appreciate the value of and need for a formal education. It is by learning and by demonstrating that learning that one's self-esteem is enhanced and one is in a position to participate in the teaching/learning of one's children.

Fifth, there is an attempt to connect the protégés to the workplace. In attempting to develop strong work habits NIRFFR focuses on seven areas. These include spirituality (the sense of knowing right and wrong); identity (coming to know who you are and learning to work interdependently with others); an awareness that one's belief system must change (learning to know and understand how you think in an effort to manage your behavior); purpose (understanding why one is here [living] and what to do with oneself); the ability to perform (going beyond simply having a purpose to performing that purpose successfully); behavior (taking responsibility for one's actions); and the environment (learning to control the environment rather than being controlled by it). As the program participants are impacted by these principles, their actions and thoughts can change. They can learn to be productive and positive contributors to themselves, to their families and to their communities. An important focus is the attempt to enhance entrepreneurial and employment skills and to recruit noncustodial fathers to the workforce. The trainees must find and maintain a job. Ballard finds that most of his participants want to work, but many are not ready to work. They have to learn to impact the job marketplace (seek and obtain a job) as well as learn to maintain that job. Work is viewed as an acceptable responsibility and men need to be responsible. This philosophy allows the trainees to learn to handle work and financial responsibilities.

The program is run in a family atmosphere, with one-on-one counseling available 24 hours a day. The work might take place in the office, at the clients' homes, on the streets—wherever and whenever it is needed. Thus, staff must be mobile and willing to serve. They have to be willing to go to the homes of their clients, they must be comfortable doing the one-on-one work, and they must understand the work is not an 8-hour-a-day job. As noted earlier, the staff is hired from the community, must know the community, must be engaged with the community, and must be available when needed.

Upon graduation from the program, the men are encouraged to model the appropriate behaviors they've learned to show other young men how to be relevant fathers. Additionally, they are encouraged to recruit others they know and meet to the training.

THE ROLE OF MEN (ROM)

The infant mortality rate (the number of infant deaths per 1,000 live births) is often used as a primary barometer of the overall health of a given community. The higher the rate, the lower the health of that community. Obviously, the goal is 0 deaths per 1,000 births. Because the infant mortality rate was so high in the African American community, in 1989 the State of California set aside money to establish the Black Infant Health Program (BIH). This program was under the able direction of Ms. Shirley Shelton from 1990 until February, 2005 and the infant mortality rate decreased from 19.2 per 1,000 live births in 1990 to 12.8 deaths per 1,000 live births by 2002. Ms. Shelton understood that while most programs dealing with Black women (women in general) tended to ignore the interactions with and the impact of men, she set about to seek support to add a male component to BIH. Shelton has been invaluable in spreading information about the need for male inclusion in families/family life. In 1994, seed monies were granted and the call went out to seek proposals that would involve men and fathers in the BIH effort.

Dr. Alvin Nelson, a public health physician working for the City of Long Beach, answered the call and submitted a proposal that sought money to develop a "best practices model" that would include men. The proposal was funded, and the author of this chapter, Michael Connor, a professor and licensed clinical psychologist, was hired to write and develop the model. My clinical work had primarily focused on children and families; I had years of experience doing work with early childhood populations (including ongoing and consistent involvement with my own children, involvement and interactions with children in my extended family network, Project Head Start, prepared childbirth training and parent training programs, as well as treating and interacting with mentally deficient and emotionally challenged children). I had been interested in fathering issues since the birth of our first child in 1967. In fact, I had sought support for funding male involvement in families across cultures for some years. In 1975 I developed an upper division, university level, interdisciplinary course that focused on men as fathers (Fathers and Fathering: A Psycho-social Perspective). For the past 28 years this class has been offered each spring semester at Cal State University, Long Beach and remains one of few classes at the college level that focuses on fathers. Additionally, in 1975 I commenced offering father-training workshops through my private practice, and began presenting professional papers annually at major conferences. Thus, I was delighted when offered the opportunity to develop a best practices model for the state.

In developing the Role of Men (ROM), I had the opportunity to travel to other locations and observe what others were doing. One of my trips took me to Cleveland, Ohio to observe Charles Ballard's work (see above). During another trip, I saw Ron Johnson's activities (see above). I interacted with "Bunny" Johnson in Philadelphia and James Johnson in Baltimore. From each of the programs visited and from each of the men with whom I interacted, I learned what was happening to/with African American men as fathers across the nation, and what some were attempting in an effort to eradicate the numerous problems. From these programs and from these men, and from my own experiences, I developed the ROM.

The Role of Men, while written in a "generic" fashion (i.e., the training components were developed to be relevant to fathers across cultures and it can be modified to include specific qualities and issues pertinent to a specific culture), has been used primarily in the African American community (at this writing, Alameda County, West Contra Costa County, Riverside County, San Diego County, San Mateo County, Santa Clara County, and the City of Long Beach have ROM programs. As money becomes available, additional health-care jurisdictions will likely include the model as they continue their work within the Black Community. The City of Long Beach had the original program).

The Role of Men embraces a "Rites of Passage" and a "Male Mentoring" approach in an effort to involve African American fathers. The program includes outreach and recruitment; screening and selection; training and follow-up. A small group approach to training is the norm; however, individual interactions are commonplace. Some of the participants are not comfortable speaking in a group context and therefore, one-on-one time must be made available. Much of this activity is in the counseling and problem-solving realm. At the Long Beach ROM program, a significant amount of this counseling time takes place after the training sessions, in the parking lot, on an adjacent children's playground, as well as in the office. It is often spontaneous as the men have not learned to postpone or schedule discussion of their issues. In the groups, it is important that the men perceive one another as problem-solving opportunities and develop the willingness to share and support one another, as in African and African American traditions of the past.

The "formal" training sessions can take place twice weekly at times convenient to the participants. However, the staff is aware that to be successful one is "always" working. As David Hillman (the City of Long Beach ROM Coordinator) notes, "we do not do drive-bys." That is, he believes wherever he may be and whatever the time, if he observes a young brother in the community with a child(ren) or with a pregnant female, he will stop, introduce himself, share some literature about the program and invite the young man to visit. Additionally, Mr. Hillman will follow up with a phone contact within 24 hours. He will also provide his business card so that the potential client can contact him. David believes, and his experience supports the notion, that most men want to be with their children and want to do what is best, but they often do not know what to do, how to do it, or where to seek help. David Hillman, a deeply religious man, has been very successful in his efforts to get men to participate and he believes his faith gives him the strength and vision to persevere.

Outreach and recruitment involves placing information in strategic places whereby potential program participants can access the materials. In Long Beach, Mr. Hillman and Reverend Larry Gann (an outreach specialist) canvas the neighborhood for recruits. Reverend Gann states: "we have a passion to impact their lives and to move the men beyond their self-imposed limitations." Additionally, previous graduates from the program are encouraged and reinforced to bring others to the program. Materials are placed in local businesses (including barbershops, fast food places, restaurants, stores, beauty shops, etc.), the department of social services, job sites, schools, the department of labor, for example. Announcements have been made on the local cable television network, public service radio programs, and in the local newspapers. And, we use word of mouth. The ROM staff makes themselves available to discuss the program at midnight basketball, at church, at school, at work, with elected officials, and with the City's Black Infant Health staff and participants. Any one and any program that is likely to attract the target population is considered and utilized.

When the men come in to complete the application process, they are screened. It is important to be sensitive to their reading and writing skills, as well as their oral communication abilities. The program is further discussed, the schedule of training is offered, and questions are answered. Men who are having difficulties with substance abuse issues are referred to a local treatment program. Names and contact numbers are maintained so contact can be reestablished, after they complete their treatment. These men are encouraged to return to the Program when they have completed their other obligations. Additionally, contact is encouraged for those fathers who have unfulfilled obligations with the local, county, and state legal systems so they might be made aware of the training as an opportunity upon their release from confinement.

The fathers who are selected enter into a four skills training module program, plus follow-up. The four skills training components include: parenting, social and legal issues, educational enhancement, and vocational training. After training, the men enter follow-up where contact is maintained for one year. To date, more than 600 men have been trained in the State of California.

1. Parenting. Parenting training is the most important aspect of the model as each of the other training components evolves around it. It is assumed that men can learn to become effective fathers whether or not they are working, regardless of their vocational status, and irrespective of their social or legal challenges. Information offered during this component is focused at attempting to provide the dads with basic information to aid and encourage them to become involved quickly with their infant and with the mother of their child. Thus they are encouraged to attend all prenatal doctor visits. The goal is to help them understand their responsibilities to their child as soon as possible and to engage in healthy behaviors early in the child's development. They are to minimize high-risk behaviors, attempt to reduce stress for the unborn child, aid in providing a healthy environment. Additionally, basic infant-care skills including holding, feeding, changing, bathing, burping, and carrying are demonstrated and discussed. Additionally, the men are encouraged to talk with and read to their young child(ren). Significant normative behaviors through the toddler years are presented. The men are encouraged to be present during the birth of their child and to establish paternity.

2. Social-Legal Issues. During the next phase of training, common social problems and legal issues are covered. Techniques of problem solving and conflict resolution are offered. Anger management is discussed. The negative impact of domestic violence is addressed and the men are encouraged to attempt to develop a positive problem-solving environment for their family. The power of learning to listen and to share is discussed. Additionally, the fathers' legal rights and obligations are covered. The men are informed as to their right to access to their child. The obligation to financially and emotionally support their child is covered and emphasized.

3. Education. California provides low-cost education. We assess the educational level of the participants and encourage them to continue their training, either by completing high school (the GED), attending adult literacy classes, enrolling in junior college or vocational school, or the university. Many of the participants have been "pushed" out of school at an early age and do not have positive feelings about their educational experiences. Many have minimal reading and problem-solving skills, many avoid the educational environment, and many have no computing skill. The participants are responsive to attempts to enhance their academic abilities, as they

tend to be bright, aware of their limitations, and motivated to improve their status. The men are encouraged to learn to read so they can read to their children and can access information required to survive. They can learn to model appropriate reading behaviors for their children.

4. Vocational Training. The fourth and final skills training component involves work readiness. Few of the participants have held full-time employment for any length of time and few of them have the requisite skills needed to impact the workplace. A distinction is made between a job and a career, with the idea that the men commence thinking about careers. The men are showed how to seek work, how to complete an application, how to interview, how to present themselves to the marketplace, and how to maintain a job once they are hired. Additionally, money management, appropriate credit card usage, living within one's means, and future goals are discussed. The point is made that they are now working to help with the support of their offspring.

After the men complete the skills training, they enter follow-up where an attempt is made to help them use their newly found skills on an ongoing basis. The men are encouraged to maintain contact with the program and to return to discuss issues and concerns they may encounter. Additionally, they are encouraged to discuss the program with their friends and family and to refer appropriate individuals to the program. To date, more than 800 men have benefited from the training.

DISCUSSION

The programs discussed are examples of models in place and working in African American communities across the nation. Many others exist and we salute them as well. Programs and activities that seem to be making a difference have several components in common. First, rather than limiting the emphasis to teenage fathers, the focus is on men *across ages* who are having difficulties. In these programs, there is a primary focus on men/fathers as caregivers and nurturers. Fathers must learn to feel comfortable caring for and directly expressing love for their children. Those working in the area are reminded that caring for and taking care of one's children represent the most masculine activities in which any man can engage. Fathers must learn to embrace and accept this aspect of their being and help those who might have rather skewed notions of what men are and what they do. Additionally, there is nothing in the literature or in the collective awareness of our people that suggests men cannot and should not be active parents. Those who work in service to men are reminded to consider this point. It takes no skill to have a child, but it does require significant resources and skills to successfully rear one's child.

Another important aspect of successful programs is the focus on education. It is important that African American men understand and develop value for education. Education can lead to mental liberation, the real and accurate definition of power. Additionally, we must understand the many limitations placed before us absent an education. In many communities, education is one of the more reasonable commodities before us and it is one too many devalue. In this sense, it is not the accumulation of formal degrees that is important, but the accumulation and awareness of knowledge that is critical. Education (learning to problem solve and think) allows one to critically analyze and reflect upon situations confronting us and to develop survival strategies that can permit us to thrive. One must begin with an awareness of oneself followed by an awareness of us in our environments. As discussed in Ballard's model, developing a sense of self-respect is critical. Finally, education should also include information about reproductive anatomy, physical health, mental health and healing, anger management, problem-solving communication skills, and the management of "at-risk" behaviors.

Successful programs should include the mothers of the fathers' children. Moms need to know what dads are doing (just as dads should be aware of moms' work). If both parents are aware of what the other is doing, it is easier to develop respect and appreciation for those activities. Children can only win when their parents work together in respectful harmony. Staff who work in those programs servicing mothers are encouraged to include fathers and fathers' needs in their activities. Additionally, those in successful marriages are encouraged to discuss their relationships and to model appropriate marital behaviors. In this sense, mentors should be recruited to model and share appropriate behaviors across the life span.

Finally, vocational activities must be included in any male involvement program as it is important that men accept responsibility for helping to rear their children and to aid in the financial provision of their families. Men must learn how to seek work, maintain their job, and grow in their effort. It is critical that a distinction is made between a job and a career, as too many vocational "opportunities" offered to men of African descent are short term and dead end. We need to consider turning jobs into careers so as not to contribute to the ongoing frustration confronting many men as they attempt to impact the marketplace. A goal is to assist African American fathers to begin to consider working toward building sustained careers. Mentors and community leaders are critical to the success of the programs, and the staff must be readily available. Finally, the staff should be trained to provide some mental health intervention, as many of our fathers are in mental distress.

Prior to closing, I want to mention the National Practitioners Network for Fathers and Families (NPNFF). According to a recent newsletter, "NPNFF's Mission is to strengthen supports for children in fragile families by enhancing the involvement of fathers, and by fostering communications, program development, education, and collaboration among service providers" (Vol. 4, No. 1). This national–international membership organization is working with the profession of practitioners to enhance meaningful involvement of fathers in the lives of their children. Their work is designed to offer training, improve communication, and develop communication between those who work with fathers (and fragile families) on a daily basis. Those engaging in fathers' work can gain valuable insights and information via this agency. Their website is www.npnff.org

REFERENCES

Ballard, C. (1999). *Prepared testimony of Mr. Charles A. Ballard,* Founder and CEO, The Institute for Responsible Fatherhood and Revitalization. http://www.house.gov/ *smbiz/hearings*

Levine, J., & Pitt, E. (1995). *Community strategies for responsible fatherhood.* New York: Families and Work Institute.

National Practitioners Network for Fathers and Families, Member Service Memo. (January 2003). Vol. 4, Issue 1.

Author Index

269

Subject Index